PARANORMAL BY REGION: EAST TENNESSEE EDITION

A.J. MASON &
MATT GEIST

COPYRIGHT

Text Copyright © 2024

A.J. Downey DBA A.J. Mason & Matthew Connell DBA Matt Geist.

ISBN: 978-1-950222-48-3

All rights reserved.

No part of this book may be reproduced in any form or by any electronic or mechanical means, including information storage and retrieval systems, without written permission from the author, except for the use of brief quotations in a book review.

This is a work of fiction. The names, characters, businesses, places, events, and incidents are either the products of the author's imagination or used in a fictitious manner and are not to be construed as real except where noted and authorized. Any resemblance to persons, living or dead, or actual events are entirely coincidental. Any trademarks, service marks, product names, or names featured are assumed to be the property of their respective owner, and are used only for reference. There is no implied endorsement if any of these terms are used.

The author acknowledges the trademarked status and trademark owners of various products referenced in this work, which have been used without permission. The publication/use of these trademarks is not authorized, associated with, or sponsored by the trademark owners.

∼

Edited and book design by Maggie Kern at Ms.K Edits

Cover art by Dar Albert at Wicket Smart Designs

AUTHOR'S NOTE

Trying to come up with the dividing lines to section East Tennessee into even smaller bite-sized chunks to make it make sense for this book was a pain in my ass, but I think I've got it.

While the state of Tennessee is divided into three sections, itself from west to east by way of West, Middle, and East Tennessee – this book just focuses on *East* Tennessee – or everything from where the time zone changes from Central to Eastern time all the way east to the North Carolina border.

To break East Tennessee down further, I divided things into three sections from north to south – so if you see "Northeast Tennessee, Central East Tennessee, and Southeast Tennessee," you now know where my thought process was with that.

I'm a damn Yankee by birth – but apparently, not entirely because I was born and raised in the Pacific Northwest. (It confuses me, too – and not every southerner agrees. I'll let you decide if I classify as a damn Yankee or not.)

Anyway, shit's confusing, and while I now live in the Volunteer State, I've always lived in a constant state of confusion.

Did I need to make this note explaining all this?

No.

AUTHOR'S NOTE

Probably not.

You, my dear little strangeling reading this, are almost guaranteed to be smarter than me. With that being said, this is my book – and I do what I want. If you've actually read this whole thing and are thinking to yourself that you feel dumber for having read this far – I can't honestly guarantee that it's going to get any better.

There's really only one way to find out though, now isn't there?

So, turn the page, and let's get our spooky on, shall we?

-A.J.

INTRODUCTION

"You should write a book!" For years and years, I've heard this as a paranormal investigator and storyteller. When I move to, visit, or somehow get hyper-focused on a location, I tend to go all out and collect every haunted story or ghostly tale surrounding it like friggin' Pokémon – *gotta catch 'em all!* Invariably, when I've learned everything there is to know about a city or region, I just *have* to tell my friends or the people around me and cue that old familiar refrain: "You should really write a book."

Funny enough – I do author books. Lots of books. Lots of *fictional romance books*. I mean, that's been my day job for *years*, and I confess that I'm not much of a technical writer. I find technical writing boring as all get out, and so, every time that refrain would come: "You should write a book about this," I would make a face and wave it off and change the subject to what I really wanted to talk about more – which was to tell more ghost stories.

Then, the advent of *TikTok* came, and a good friend told me, "You should do *TikTok* to advertise your books!" You know, my other books, the spicy romance books I've been writing for the last ten years. I'm always looking at new ways to push it to a broader audience. So, I

INTRODUCTION

knuckled under, downloaded the app, and then I was like – doing *TikTok* for my spicy books is a lot of work and kind of boring, but then the lightbulb went off.

You know what's not boring? Talking about dead things! I can talk about cemeteries, death practices, ghosts, and all things spooky all damn day and even more on Sundays, if you'll let me. Now, I had a portal open up in front of me with not just a captive audience but an audience of *strangelings like me!*

I always wanted to do more with my passion for the paranormal. So I started up Sound Paranormal – not intending to draft a book, but rather with the intention of starting it up into a podcast where I could talk spooky shit to my little black heart's content.

But then the comments started coming in… things that flattered and made me giggle. Things like: "Wow! You're a great storyteller!" and then the oft refrain started *again*… "You should write a book."

Of course, I pushed that shit off as long as possible, but then, alas, the seed was planted, and damned if it didn't start to grow like a weed.

Still, as much as I didn't want to do a podcast alone and wanted someone to do it with, I also didn't want to author a book alone. Of course, just my luck that I found a spooky homie! Right in the nick of time – no, not to record a podcast, although the intent is still there. No, I met Matt thanks to *TikTok* and discovered not only were we a matched pair when it came to our thought processes on espookies, but we were also both writers. I got Matt to come on board to help write and record spots for *TikTok* on cryptids, and one day, I guess, I'd been assimilated because I was like, "Hey, spooky homie, you wanna write a book with me?" and Matt was like, "Bet!" The rest was pretty much history. So here we are, a *TikTok* channel created to support a podcast called *Sound Paranormal*, and still with no podcast, but hey, we got a book instead!

Someday we'll get our shit together, and the podcast will be a thing. Hopefully, by the time you have this in your hot little hands, it will already be out there and picking up a listenership. Still, if it's not a thing yet, and you find yourself jonesing for more ghostly tales, you

INTRODUCTION

can find us working hard on the *TikTok* that's been going strong for over a year now as of writing this.

Just hop on over to *TikTok* if it's your thing, look up @soundparanormal, click that plus sign, and become one of our strangeling crew.

-A.J. Mason

PART 1:
GHOSTS & HAUNTINGS

This book wouldn't be a book without the spooky factor of ghosts and hauntings. It's the backbone of all things paranormal, those lingering spirits and shades from tragic events and beyond.

What exactly *does* life after death look like?

Is it even "life after death," or are we just seeing an echo through time and space, or getting a glimpse into another dimension with some of these stories?

One of the more frustrating things when looking into the paranormal is starting out with questions like these, doing your research, reading stories, finding new or coming up with new theories of your own, only in the end to wind up with even *more* questions than you started with.

It's a frustrating world, the world of the paranormal, and rewarding at the same time. It's always fun to challenge yourself and your beliefs. The mind, as always, is much like a parachute – it works best when open.

So, without any more preamble, let's get into the ghosts and hauntings of the East Tennessee Region and see if your horizons get expanded or if your focus narrows. Either way, we're about to get into some fun stuff. At least, if you're a regular *Addams Family* type like I am, which of course you are, aren't you, my little strangeling?

You're here, aren't you?

Northeast Tennessee

NORTHEAST TENNESSEE

We start our adventures in weird by taking it from the top – literally, the top of the region of East Tennessee, from the Kentucky border on down to just above Knoxville and what we're calling Central East Tennessee.

At first, this portion of the region was a pain in my ass for digging up any stories, but the more I dug, the more I realized I done fucked up. There were actually more stories than I could possibly cover up this way. Easily enough to fill out their own book! I was pretty much buried in an avalanche of spooky bullshit. To say I was on cloud nine is an understatement, but it also posed a bit of a problem for me.

One, it's hard to get up and out to some of these locations from where I live in Central Tennessee – not that I would let that stop me.

Two, I have made it my mission in this book to try and cover that which has not been covered before. Which is a lot harder than it sounds, my little strangelings. These hallowed haunted grounds have been walked by paranormal investigators before me simply so that I could run. I want to take full advantage of their trailblazing, and thus, most of those notable folklorists and parajunkies are in our bibliography. I highly encourage you to check their books out in addition to this one.

Three, barring going over the ground that's already been traveled in those books that have gone before mine, I was, and still remain, determined to find *new* and personal firsthand accounts from people who have lived and worked in these haunted places. Gathering encounters that have happened since the publication of those books that have gone before and trying like hell to bring some kind of *new* aspect to things, even though many of these stories are founded in repetition and not much new has happened since those initial experiences.

Hopefully, I've done you proud in that aspect. Hopefully, in addition to some new uncovered information about the places you *have* heard were haunted before, I bring you some locations that you *hadn't* heard about and are new to you.

Hopefully, I've done my job satisfactorily, in other words.

There's really only one way to find out if I have, and that's to turn the page and join me on a deep dive into the ghosts and hauntings of the northern third of East Tennessee.

A Residual Haunting in the Unakas, Northeastern Tennessee

So far east in East Tennessee as to almost be North Carolina, just outside what is now Johnson City, TN, the land was a rich and fertile tract and, once upon a time, home to the Cherokee Indigenous tribes. That is until a bunch of White colonizers showed up and fucked everything up – which isn't that always the way?

For real, though – it was the 1700s of it all, and the Cherokee and White folks started off as decent enough neighbors. That is until the Cherokee realized their miscommunication in that the White settlers thought they had somehow *bought* the hunting land from the Cherokee and now *owned* it. The Cherokee were like, *wait, what?* As they lived under the impression that owning land was freaking ludicrous, no one *owned* the land! The land was just the land, and we all were just passing through and should be grateful it provided like it did for us.

So yeah, things escalated quickly, shit got real, and the next thing you know, everybody was killing each other. You know how all that goes.

That's where our ghost story begins. You see, there was a family of colonizers chilling on a tract of land in the heart of Cherokee hunting grounds. The Cherokee, disgruntled with these White folks and how they were altering the natural landscape to grow crops, etc., and their audacity at being told, basically, *fuck you*, we *own* it now – said "bet" and slaughtered them all. Man, woman, and child were put to a brutal and violent end. Their cabin and outbuildings were torched, and it was, unfortunately, weeks or longer before a group of White hunters came along and found the absolute horror show of what was left after the incident.

There really wasn't a whole lot left behind except the scar of where the White settlement had been, the trees cleared, the earth churned, and the crops left to wither where they weren't burned.

Well, that, and apparently, the *un*settled ghosts of those White settlers.

Legend has it, on the banks of aptly named "Indian Creek" in Unicoi County, Tennessee, when the leaves are starting to turn and the nights are starting to crisp with autumn, the events of that fateful night when the settlers were slaughtered will begin to replay under the light of the moon.

How do we get this legend? A pair of apparently enterprising boys, who in the intervening years between then and now, and with little else better to do, crept out of their home to see the phenomenon for themselves.

The story goes that they asked their parents' permission first and were resoundingly denied – but, in one of the few exceptions where "boys will be boys" is used rather appropriately, they fucked off into the night and went to do it anyway.

They crouched down in some bushes at the edge of the old and abandoned homestead, and it wasn't very long before they saw something.

A woman, dressed in white nightclothes – a long white gown – was seen fleeing in terror from the direction of the tree line somewhere out in front of the boys. She did so noiselessly, and then, a boy their age, around twelve or thirteen, burst from the underbrush behind the woman, who could have been his older sister or his mamma. There's no real way to know today.

One of the boys craned his neck and came up out of his crouch to get a better look at the unfolding drama in front of them, but he was quickly pulled back down behind the shrubs by his friend.

A twig snapped nearby as two Indigenous men emerged from the trees, both painted fiercely and staring *right* at the boys. The boys yelped, splitting the night air in their terror, as they fled the clearing, lighting off like a fire had been lit under their little asses at the imposing sight of the war-painted "Indigenous" men – who fell out laughing at their sons' terror.

The boys' two fathers high-fived one another at a job well done in teaching their boys a damn lesson about sneaking out at night against their wishes. One congratulated the other, telling him that the prank had been made all the better by his recruitment of the other two, the woman and the boy.

The one father blinked in surprise at the other and said, "I didn't recruit them. I thought you did!"

Both men turned uneasily and watched in horror as the scene of that terrible night was played out in front of them, in the form of a residual haunting – screams rending the air as a pack of Indigenous braves brutally murdered every man, woman, and child of the homestead.

While their prank had started off innocently enough and had certainly taught their boys a lesson, the men themselves learned a lesson of their own – how instant karma worked.

ROTHERWOOD MANSION, KINGSPORT

Located in Kingsport, Tennessee, Rotherwood Mansion has a deep and troubling history that is pretty much low-hanging fruit, ripe for the picking, where paranormal legend is concerned.

Built in 1818 on the banks of the Holston River by Frederick Ross, Rotherwood is a beautiful antebellum brick home that has no less than four ghost stories attached.

The first is of your classic "lady in white" ghost but with a twist. It centers around Fredrick's daughter, Rowena Ross. Rowena was to be married at Rotherwood. However, just before her wedding day, her fiancé drowned in the Holston River while Rowena helplessly watched from the bank.

Despondent, Rowena fell into a deep depression and remained in it for a long time before eventually going on to marry, leaving Rotherwood with her new husband. Years later, and after having a daughter of her own, Rowena and her family returned to Rotherwood. It is said, that night, Rowena heard the call of her first and lost love, and, looking out the window, saw him waving from the riverbank.

It is said that she donned her wedding dress, which she was originally supposed to wear the day of their wedding to one another, and she slipped from the house down to the banks of the river to join her lost love. It was there that she waded into the black waters of the icy Holston and drowned herself.

Devastated by his daughter's death, and in a bid to save the plantation, Ross sold Rotherwood to a man by the name of Phipps.

Where Ross had been considered an almost kind master, for a man who thought it was cool to own other human beings as cattle – Phipps was a straight-up *asshole*. Indeed, Phipps had a widely held reputation for his utter cruelty where his slaves were concerned. Forget any pretty language about a "firm hand" or whatever. This guy was straight-up *abusive as fuck*.

While Rowena Ross would become Rotherwood's first and most enduring ghost – spotted wandering the mansion and grounds in her white wedding dress, eternally searching for her first love - she's regarded as sad and harmless.

Phipps is the mansion's dark entity, even though there isn't anything remarkable about Phipps's death, and his ghost wouldn't be encountered until sometime in the 1940s.

It was during renovations on the place in the '40s that one of the workers reported that he was speaking to some of his fellow crew members when he first saw Phipps's ghost.

The crew members said they were talking to the fellow and that he just sort of stuttered to a stop mid-sentence, went deathly pale, and booked it, screaming out of the mansion, getting into the company vehicle, and driving away, leaving the rest of the crew scratching their heads in confusion.

When the dude calmed the fuck down, he returned to Rotherwood and explained to his colleagues that behind them, he had watched a man in a dark suit materialize out of the wall, holding the collar of a huge black dog with glowing red eyes. He said the man had stared a hole through his soul and had the most malevolent and evil, absolutely vicious grin spread across the ghost's lips in the ghastliest of smiles. He had ominously pointed at the worker and let loose the dog. What is now being called the hellhound of Rotherwood chased the man out of the mansion, screaming.

In a bid to escape the snapping jaws of the angry black dog, its eyes alight with the fires of Hell itself, the worker'd leaped into the company vehicle and had taken off, hauling ass out of there.

Truthfully, I would have probably noped right the fuck out of there, too. Dogs scare the shit out of me – ghosts? Not so much. But dogs? Yeah, fuck that. I'm out.

Everyone believes this malevolent spirit with his "hound from hell" to be that of Phipps, the mansion's second owner. I mean, he was a son of a bitch in life, so it isn't exactly a stretch to assume he's one in death, right?

Also reported on the mansion's grounds are the apparitions of enslaved peoples – which I really hope are just residuals and not sentient – but nothing I've read or seen has led me to believe they are anything but.

So that's it: a lost and lonely bride, an evil slave-owning piece of shit, his foul and evil mongrel dog, and the visage of slaves still toiling the land surrounding the manse.

It all makes for a sad and sordid legend, which is honestly the best kind – don't you think?

As with a lot of places in this book, I went to check the veracity of these legends and claims for myself, which oftentimes means speaking to front desk staff, waitstaff, historical societies, museum staff, or theater staff.

In the case of Rotherwood Mansion, it was pulling on my big girl panties and doing something that I really loathe doing…

Ringing the doorbell and hoping for the absolute best, but expecting to get yelled and screamed at for trespassing, and rightfully so. The Rotherwood Mansion is now a private residence, and I hate knocking on any stranger's door if I can help it. I also recognize that a lot of paranormal investigators *don't* have the same scruples that I do, and thus, residents of knowingly haunted places are sick to death of us bothering them.

Still, for this book, I rolled the dice, and I got *very* lucky.

The homeowner was home, answered the door, was polite but firm that it was a private residence and that she had never encountered any of the supposed hauntings since moving in. Which, I believed her, my little strangelings. I really did. She was gracious enough to allow me to take photos and video of the outside of her home for social media but did ask that I stringently let everyone know – this is private property, trespassers are unwelcome and *will* be prosecuted, and to please *don't* randomly knock on her door.

I was grateful for her polite understanding, told her I would happily relay the information, and promised I would never darken her doorstep again, and I absolutely shan't. That's *respect*, my little strangelings.

Please don't bother me, was the message, and the message was received loud and clear. To the lovely woman I met at Rotherwood, if you're reading this bit about your home, I really appreciate you and how gracious you were that day! Especially after my encounter at another haunted location only days before, which was totally uncalled for.

May your pillow always be cool on both sides at night and may your coffee order ever be perfect. I really do wish you all the good things in life! I mean, you already are rocking one of the best things ever, living in a mansion that's over 200 years old and supposedly haunted. I'm super jealous about that one. I'm just going to go out on a limb and say the spirits within Rotherwood are pleased with you and how you're taking care of the place. I don't think they'd be quiet otherwise.

Sensabaugh Tunnel, Kingsport

Built in the 1920s, along Sensabaugh Hollow Road, by a man named Sensabaugh, no less lies Sensabaugh Tunnel. It's a ramshackle, 200-foot cement tube, punched unceremoniously through a ridge rather than engineers building around it. The walls of the tunnel are a veritable rainbow of modern-day rattle-can-induced graffiti, and the road within the tunnel itself is a bumpy ride filled with potholes that have gone too-long neglected, much like the tunnel itself.

Overgrown on the outside, the lane narrows and is really only fit to accommodate one car or truck at a time. This place has kind of a funky and cool sort of vibe during the day – one that I'm told turns wholly sinister after dark.

There are a myriad of legends surrounding Sensabaugh Tunnel, the most prevalent of which is that at night, you can hear the ethereal cries of a tiny baby echoing through and around the tunnel. The story goes that these are the cries of a wee little babe, murdered brutally by a full-grown man.

The story goes that at the height of the Great Depression, when many a hobo rode the rails looking and scraping for work wherever they could find it, one of them wound up at a local home near Sensabaugh Tunnel.

The man and woman of the house agreed to let him chop firewood for them for the day, for a small payment and a hearty dinner.

The couple weren't rich by any stretch of the imagination, but they were doing alright for themselves during the trying times of the Great Depression and *did* have some things of value lying about the house.

The hobo finished his task and joined the couple in their home for dinner. At some point, during the meal or just after, the couple found that the hobo had attempted to steal a family heirloom silver cup of some sort. An argument ensued, the man of the house running to fetch his pistol.

Not wanting to be shot, the hobo snatched the couple's baby from its nearby cradle and dashed out the door, using the babe as a meat shield against the dad taking any shots.

The hobo ran for it and found himself running through Sensabaugh Tunnel, where he stopped to hide.

Realizing that the baby had helped facilitate his escape, and yet having no desire to keep on with it, the hobo made a terrible choice. Rather than leaving the child for better or worse and giving it the chance to be found, he opted to hold the babe under the waters of the creek that flowed near the mouth of the tunnel. Drowning it and its cries in the brackish waters.

That's some really foul shit, my little strangelings – desperate times or not.

While Sensabaugh Tunnel was a main thoroughfare in its heyday, as more roads and eventually highways were built running around and through Kingsport, the tunnel was increasingly only being used by locals and eventually fell into the state of disrepair of barely functional that it is today.

Still, it is reported that late some nights, you can hear the screaming wails of that long-ago infant, echoing and emanating from the tunnel, a throwback to that long-ago night and the foul deed committed against it.

Given enough time, the area around the tunnel became a popular spot for teens and young lovers looking for a bit of privacy, and I can see why. The road here is rarely traversed and does have a couple of spots good to park alongside at either end of the tunnel itself.

Young lovers have been known to park to get a little privacy, and the tunnel has a particular draw for young men who like to tell their girls the wild, ghostly tales of the place in a bid to get them to "Come closer, baby. I'll protect you."

But there's more that goes on here than the phantom cries of that long-ago murdered baby.

It's not just a residual haunting but also an interactive one in that if you hear the baby cry, there's a good chance your car will fail to start.

Many stories are told of young lovers getting hot and heavy, the crying starting outside of their car. Thoroughly creeped and wanting to leave, they try to no avail to start the vehicle while the wailing intensifies outside.

In another version of Sensabaugh Tunnel lore, if you stop your car halfway through the tunnel and turn it off, it will fail to restart, and then you must push it to the end, and it will miraculously start once you're outside the tunnel again.

When I went with two of my friends on a daytime excursion, you bet your ass I told them this bit. Midway through the tunnel, I threw it into park and shut off Eliza, my 2020 Nissan Rogue.

My friends yelled at me, I laughed, and I turned the ignition. She started right up, of course. I guess they weren't paying attention to the qualifiers that it had to be at night and when the phantom baby cried.

Yes, I am the asshole, but it was amusing, so at least there's that, right?

If you wander out to Sensabaugh Tunnel, do be careful. It is old and decrepit, and locals tend to speed through it. It is also incredibly narrow, with no place to go should you be walking through it and someone tries to pass through with a car. Indeed, if two vehicles slip into the tunnel from either side, one's got to put it in reverse and back all the way out to let the other pass.

In short, I do not recommend this place for any nighttime excursions or investigations. There are no streetlights, it's remote enough that it's pretty much local access only, and there are too many factors that make this an unsafe place to be. If you decide to ignore my warnings, that's all you, and I can't, for legal reasons, be held accountable if you're injured. I told you to stay away for a reason.

That concludes this story, and me having to be a helicopter mom/Karen about it.

PARANORMAL BY REGION: EAST TENNESSEE EDITION

Just trust your Auntie Strange on this one, yeah?

The General Morgan Inn, Greeneville

Before the grand brick building that stands here today in the form of the General Morgan Inn, this spot used to be occupied by a ramshackle, roughhewn, log cabin-like building known as the DeWoody Tavern.

This janky wooden structure of yesteryear was built by a man named William Dunwoody in the 1790s. It was known as a good spot to stop for food, lodging, and to resupply for pioneers moving westward along the old wagon trail that would, many, many moons later, become US Highway 321.

Greenville was an ideal stop along the trail for many reasons. Chief among them, the abundance of fresh spring water from Greenville's Big Spring – which, as we all should know by now, where there's an abundance of water, there's sure to be hauntings. From lakes to rivers to springs – it's unknown *why*, but it *is* known that where there's an abundance of moving or even stagnant water, hauntings seem to pool and collect just like this natural resource.

So, if you didn't know that fun paranormal fact, today you learned!

The DeWoody Tavern was a long-lasting fixture in Greenville, TN. It changed ownership and names over the years, going from DeWoody to the Bell Tavern from 1820-ish to 1860-ish and winding up the Lane Tavern after the Bell, sometime during that same timeframe when Joshua Lane bought it.

Lane owned it during the Civil War and declared his tavern a sort of Switzerland at the time – that is, to say, neutral. He served both

Union and Confederate troops alike in his establishment and didn't care who you were or where you came from, or even where you were going. He figured all coin was good coin and, especially if it was jangling in his own pocket. So come one and come all, which worked for the most part, right up until it didn't.

It was during this tenure as the Lane Tavern that the building and the land it sat on entertained one of the most infamous skirmishes.

It was the morning of September 4th, 1864, when the guests of the Lane house witnessed a ghastly knock-down drag-out fight. You see, the "Thunderbolt of the Confederacy," General John Hunt Morgan, had come into town and had arranged to stay at a friend of his place, the home of one Mrs. Catherine Williams.

Union Troops, eager to apprehend this guy, were tipped off that he had arrived the afternoon before. They moved out from the Tavern where they were quartering at around dawn of the 4th, to be set and ready to cut him off from escape and to nab him that day.

Mrs. Williams and family did their best to help General Morgan but were too late. Their home in the center of town was already surrounded, and a bloody skirmish ensued in their big yard full of trees and vineyards surrounding their house. The Union had successfully outnumbered the general, his men, and Catherine's family and ambushed the general as he had tried to escape. He was shot dead by Union troops as he ran across the yard from the house to the stables to get to his horse and was later buried in Lexington Cemetery.

Change came to Greenville and the Tavern when, in 1886, the East Tennessee and Virginia Railroad built a new train depot in town. It revolutionized the little town and surrounding area, and it was a man by the name of Colonel John Doughty, a local businessman, who recognized that with the passenger trains now running through Greeneville, an intense need was there for a hotel to accommodate them. So, to that end, he started planning to build one.

He bought the old Lane Tavern and the property it sat on, demolished the wood structure, and had a grand vision for a four-story brick hotel that he would later name The Grand Central. Boy, was it grand – state-of-the-art for its time and trimmed beautifully in marble. It was classified as one of the most luxurious accommodations between

Roanoke, Virginia, and Chattanooga, Tennessee, in its heyday with its wide hallways and stunning top-tier furnishings. It was unique in that it had an upper balcony that spanned the entire front of the second story with its own set of steps that let out directly onto Main Street of the town. Not that you had to really leave the hotel to do any shopping – as its entire first floor was a set of luxury shops and boutiques, making the Grand Central Hotel a veritable oasis of finer things smack in the middle of town.

After its construction, the hotel only changed hands once, from the Doughty family to the hands of the Brumley family, where it remained until 1981, when the crown jewel was finally acquired by a group calling itself the Olde Town Development Corporation. They had spent a lot of time and money buying up old historic properties around the hotel for restoration.

It took nine excruciatingly long years of planning, fundraising, and restorative and code compliance construction, but they made it and finally opened their doors to the public on September 18th, 1996. However, The Grand Central Hotel does not bear the same name as it once did. Today, it is known as the General Morgan Inn and Conference Center. Not sure why they felt the need to name it after the fallen Confederate general, other than it makes me side-eye the people involved for obvious reasons, but that's where we're at with it.

Today, the General Morgan Inn still stands proud, as do the legends associated with it…

It's said that the General Morgan is haunted, my little strangelings, and not by just a few ghosts, but word has it, *over forty.*

I'm a little skeptical of that number, but here's what I can tell you…

The hotel has a few named ghosts, from General Morgan himself to one they call Green Room Grace, and another they call Front Desk Bill.

It is said that Grace is a former server and is most often seen by the staff of the hotel's restaurant. Not that she's just *seen*, but the article that I read specifically mentions that she is *seen every day.*

She is notorious for stealing flatware, spoons to be specific, and the strange part of that is that she only steals the spoons from her preferred setting – the Green Room – hence the staff calling her Green Room Grace. Much to the establishment's frustration, they find themselves having to order spoons more than any other piece of silverware due to Grace's kleptomania of the piece. Because once Grace does pilfer the spoon, it's gone for good, never to be seen again.

She's also attributed to the fact that all the paintings will find themselves crooked on the walls by morning. That she tips them sometime during the night.

Somehow, Grace made it known to some guests of the hotel that she had been haunting the place for over 75 years and that she wasn't the only one trapped there. She has at least nine other ghostly homies with her. One of these spectral homeboys was spotted by some of the staff at the hotel in an experience they swear they will *never* forget.

The staff members were prepping food in a small group with their living colleagues, when, out of the corner of their eyes, they saw movement, a shadow passing by. They all turned as one to see just the black outline of a person move across the kitchen!

There's also poltergeist activity mentioned within the kitchen as well, with heavy objects reportedly moved by an unseen force or hand. Some of those objects have been seen flying across the kitchen, specifically metal serving trays, as though someone has angrily flung them off of their resting place atop the ovens.

Indeed, apparitions have been reportedly seen in the kitchen almost daily, like Grace in the dining room.

That's all I have been able to find for now regarding the General Morgan Inn. It's said that the abandoned Depot Hotel right next door is *also* haunted, and that some of the ghosts from The Depot Hotel are interchangeable and visit the General Morgan's property. That's where we'll get to Front Desk Bill, who apparently is happy to still be at the front desk of what was The Depot Hotel next door. Investigators claim that he's told them he is accompanied by at least twenty-six other spirits that move between this building and the General Morgan Inn.

Back on the second floor of the General Morgan, the building's namesake is said to haunt with a vengeance but is also very vain for being dead, supposedly refusing to be photographed without his general's hat present on his head. It's said that John Hunt Morgan's vanity extends beyond that, however, in that he only tends to haunt the finest room in the hotel, the Presidential Suite, where his photo hangs on the wall.

Guests on other parts of the floor have been known to report the sounds of screaming coming from the room to the front desk, who say they will handle it. However, there's really nothing to handle as room 207, the source of this particular haunting, will be standing empty at the time of the calls.

When attempts to communicate with the ghost in this room were made, it is said that the spirit reported being shot in the back and that he had died on the premises – which does sound a lot like the general's story, doesn't it? However, could it be him? How close was Mrs. Catherine Williams's home to the old Lang Tavern, because wasn't the Morgan built on *that* location?

Things that make you go *"hmm?"*

As a last note, there are, once again, supposedly over forty spirits that haunt this location, and some of the other activity attributed to the General Morgan Inn and Conference Center are ghosts that like to play on the elevator. Some consist of full-bodied apparitions that are seen in the restaurant, sipping coffee, and reading the newspaper. These activities are considered so commonplace that the staff tend to forget that seeing ghosts, moving objects, and disappearing silverware aren't considered normal parts of everyday life.

Sort of me and how swearing is so commonplace, that I literally forget that it offends some people. But that's pretty tame by comparison to the hauntings mentioned here, don't you think?

I went to the General Morgan Inn and Conference Center personally, as I worked to write this book. It was July 8th, 2024, and while I understand that some locations don't want a haunting associated with them, here's your friendly reminder about a few things.

1. Treat everyone you meet with kindness. It costs nothing.
2. You never know who you are talking to, so always keep it professional, especially if you are running the front desk of an establishment such as the General Morgan.
3. It's okay if someone doesn't believe the same things you do. You don't have to be nasty… because you never know if the

author that you're speaking with in that tone is going to be as petty of a bitch as I am.

So, here's how this went down, keeping all of the above in mind.

I went into what was a very beautiful and opulent lobby of this establishment. I'll tell you right then, my first thought wasn't at all about ghosts and hauntings, but rather my day job, which, if you don't know, is as an accomplished independent romance novelist going nigh on a decade as I write this.

So, my first thought upon walking in was – *I need to call so-and-so. This would be a great event space for a signing.*

Romance is big, my little strangelings, and signings are a big part of romance reading and writing culture. To hold a signing at a venue could bring in *thousands upon thousands* of dollars, both in renting out rooms to signing-goers and authors alike, as well as all the money poured into holding an event of that size and magnitude in the first place.

I know a lot of hotels that would make huge grabby hands for something like that to come through.

After how I was treated, so-and-so never got that message or call, which hurts my heart more than a little. This venue would have been perfect.

I went to the front desk and waited back a bit patiently for the front desk staff person, Barbie, to get off the phone. One of the hotel and conference center's maintenance personnel was standing nearby, and I waited to see if there was something pressing he needed an answer on before I even approached, but he waved me up with a big smile.

I smiled and told Barbie of the front desk, "Hi, I'm A.J. Mason, and I'm an independent author currently working on a book about ghosts and the paranormal in East Tennessee. As I understand it, The General Morgan might have some stories to it. Is there someone I could talk to about that?"

Barbie's smile was gone in a flash. She took my card, and both her expression and her tone dripping with absolute contempt, said, "No, it's not haunted."

"Not at all?" I asked.

"No," she repeated sharply.

"So, no one has ever had any kind of experience here, whatsoever, despite the numerous writeups and articles I've found about the General Morgan?" I asked, hoping against hope that the maintenance man nearby would pipe up and save me from Barbie's death glare she had leveled on me.

"I already told you it's not haunted!" she snapped. "What more do you want from me?"

I blinked in surprise. The maintenance man had an uncomfortable smile on his face that was more a rigid baring of teeth than an actual smile.

I stood up for myself and said, "Wow. This has to be the rudest interaction I have had to date in any of the hotels I've been to so far."

Barbie muttered something like "Whatever," as I turned back to both my friends who had accompanied me and hung back, having taken a seat on one of the couches in the lobby. At the look on my face, where I was honestly trying not to cry, because as much as I like to think of myself as a badass – my feelings were genuinely hurt – they got up, and we went for the door, both of them asking me, "What just happened?"

I told them, "While she didn't swear at me, I was just rudely told in no uncertain terms to get the fuck out of her hotel."

We left, I was upset, and the three of us decided that the entire interaction was *not* okay. I tried calling the hotel and shakily asked for the manager or someone in the events sphere, still thinking about how this would be a grand space for a signing.

It was Barbie on the phone, and she clearly recognized *my* voice because she flat-out said that no one was there or available today. No management and no event planning staff was on the premises – and then she hung up on me before I could even finish getting my polite, "Okay, thank you," out of my mouth.

My friends stared at me, stunned, and twisted around in the front seats of my friend's car. My friend and research assistant, Ellie, said, "Oh, now that's not right. Give *me* the goddamned number."

I gave it to her. She called in her beautifully lyrical and clipped

British accent and asked for the manager to speak about an experience she'd had at the hotel.

For her, Barbie put her right through to the manager's office, stating he was in, but alas, he didn't pick up. As soon as his voicemail came up, Ellie handed me the phone.

I summarized the abysmal experience I'd had at the front desk earlier, told him who I was as the author of this book, gave him my legal name as well as my *other* pen name, and asked for an opportunity to have the situation rectified by having someone call me back to at least discuss the history of the building and any potential reason why anyone would *think* it was haunted for the book.

I told the truth, that I would be writing and publishing the accounts of the General Morgan either way, and I would much prefer that the hotel management and owners get it on record their views on the whole "is it or isn't it" haunted thing politely, and amicably. I told him, in short that I didn't want to walk away feeling like this and that I was offering a do-over.

If you're reading this, I never heard back from the manager at the General Morgan Inn, and that's honestly all I am going to say about it other than just leave the place alone. Our kind are clearly not welcome there.

The Ghost House Trail, Big Ridge State Park

Twenty-five miles north of Knoxville, located in Big Ridge State Park, is one haunted hiking trail you won't want to miss. It's known by a couple of names: The Ghost Loop Trail, noted for its 1.2-mile loop through the woods, and The Ghost House Trail, as it runs past the ruins of the Hutchison Family Farm and the small family cemetery that was a part of it.

The stories about this trail are pretty low-key and cut and dried. It's said that it's possible that you could encounter the eerie sound of a dog panting – which, if you're scared of dogs in general, like me, could definitely raise the hair on the back of your neck – but actually has a bit of a sad, and wholesome tale attached to him.

It is said the ghost dog first appeared when poor Mary Hutchinson finally succumbed to the white death, or more commonly known in its time as the consumption. Today, we know the disease by its more commonly known and closer to its scientific name – tuberculosis.

A far less wholesome and more terrifying spirit that has been encountered on this trail is the spirit of Peter Graves, a White man known to appear near what is called Indian Rock, where he was murdered by the local Indigenous population and scalped. It's said that when you encounter poor Peter, it is in the visage of *after* his mutilation. I think seeing an individual, sans his scalp, dripping copious amounts of blood, would be enough to catch anyone off guard.

Another legend says that if you stop and take photos in the old family cemetery within the park along this trail, that you have a good chance of capturing past loved ones standing behind you in the photographs you take.

Another legend associated with this trail is that a young witch was supposedly hung to death by her father, and her lonely, aching, and rejected spirit has been seen wandering around the old grist mill along the trail.

This is honestly one of those haunted places within Tennessee that is often times touted as "terrifying" and "frightening" and one of the "scariest", but I don't really see how. I mean, other than the potentially startling appearance of Peter Graves, I don't really see how anyone could find this 1.2-mile loop of a trail anything close to scary. I imagine it to be somewhat somber in nature, and indeed – in all the accounts that I have read both online and in books, there is seriously one common theme: this trail is breathtakingly beautiful no matter what time of year you hike it, and even more spectacular in the fall when the leaves are a riot of color.

It's the middle of summer as I write this, and honestly, 1.2 miles doesn't sound awful to me, and I happen to have a permanent spinal injury that makes most hiking trails disappointingly a no-go. This one, though? This one, I'm going to have to try.

If I do attempt it, and ever get around to updating this book into a second edition, I'll be sure to let you know if I encounter anything. If *you* have encountered anything on this trail, my little strangelings, I would love to hear from you. You can reach me through the contact section of this book.

DRUMMOND BRIDGE, BRICEVILLE

In 1891, there was something known as the Coal Creek War of East Tennessee. It wasn't a war between states or a foreign war, but rather a war between employer and employees. It began when the coal mine owners in the Coal Creek watershed area began replacing their company-employed private coal miners with cheaper convict labor leased out by the Tennessee state prison system.

The former wage-earning coal miners were pissed, and understandably so, watching their livelihoods and the ability to feed their families being subsidized out of existence by convicts. Talk about adding insult to injury.

The miners repeatedly attacked and burned both state prison stockades and mining properties in protest over losing their jobs to the convicts, all while releasing hundreds of convicted felons out of their bondage and out into the wild. They set the prisoners free so they couldn't be used to undercut and take their jobs.

Many of these miners wound up bloodied and worse when the Tennessee state militia was called out to handle them and put down the insurrection and stop the rioting. The militiamen didn't fare much better, losing a dozen or more of their own ranks during this – one of the earliest and most important fights for labor rights in the United States.

The Coal Creek War was only part of a greater struggle with the labor market and the whole concept of convict leasing for labor across the US. This was some bullshit that rich people came up with in order to get richer, and it was definitely and apparently at the cost of the American People. Not only were the civil rights of the convicts being taken into question, but there was also the whole matter of *didn't we just fight a whole-ass Civil War over enslaving people? Because this shit feels a whole lot like the Diet Coke of slavery, and we don't like it.*

For the rich people, why pay a person a living wage to do a job when we can pay the state for a convict to do it for pennies on the dollar?

Pretty soon, this turned into "we're going to pay the working man less because meh, we don't really have to pay them when we can get a convict from the state to essentially do it for free."

People were suffering, and not just the convicts. Those people had a right to be angry about it.

Thankfully, the Coal Creek Wars ended with the arrest of several of the coal mine owners for corruption and shit and led to the downfall of then Tennessee State Governor, John P. Buchanan. The protestors didn't really win the day, though, until the state of Tennessee refused to renew the convict labor contracts with the coal mines, at which point this thing finally got put to bed, but not without a substantial cost in lives lost and men maimed.

Thus, we come to how exactly Drummond Bridge managed to become haunted in the first place.

Well, in order to have any sort of haunting begin, it has to start with someone's death. Unfortunately, that death came by way of the demise of twenty-five-year-old Richard Drummond, for which the bridge gets its name.

Richard Drummond was a coal miner during the Coal Wars and, amid the skirmishes, was accused of murdering one of the militiamen sent to put down the employee uprising.

Instead of waiting for the law to get involved, one man, a member of the militia, took matters into his own hands. He took Richard Drummond to the railroad bridge used almost exclusively to transport coal and mining supplies back in the day, tossed a rope over one of the steel supports for the bridge, and hoisted Richard up off his feet to strangle.

It was a horrible way to go, and rumor has it that it honestly had nothing to do with Richard killing one of the militiamen at all, but rather this murder was *personal*. The product of a love triangle. The man who hung Richard and Richard having been involved with the same woman.

Eventually, sixteen officers and enlisted men of the Tennessee state militia were arrested and tried for the murder of Richard Drummond, the trial lasting for weeks, in an exhaustive preponderance of the evidence. But really, more because the whole damn state was walking on eggshells about what Drummond's coworkers and fellow miners would do if they were dissatisfied with the verdict the judge handed down.

I haven't been able to find anywhere what that verdict was, much to my annoyance.

Whether guilty or not guilty, Richard's ghost doesn't seem to be satisfied, as he still haunts the bridge today.

Visitors to the now-defunct railway bridge, which is slowly being reclaimed by nature, say that they hear the gasping, struggling, wheezing breaths of poor Richard as he struggles to breathe with the noose around his neck. Others report the shadowy, spectral image of a man pacing back and forth along the railway bridge above where he was hung.

Local animals and people alike tend to avoid this bridge, but when I visited, there was apparent evidence of plenty of local teens or young adults using this as a place to drink. The area was littered with beer cans, which was disappointing, to say the least.

Seriously, clean up after yourself, people! You pack it in, bring a damn trash bag and pack it out!

It is said that local cattle avoid going near the bridge and that dogs refuse to cross it, while some visitors report the atmosphere around the bridge as just feeling *off*.

It was a particularly bright and sunny day when my friend Ellie and I went to check it out. We parked and walked along both the bridge and along the water beneath it, which I warn you, the railroad ties comprising the bridge are spongy and covered in moss. I don't recommend walking on them at all. Seriously, I am your paranormal mother and I'm saying do as I say, not as I do, on this one. Keep yourself safe!

We didn't encounter anything out of the ordinary when we were there, but that doesn't mean no one has.

Indeed, in one account that I've found and read, it was a sunny and idyllic October day when the narrator and her friend stopped for waffles on their way down to the Smoky Mountains. Another patron of the restaurant overheard their conversation about the paranormal and asked to sit with them. The girls consented, and this woman told them that if they were headed to the Smokies for some paranormal and a spooky fix, that they should make Drummond Bridge one of their stops. The girls listened to what she had to say and enthusiastically agreed.

They set back off on their journey, making Drummond Bridge one of their new stops.

They said that before they even saw it, they felt a sort of strange sensation as they drove into its general vicinity – like the air was somehow charged or electrified. They also found it odd that even though it was mid-autumn, none of the trees in the area seemed to be losing their leaves. They were in a riot of fall color, just no leaves were falling.

They sat a while when they found the bridge, on some nearby rocks or stumps, and listened, but nothing occurred. As they left, the girl telling the story could *swear* she heard a faint, "Wait!" As she turned around, she said that she had seen a golden ball of light shoot behind one of the trees standing near the bridge.

Something she didn't tell her friend, for she knew her friend scared easily.

HISTORIC SCOTT COUNTY JAIL, HUNTSVILLE

I almost missed this one, my little strangelings. No, really. As I was researching this book and struggling for places to come up with for Southeast Tennessee, this one came up on one of those random "9 haunted places you just have to visit in Tennessee" lists. While there are a shit ton of those lists all over the internet, (believe me, I've read through the same locations over and over until my eyes bled), this one really only came up on one of them – and I didn't encounter it at all in any of my other book research, so you just know I had to cover it.

In operation from 1904 until 2008, this jail served the local community of Huntsville, TN, for over 104 years before a newer, more modern facility was built nearby, with even better surveillance capabilities, etc. During its tenure as a functioning jail, it gathered quite a few stories and ghostly legends. These tales were brought back to life when, in 2021, the jail was leased by a pair of women who put in the work to turn this historic site in their county into a working living history museum.

It wasn't long before the building's past came back to haunt things, however.

There are a couple of incidents that stand out among the jail's history as an explanation as to who some of the spirits still present are:

The first concerns a Mr. Richard Ellis. Mr. Ellis was the Scott County Sheriff and has become quite a bright spot in the jail's storied past. It was the height of the era in America known as Prohibition, which ran from January 17th, 1920, until December 5th, 1933. Just a quick recap on that: the prohibition period in American history was the period in time when the manufacture and sale of alcoholic beverages were strictly forbidden, and the whole of the country was forced to surprise their livers by drinking water.

It was miserable for the average American, and illegal operations were at an all-time high. From moonshiners and bootleggers up in the hollers and hills distilling things on the down-low to speakeasies and underground bars. Again, all of it was strictly forbidden by the 18th Amendment to the United States Constitution, and it was something Sheriff Ellis prided himself on being a hard-ass about.

It was the night of August 11th, 1925, that Sheriff Ellis had caught himself a ner'er-do-well. He was bringing him in to booking, coming up the street out in front of the jail, likely before making the turn to bring his quarry in through the back as was the custom at the time. Little did Sheriff Ellis know that two men lay in wait beneath a tree at the edge of the woods near the jail. These men unceremoniously ambushed Sheriff Ellis just outside the building, right there in the open street in the middle of town! The gunman fired three times at the lawman's back. Mr. Ellis took a shotgun blast to the back of his head and was killed instantly. The prisoner he had apprehended didn't even try to escape but rather sounded the alarm, screaming that the sheriff had been shot and killed.

Unfortunately for Sheriff Ellis, he would receive no justice for this heinous and cowardly crime committed against him.

You see, at the very same time, two youths were being held within the Scott County Jail on criminal charges of murdering an old man by crushing his skull in a brutal attack with a hammer or an axe.

Folks were mighty upset with them, and an angry mob had formed. There was talk of storming the jail and teaching the two young men a permanent lesson – what many around here affectionately refer to as "Mountain Justice."

To that end, there were two extra guards posted at the jail, standing guard on the jail's roof.

When they heard the three shots that took out Sheriff Ellis, they thought it was the mob coming and thus didn't mobilize right away. It wasn't until the prisoner in Ellis's custody started hollerin' that the sheriff had been shot and was dead.

The mob that was about to accost the jail turned into a posse, hell-bent on apprehending the killer responsible for Sheriff Ellis's cold-blooded murder, but it was too late. The delay in anyone getting started on the hunt was enough to allow the two killers to slide down the embankment behind the jail and make their escape down the river that flowed behind it.

No one was ever caught or tried in the murderous ambush of the preacher-turned-lawman, and to this day, it is one of Scott County's greatest unsolved mysteries.

One thing that no one argued was the fact that Ellis was murdered by the local moonshiners and bootleggers in the area. Ellis took a hard line against them and was the recipient of many threats on his life for destroying stills and arresting locals making their living on the manufacture, distribution, and sale of alcohol.

It locked these men into a permanent game of cat and mouse with law enforcement at the time, and it was a game that, by all reports, Richard Ellis was winning. Winning to the point that someone made a very permanent solution of what would amount to a temporary problem, as it would only be eight more years before the manufacture, distribution, and sale of alcohol became legal again, and prohibition went down in American history as an epic failure.

Fast forward from then to now...

It is said that you can still catch Mr. Ellis performing his duties within the Scott County Jail today. His echoing footsteps can be heard moving up and down hallways and stairs when no other living soul is present, closing doors left open that are meant to be secured, and sometimes, just sometimes, you can hear him softly singing or whistling to himself as he drifts up the hall in accordance with carrying out his duties.

I asked Kristy Sumner of Soul Sisters Paranormal and one-half of the dynamic duo that runs the Historic Scott County Jail as a museum and paranormal research beacon some questions about that.

Specifically, I asked how anyone knew for sure that it was Sheriff Ellis, and to that, I received the answer: "...we do suspect that the spirit of Sheriff R.D. Ellis still lingers at the jail, as various questions and trigger items directed toward him seem to get interesting results, from unexplained pictures of shadow figures to an assortment of activity on various pieces of 'paranormal investigation equipment.'"

As for that "paranormal investigative equipment," that's a pretty broad umbrella. Without further clarification, I can think of several items that may have yielded some positive results in identifying a specific specter in the jail – from a captured EVP or Electronic Voice Phenomenon to a Yes/No Question & Answer session utilizing a K2 or other electromagnetic field detector. There are several options out there for making communication with the other side easier than ever. However, the dead are people, too, and everything must be taken with a grain of salt when it comes to people – especially of the criminally enterprising sort. Liars gonna lie is what I'm saying here, my little strangelings. Still, if there was any reason for a spirit like Mr. R.D. Ellis to hang around, his unsolved ambush and cold-blooded murder right outside the jail's doors is undoubtedly a big one.

Sherrif Ellis isn't the only spirit to linger here, however.

The year was 1933. A man by the name of Jerome Boyatt had allegedly killed a couple of lawmen, Sheriff G.B. Winningham and his son, Floyd Winningham, up over in Pickett, Kentucky, and had gone on the run.

It's a story eerily similar to Harvey Winchester's, which we'll get to in a moment here.

Story goes that both Winninghams were headed out to a disturbance at a rail yard, and as they approached a boxcar, Jerome Boyatt is said to have fired on the two and killed them.

After allegedly killing the two lawmen, Boyatt immediately went on the run, and he ran right back home to Scott County, Tennessee. It was a couple of weeks between the slaying and when he turned up at the Scott County Jail to turn himself in, but that's how that went. I think he was smart in one regard, knowing that he wouldn't get anything close to a fair trial in Kentucky and bolting for home.

Unfortunately, the only trial Boyatt would receive was in the court of public opinion. He only made it eight days in the jail before an angry mob of 25 men wearing bags over their heads, in a furor, stormed the Scott County Jail. They pistol-whipped the jailer, stole his keys, and marched right on up to the third floor where Boyatt and another man, Harvey Winchester, were being held.

They hauled Boyatt and Winchester into the street, cutting the phone lines to the jail on their way out, and stuffed the pair into one of four cars that all swiftly left the scene.

Now, about Winchester…

Harvey Winchester was in the Scott County Jail, awaiting trial for the alleged murder of Namon Terry, aged 40, and the sheriff of Scott County's son, a boy by the name of Esker Thompson, who was tragically only 19 himself at the time of his death.

The Chattanooga Times wrote the story up. Here's the CliffsNotes' version:

Apparently, on the night of November 26th, 1932, the Scott County Sheriff, J.M. Thompson, had received word that four men were blocking the highway at Bear Creek Junction. He then deputized Namon Terry and his own son, Esker Thompson, and sent the duo out to the scene.

No sooner did they reach the location in question, it was later reported that Harvey Winchester, also 19, allegedly opened fire on the newly minted lawmen, hitting them both. The sheriff's son, Esker Thompson, returned fire before going down but didn't manage to hit any of the other three that were there, nor his assailant, Winchester.

Winchester got away, but his freedom was short-lived. He was apprehended and had been in the Scott County Jail about five months before Boyatt showed up.

Again, only eight days after Boyatt became a resident of the Scott County Jail, the mob showed up, and they got themselves a two-for-one deal on alleged cop killers when they stormed the jail, kidnapped the pair, and disappeared up the road in their four vehicles.

My little stranglings, I am here to tell you, after extensive research on the subject, that lynching is such a small and innocuous-sounding word. That it is far, far more than a man taking a few hits before being strung up to hang by an angry mob. It is a subject we will get into the gory details of in the next book we have planned in this series, and it's not for the faint of heart. Also, to be clear, the lynchings from the Scott

County Jail were not based on race (as all the inmates mentioned were White), but rather it was based on a belief that "mountain justice" was swifter than going through the channels of the proper legal system.

Now, all that being said, there are no reported gory details of what happened to these two men, other than the condition their bodies were found in.

It was the next morning after their abduction when the bodies of Winchester and Boyatt were found.

Winchester was found first, by a man named Archie Lewallen, who just happened to be walking down the roadside where the men's bodies were dumped the night previous.

Winchester's body was found fully clothed with six bullets in his back.

There were several extra articles of clothing found near his corpse, and a further search was conducted. Several hours later, law enforcement found Boyatt's naked body further along in the woods, about forty yards from Winchester's corpse. He had been stripped and likewise had taken seven bullets total to the back of his body, one of them to the back of his head.

To me, it is a bit of a wonder that Jerome Boyatt is the one held primarily responsible for the bulk of the paranormal activity taking place on the jail's third floor. After all, he only spent eight days in jail on the maximum-security floor. Winchester, on the other hand, was incarcerated there much longer, at over five months.

I asked Kristy and her partner in spooky, Miranda, about experiences they may or may not have personally had on the third floor, and this is what she had to say.

Kristy had the following to say: *"Yes, I have personally seen a shadow image on the 3rd floor of the jail. It was one morning when I was opening up, and as I turned into the jailer's walk, I saw a black shadow standing in the corner. I stared at it for a few seconds and then it zipped down the hallway and out of my view."*

Meanwhile, Miranda had this to impart: *"The jail has several shadows and apparitions that have been seen, and I have experienced several of them. I personally saw an apparition of a man on the 2nd floor as I was closing up after a paranormal investigation. I typically work the night investigations,* and I like to lock the cells and clean up so that everything is ready for Kristy when she opens the jail for the day tours. The teams leave at 3 a.m. and this task usually takes me about 20 minutes to do. I had just cleaned the three 2nd-floor cells, and upon walking into the 2nd-floor kitchen, the reflection of a man standing in the doorway caught my eye as I looked at the glass on a display case. It took a few seconds to register what I was seeing. When I realized it was a man with a mustache, wearing a low hat, I turned and looked behind me, but there was nobody there. Shadows are very commonly seen on all floors of the jail. I don't know exactly who this man was, but I believe he was either an inmate from back when the 2nd floor was used as maximum-security or a former sheriff helping me 'make the nightly rounds.'"

Personally, I wonder if it was Sheriff Ellis, who had been noted to whistle or sing while wandering through the jail as it is today. Here's Miranda again with something eerily similar to these reports:

"Between Kristy and I, we are always at the jail and have had quite a few personal experiences. We often hear footsteps, disembodied voices, and see shadows on all three floors. After one of our first paranormal investigation teams left for the night, I was downstairs cleaning up and gathering my things to leave. As I walked from the 1st-floor gift shop to the booking room to drop off some paperwork, I heard what sounded like a deep, rich male voice humming on the 2nd-floor stairwell. I wasn't sure if I was actually hearing what I thought I was hearing until he stopped humming, cleared his throat, and continued on for another 3-4 seconds. After leaving, I texted Kristy the timestamps and asked if she would review the security camera footage to see if it captured the hum. The cameras were too far away to catch the hum, but what it did capture were two voices... One saying, 'there she is' and 'not so loud next time.' We believe that these two spirits were intelligently talking about what just happened and were telling the humming spirit on the stairs not to be so loud next time."

Hang tight, my little strangelings, there's more, but first, I'd like to take a moment to make an aside.

Boyatt and Winchester are not the only men to have been lynched by an angry mob here. There have actually been seven lynchings over the Scott County Jail's long and storied history – more than enough traumatic deaths of some individuals who were clearly and, on the record, as being rather nasty in life. Again, it's important to note before anyone tries to go there, these lynchings were not racially motivated. All of them happened to be White men, but that doesn't preclude the level of violence involved with their deaths, and as we all know – the more violent and traumatic the death, the more likelihood there is for a haunting to result.

That being said, you don't go to jail for being nice… you go to jail, most of the time, for doing some fucked-up shit. Likewise, you don't have an angry mob descend on your head and lynch you if what you are accused of isn't some of the worst of the worst.

Which brings me to a point I would like to make.

When it comes to haunted locations such as jails, hospitals, asylums, or prisons, there are a lot of big and heavy emotions being bandied about. Especially when it comes to things that people have done to land in such places, and in the case of jails, prisons, or asylums specifically – incarceration or involuntary commitment does something to a person.

Anger, sadness, hopelessness, guilt, depression – it's a veritable melting pot of mixed negative emotions and, as such, there are certain people and entities who thrive on that kind of energy.

It's sorely tempting to believe that just about every place like this is home to a gaggle of demons – but guess what?

People can be horrible people without demons coming into play. Horrible people die every day, and they keep on keeping on, being dreadful in the afterlife. Some of these assholes probably think it's mighty damn funny pulling the living's leg and giving them a ration of shit – lying and getting them to believe they're really bigger, badder, and more important than they are.

To that end, I'm here to tell you – not everything is a thing.

I honestly like to call it the Warren Effect, which probably gives you a pretty strong indication of where my feelings lie on the subject of the Warrens. I know, I know, they have a pretty big fan base – but I don't like them. It seems that everywhere they went, the cry became "It's a demon!" and I'm sorry, I can't chalk every bit of nasty in the world up to there being a demon involved. Actually, the rate of demonic anything is actually pretty rare.

My point is, there's no need to sensationalize a place like this, by screaming bloody murder that there are demons everywhere, when there has been absolutely zero evidence to suggest it.

What there are, and were, are people accused of and who were guilty of committing horrible acts when they were alive. Whether out of some brain chemistry malfunction or personality disorder is neither here nor there. People do awful shit, and it has nothing to do with heaven, hell, or anything in between, especially in the case of the Scott County Jail.

Why am I saying this? Because the Historic Scott County Jail is an amazing example of a location that has pure, unexplained activity, where the word "demon" does not need to enter the vocabulary. In fact, paranormal investigators and YouTubers are encouraged and welcomed to investigate during the night but must sign waivers acknowledging that "demons" are not present in the Historic Scott County Jail. Were there bad inmates? Yes. Do the spirits of those inmates occasionally say things like "get out," "go away," or "I hate you!"? Yes. But that is the nature of a place that has seen so much violent history. The current ownership embraces its paranormal investigators. In fact, the revenue generated by overnight guests has allowed the building to be preserved and its history to be displayed for the general public to see. But make no mistake, Miranda and Kristy are staunch defenders of the building, its history, and its paranormal inhabitants.

Just a point that Kristy, Miranda, and I had to make – and this is my book, so again, I do what I want! The three of us are in total agreement on this, so I absolutely didn't mind lobbing this grenade. The joys of self-publishing, am I right?

Anyway, I've beat this dead horse enough, and my point stands. These were some bad people that were incarcerated here, awaiting transport or trial – and just like any other energy, negative energy can, and will, linger. It doesn't make it special. It doesn't mean it automatically becomes demonic. It just is what it is. Bad people become bad ghosts; good people become Casper. It really is just that easy.

At any rate, some of that energy is still here and for sure scary, but there has been no indication of the demonic whatsoever.

Now that I've made that abundantly clear, I'd like to go back to another story from Miranda:

"In 2014, as the jail sat vacant, I was invited by a local officer to investigate it. During that initial investigation, I captured evidence of a female in the drunk tank. We heard disembodied sobbing as well as captured EVPs of what sounded like a distraught woman. It was quite an active night! When I approached Kristy about going into this business endeavor, I knew the jail was haunted from the stories I had heard and what I experienced firsthand on that investigation."

"The jail housed both men and women during its operation. Early on, after the 3rd floor's construction, women were housed on the second floor. Then, in the '90s, they were moved to a section on the 3rd floor. A disembodied voice of a woman can often be heard saying "help" on the 2nd floor. We've also captured several names of women who were held on the 3rd floor in the designated women's maximum-security cell."

One of the more chilling things noted about the jail has come from the 9-1-1 call center's dispatchers across the street.

While the museum's hours typically run from around 11 a.m. to 4 p.m., the 9-1-1 call center is a 24/7 and 366-day-a-year operation. (Yes, I'm including leap year days in that count. There's no rest for these civil servants.)

Kristy, one of the museum's owners, told me on my visit that she has, on more than one occasion, come into work to open the museum while a dispatcher has been outside taking a smoke or fresh-air break from the call center.

The operators have told the museum personnel that they were well aware that no one was in the jail the night before, but nevertheless, they heard screaming coming from the third floor. Other times, they report shadowy figures moving behind the windows up there. In either case, it is such a common occurrence that no one even bats an eye about it locally anymore.

Back to Kristy's own words:

"In addition to the shadow figure that I mentioned above, it is very common for both Miranda and I to hear footsteps, whistling, and disembodied voices coming from all three levels of the jail when we are alone in the building. These are all common both during the day and during the night. In addi-

tion, our security cameras have captured doors opening, and our jail mascot, Celly the Jail Cat, sometimes seems to act as if she is interacting with something that we cannot see. Various pieces of electronic equipment also seem to indicate that some type of energy is present in the jail, as Miranda, myself, and other paranormal investigators all have various accounts of this occurring."

The Old Historic Scott County Jail is paranormal investigative friendly, my little strangelings. It's a delight to live in this region, as there are several locations like it.

Like so many of those places that will follow, however, the Scott County Jail needs the funds to keep it in tip-top shape and running smoothly. The lights must be kept on, repairs to HVAC units and roofing must be done, and so they have to put a price tag on things. Still, as far as that goes, they've kept that price tag extremely reasonable.

To book your flashlight tour, guided ghost hunt, or paranormal investigation with this hidden gem, you can go to their website at: https://www.historicscottcojail.com/ for their hours of operation, booking, and contact information should you have any further questions about pricing tiers and private parties over public tours.

I can attest that the staff here are friendly, more than reasonable, and accommodating and it's great. Just like anywhere else, asking permission, remaining polite, and following the rules aren't that hard and will net you a better experience more often than not.

If this spot isn't on your haunted location bucket list, I strongly advocate that you add it! You won't be sorry.

Brushy Mountain State Penitentiary, Petros

I had a hard time deciding whether Brushy Mountain State Pen is more Northeast Tennessee or Central Tennessee and decided to split the difference by making it the end of the line for the section on Northeast going into Central East.

It's fitting because this prison was known throughout its tenure as being fully operational as *the end of the line* for many.

The website for Brushy Mountain State Pen and its current iteration as a tourist attraction touts that the "Gates of Hell" first opened in 1896.

It's not lying. Brushy Mountain was the state of Tennessee's first maximum-security prison and, throughout its tenure as a working prison, was known both for housing the worst of the worst when it came to violent men, rapists, and murderers. For many of them serving 200-years-plus sentences, it quickly earned its aforementioned moniker of *the end of the line*. Now Brushy wasn't just known as the *end of the line* for the weighty sentences far outstripping the average human lifespan, but it was also known for the fact that prison violence was commonplace and ruthless; prison justice meted out here even though executions were not.

Slow of natural causes such as disease, illness, and old age, or quick due to prison violence, Brushy Mountain is estimated to have seen over 10,000 deaths within its walls and fences over its tenure as an operational correctional and penal facility.

That's a whole fuck of a lot of death to be attributed to one location.

Back to the very beginning, though. As I said before, it was 1896 and just after the Coal Mine Wars of East Tennessee, that Brushy Mountain State Penitentiary opened its doors. It was built, in part, to hold some of the more violent rioters and coal miners who participated in the uprising against their employers – ironically, the same employers who were stripping the senior coal miners of both work and pay in order to put prisoners to work as virtual slave labor. They had a deal with the state in order to score uninitiated and underqualified workers on the cheap by paying them pennies on the dollar and essentially leasing them and their forced labor from the state of Tennessee in the form of prison work programs.

Makes me wonder how many of the seasoned coal miners wound up within Brushy's walls, and how many of them were forced back into their old jobs for mere pennies before the Coal Mine Wars were essentially over and the work programs through the Tennessee Department of Corrections were halted.

Gotta love big business. Not much has really changed, has it?

At any rate, Brushy's tenure as a fully functional and operational prison spanned over 113 years until its doors were permanently shut, and the last inmate was either released or moved to another Tennessee prison in 2009.

That's a long damn time, my little strangelings. And, as we all know, there's nothing romantic about prison life, and Brushy housed the absolute worst of the worst throughout its years of operation.

Men like James Earl Ray, the man who assassinated Dr. Martin Luther King Jr. in Memphis, Tennessee, in 1968.

Ray was stabbed twenty-two times in the year of my birth, 1981, within Brushy's walls. He didn't die there, though. No, he was removed from Brushy in 1992 and relocated to a facility in Nashville, Tennessee, and died there six years later.

Very rarely do you get to look into the face of true evil, but when Brushy was operational, it held prisoner the sheer embodiment of evil in a man by the name of Paul Dennis Reid.

He's a spree killer they dubbed the Fast-Food Killer for his penchant of robbing and killing the teens and twenty-somethings working when he'd happened to hit the joint. It was in the late 1990s, and the killings were both brutal and heartbreaking. So much so, that he was slapped with seven death sentences – the most handed down in Tennessee State history.

Unfortunately, he died of pneumonia in the Morgan County Correctional Complex in 2013 after Brushy closed.

Brushy Mountain was also home to Byron (Low Tax) Looper, a politician who stupidly changed his middle name to (Low Tax) parentheses and all. He was a blowhard who swore up and down he would eliminate political corruption in Putnam County, TN, all the while being as corrupt as they come himself. It was during an election for Putnam County that Byron the blowhard decided it would be a good idea to blow *extra* hard when he went to his political opponent's home and farm and blew his head off.

Like, dude, just drop out of the race, you gobshite.

Anyway, this was in 1998, and like many murdering douchecanoes of yesteryear, he found himself, likewise, imprisoned within Brushy's walls. He was somewhere around 33 when he murdered Senator Tommy Burke. He died in the Morgan County Correctional Complex at age 48 from a heart condition in 2013, right along with the Fast-Food Killer mentioned above. It surprises me that he even had one – a heart, that is.

So, A.J., if all of these guys died in Morgan County or Nashville, or whatever – how does that make Brushy haunted?

Well, my little strangelings, I'm glad you never asked – because these are just three of the more infamous inmates that Brushy housed. After 113 years in operation, there are a lot more men than just these three that passed through Brushy's gates and lived in its tight cells.

Not to mention, just because you die somewhere else doesn't mean you haunt where you died. Some hauntings occur in a residual aspect, other intelligent hauntings happen to be where the person spent the most of their time in their life, or perhaps they haunt a location that they had a permanent tie to with unfinished business...

The fact of the matter is, we don't know *who precisely* haunts Brushy Mountain with how many people, both prisoners and correctional staff, have passed through the building over its lifespan.

I was just trying to give you examples of a few of the low-lifers that were imprisoned there.

What we're all really here for, though, is what happens *after* death, and to that end, I'll tell you a little personal story I had in August of 2023 at Brushy Mountain State Penitentiary.

After Brushy closed in 2009, the land and the prison were purchased to turn it into a sort of interesting little touristy complex. The prison still squats at the top of a hill, surrounded by the steep pitch of forested mountains around three sides. It's an imposing sight as you roll up to what is now the gift shop, distillery, and restaurant that's been built lower down on the property.

Here, you can buy a drink, have a bite, and listen to music – and also buy your ticket to head on up to the prison for your historical or paranormal tour, should you so choose.

On the day I was there, I wasn't there for any of those things.

I was asked by a haunt actor friend of mine to help facilitate a photo shoot for a haunt actor friend of theirs on Brushy's grounds. Something that didn't happen due to some misfortune and miscommunications, but that is neither here nor there.

This was a solid month and a half to two months before I purchased Eliza, my 2020 Nissan Rogue, and I was still driving Ruby, my 2013 Jeep Patriot.

I was parked at the top of the hill, the prison at my back, nose pointed down the wide, sweeping driveway, watching for my haunt actors to arrive. There was absolutely *no* phone signal up there – which was fine. They knew where I was at.

It started to rain, the patter falling softly – and there was no wind. I happened to look up from my book, and out of the corner of my eye, I watched the antenna on the passenger side of my Jeep pull down, arching as though someone had hooked it with their finger and pulled it down before *thwack! Whip-whap, whip-whap, whip-whap* – it was as though the invisible hand had let go, sending the antenna whipping back and forth on its own.

My little strangelings, I am telling you; it was *not* raining hard enough for an errant raindrop to somehow cause that violent of a motion in the antennae. Nor was there anything else out there to cause it. No birds, no critters, no other living soul except little ol' me.

My friends eventually did show up to fetch me to a different location, and as of yet, I haven't been back to Brushy. But before I'd gone up that way and had my very own weird little experience, I did talk to the woman who was running the tasting counter of the gift shop portion of the new building on the property and asked her if she had any experiences.

She told me, "Down here? Oh, yeah. All the time." She went on to regale me with tales of apporting items behind the distillery counter. Things disappearing, only to suddenly reappear as though they'd never been touched or showing up in odd places that there was no way they could get there.

For example, she said that she was opening a bottle of something and dropped the cap among the other bottles – heard the cap plink off of the glass of another bottle in the rack and went searching for it diligently but couldn't find it and didn't want to keep the guests at the tasting counter waiting. She poured, she chatted with them amicably, and when they decided to purchase – she rang them up, and when the register drawer popped – there was her bottle cap in one of the change wells.

Another often reported activity in the distillery and restaurant that concerns the restrooms in that building.

Toilets will flush, faucets will turn on, and the hand blowers *especially* get going when no one is there to trigger them, oftentimes refusing to work for no discernible reason when someone *is* there and needing them. (Ghosts got jokes.)

There's a more sinister story when it comes to the restroom shenanigans in the distillery/restaurant.

It happened back when the building was still being worked on and hadn't quite opened to the public yet. One of the owners, a woman, went to use the ladies' room, and she shut herself into a stall. She was doing her business when she heard distinctly male and heavy footsteps outside the bathroom stall she was in. She hurriedly finished what she was doing and steeled herself for a fight, but when she exited the stall – there was no one there. There *was*, however, a heavy, uneasy presence within the restroom, and she felt distinctly as though she was being watched.

She rushed through washing her hands and raced out of the restroom without even drying them, so pervasive were the bad vibes.

Brushy has been featured on a couple of paranormal investigative shows. *Ghost Asylum* with the investigative group, The Tennessee Wraith Chasers, as well as on *Destination Fear*.

You know I watched both of them and took copious notes about the reported activity within the prison's walls.

I'm going to CliffsNotes it here because this section is liable to run on into oblivion and you guys into boredom if I do a whole-ass detailed breakdown – and why? Let's just skip to the good part.

One of the historical stories told by a former inmate that served time at Brushy when it was in operation on *Ghost Asylum* concerned a man who was pretty damn diminutive in stature, being under five feet tall. His name was Jack Jett, and he was a nasty piece of work with some serious small-man syndrome and a mouth that was prone to writing checks that his ass couldn't cash. He pissed off the wrong people, as most types like this are wont to do, and ended up getting shanked to death.

The former inmate telling the story said it happened just outside C Block and that the man took the shiv right to the side of his throat, the improvised blade going clean through his neck, tapping a major artery or vein. It was a gory scene, blood shooting out of his *eyes* and mouth, Jack bleeding out before anyone could even attempt to help him. Not that they could get close. The inmate who had stabbed him in the neck was going absolute *ham* on poor Jack, stabbing him a further eighteen to nineteen times.

Another story was related by a former correctional officer of the facility, about how she was tasked along with several other COs to sit in the dark of the prison's movie theater with about 200 of the inmates, all watching movies… She said that one time, a man jumped up out of his seat and went running past her, clutching his throat, which had been laid open from ear to ear in a gruesome slit.

No further information was given on whether this inmate survived or died from the attack, but it's a pretty damn good indication of what went on daily at the prison when it was in operation. Indeed, it was estimated that a body dropped at least once a week within the prison walls and yards for each year it was open – fifty-two weeks in a year, one hundred and thirteen years in operation… that math leaves quite a bit to be desired when the estimate is ten thousand or more dead… at that rate, it was significantly *more* than just one a week. I suppose, though, one per week from *violence* is a decent estimate.

Still, all that aside, you can easily see why prisons like Brushy are haunted AF. Emphasis on the *AF*.

During the course of the investigation on *Ghost Asylum*, one of the investigators claimed to have discovered a hole burned into the hem of his tee shirt like a cigarette or a cigar had been held against it. This was at the same time a piece of their equipment blurted out the name *Jack*, and a little further in the show, it was revealed that Jack Jett smoked stogies or cigars…

It all seems more than a bit contrived for ratings to me, but I'll let you be the judge if you watch the show yourself.

Some of the activity reported in the prison itself includes shadowy figures moving within cells and along catwalks, disembodied voices, and the sound of slamming cell doors and locking mechanisms clicking home. Phantom smells of cigarette and cigar smoke can sometimes be smelled. Apparitions have been seen of inmates and correctional officers alike. Most of all, is the pervasive feeling of a presence unseen. Of malevolence and violence, just beneath the surface, a creeping sensation that leaves the living feeling uneasy, that kind of signal you get from your lizard brain that you're being stalked, that you're prey, and that you'd better get the hell out of there if you know what's good for you.

Electronic equipment such as digital voice recorders, flashlights, and cameras have been known to fail. Their batteries going from full to empty in the blink of an eye – which doesn't surprise me and likely doesn't surprise the seasoned paranormal investigators and enthusiasts reading this. For those of you not in the know, it's because the spirits present likely have sapped that energy in a bid to make a push to break through the veil. To make something move or to get their voice to be heard. To manifest in some corporeal or physical way... in the case of a place as dark and steeped in violence as Brushy, I'd imagine to attempt to physically harm the living by scratching, pulling hair, or on clothing, or even giving an opportune shove while someone goes up or down one of the prison's many staircases.

People have reported feeling intensely negative emotions inside the prison walls. Things like anger and a misplaced incendiary rage. Others have reported feeling a deep depression or sense of loss. Sadness, hopelessness, and an overwhelming sense of fear or dread.

Perhaps these feelings resonate from the very stone walls and metal bars of this place. After 113 years of exposure to these feelings, I can only imagine their echo seeping from the very layers of institutional colors of paint, the cracks between the bricks, and up through the cement floors.

Now, one thing that *Destination Fear* had going for them that *Ghost Asylum* did not, which I was interested to see how the prison treated them, was a *woman* on the team.

During the course of the *Destination Fear* episode, we learned more about the brutal history behind the prison – about the rapes, murders, assaults, and cruelty behind its walls, up to and including the hole or what are the solitary confinement cells. Men were kept here indefinitely until they were rendered blind from too much time spent in the dark. An act of unspeakable cruelty that has left its mark indefinitely here. More importantly, we learned more about specific entities within the prison.

The landowner and one of the former landowners of the prison call one, in particular, *the creeper*, and they say it's mostly held within the prison's old auditorium. They say it's a shadow-like figure, dark, almost an absence of light or a manifestation of the dark where light goes to die, and it crawls and slithers and, well, *creeps* its way across the floor at you along its belly.

The auditorium is where they showed movies to the inmate population. As you'll recall, there was the firsthand account from a CO in the *Ghost Asylum* episode where she recounted an inmate having their throat cut while the lights were low and a film played.

Another area of concern is D Block on the second floor, where a general manager reports that she was physically scratched to the point that blood was drawn on her arm.

During the explorations of the prison by the *Destination Fear* crew, loud slamming and bumping were heard emanating from inside the locked auditorium, the supposed lair of the entity known as *the creeper*. Crew members reported feeling dizzy in parts of the prison and in the hospital portion of the prison, and large temperature drops and fluctuations accompanied those uneasy and heavy feelings.

When the crew found their way back around and down into the auditorium on the other side of the locked door, they all took a seat and went quiet. Footsteps were heard, and one of the investigators started having trouble with their throat and breathing.

On D Block or Death Row, which is separate from the main building of the prison, the team found all of the cramped cells open. Scratching sounds and shuffling were heard, with no discernible origin.

In the last building, or the hole, the team found carvings in the concrete walls. Disembodied voices were heard. Thumping and banging emanating from up above them had them running to check things out.

They, of course, found nothing.

Later, the team broke apart and went their separate ways. A practice I do not advocate doing *at all* for safety reasons.

The team member down in the hole thought he saw the head and shoulders of a shadow person peek at him from behind a door and heard a disembodied voice call out to him. A huge crashing noise caused him to scream like a little girl, which didn't honestly impress me much, even if I probably would have done the same thing.

Another team member, while up in the hospital wing, was disconcerted by rapping and three consecutive and intentional-sounding knocks.

The rest of the episode devolved into a whole lot of screaming, whining, and crying when their equipment gave them exactly what they asked of it and what it was designed to do, which I found to be more than a bit silly… but overall, what it *did* do for me was give me a deep desire to return to Brushy myself to check things out.

So, I did.

Just so happened I returned on the wrong day, but that was okay – I still got a juicy firsthand account or two from Sarah Seiber at the prison's ticketing window.

The first personal experience Sarah shared with me took place in the kitchen of The Warden's Table Restaurant, which is combined with the gift shop, and the first building you come to as you drive onto the property.

She said it was after hours, and she was in the kitchen alone when she heard a man's voice say her name, "Sarah." She, of course, turned around, this way and that, but saw no one.

She also said this didn't happen once but twice, on two distinctly separate occasions.

That was enough to raise my eyebrows, but the story she told me *next* really got me excited. She said she's been at Brushy for six years now, and aside from the voice calling her name down at The Warden's Table, which used to be the prison's old maintenance building before being retrofitted and upgraded to restaurant and retail space, she had *another* experience just a few weeks back when taking tickets up at the prison itself for the recent 2024 Travis Tritt concert that was held there.

She said she was sitting, and her husband happened to be helping work the event with her, so when someone came up behind her and slipped their arms around her middle, she thought nothing of it, likewise, when they rested their chin on her shoulder. Except when she turned to talk to her husband? You guessed it. No one was there.

Later, when she saw him, she asked him, "Honey, was that you?" and he shrugged and told her he had no idea what she was talking about. He hadn't been anywhere near the ticketing area.

While I was there, another employee gave me the number for Brushy's Paranormal Research Coordinator, Jaime Brock. Unfortunately, Jaime wasn't there the day I was, but she asked if I could be there the next day, a Saturday when she would be in.

I told her enthusiastically, "yes!" and dragged everything I had written about Brushy with me thus far, eager for her to correct any misconceptions or details that I'd been misinformed about. What's more, I desperately wanted to gather any more firsthand experiences she wanted to share with me in her own words. I'm kind of a paranormally greedy ho – I fully admit it. I want to give the best, most accurate depiction of a place I can put on the page for you guys, and I love to do it when I have the full cooperation of the people to live, work, and love the location as much as they do to dedicate so much of themselves to it.

To that end, I sat down with Jaime on the following sunny, if muggy, Saturday in the breezy open area of what was once the old prison yard under a shade-giving pop-up tent.

I let her read what I'd written so far from all the sources that had been readily available to me thus far, waiting for the inevitable chuckles at the things that were hammed up for television or were just plain wrong – it happens – and I was an equal mix of pleasantly surprised and a wee bit chagrinned when she said that most of it was right, but some stories were *wildly* off base – something she assured me wasn't my fault, but the story about the women's room? There was more to it than that, and it was told to me inaccurately – but you know what? That's okay! Because she was *there when it happened*, and she proceeded to set me straight!

This is what she had to say…

There was much more to the bathroom story than what I'd been told. She said that the wife of the owner had gone into the women's room in the newly built giftshop, distillery tasting area, and restaurant The Warden's Table. It wasn't open to the public yet at the time. She went into the ladies' room, picked a stall at random, and sat down to do her business – and it was *as she was doing her business,* some invisible force savagely yanked her hair, forcing her head all the way back.

She cried out, quickly got up, and left the restroom.

I mean, the only silver lining to that is if you're going to piss yourself, it's a good thing to already be on the pot, I guess – I know if it were me, I'd be getting into some damn fisticuffs with the ghost of whatever past.

No, sir! Not cool!

She also let me know that the hand dryers going off in the women's restroom at The Warden's Table were especially extra now, considering they were unhooked from their power source. So, if you're in there, and they go off – it really is a *holy crap* moment. Likewise, if you're trying to use them and they don't work when you try them – that's why.

Mostly, she went into a deeper understanding of the history of Brushy – making certain that I understood its sheer unfairness and brutality.

About how many of the men incarcerated here were incarcerated not on any actual *crimes* committed – but out of sheer pettiness. For example, there were men incarcerated at Brushy for extended stints of hard labor for lying, for *dancing*, black men are on record as having been incarcerated here for, and I shit you not, *sassing a white man*.

She went on to point out that Brushy was a bastion of cruelty and had always been intended to be – how the building was intentionally built in the design of an upside-down cross, the stone for its walls quarried out of the mountain that sits behind it and how for a long time, the prison was little more than a work colony – men forced into hard labor day in and day out mining coal direct form mines surrounding the property on which Brushy sits.

These men were slave labor. Mercilessly beaten when they didn't meet their quota of coal – which was often, as the goalposts were consistently moved to remain just out of reach. Men were crippled from this back-breaking manual labor just as much as they were from the beatings.

The original prison didn't even have *walls*, my little strangelings. The prison officers opted to shoot any men daring to try to escape in the back instead.

Here at Brushy, there wasn't even any peace in death.

Over two thousand men were buried here – many of their family members never even told or given the option to claim their bodies and have them buried elsewhere.

Adding particular egregious insult to injury, many of these men who identified as Christian were buried in western-facing graves. It is the Christian tradition to bury the faithful facing East to face the direction in which Christ is to return – the men who toiled and died in Brushy weren't even given that. Just a further insult, a further *fuck you* by the prison officials to beat these men down spiritually and emotionally, as well as the physical beatings they endured here. A way of ensuring they knew, beyond a shadow of any doubt, that they were *not worthy*.

While caskets were built on-site for these men on the property, they were built in a uniform one-size-fits-all approach. If you were a man over six feet tall, it wasn't just enough to break your legs and fold you – no, they hacked them off.

Jaime had one theory as to why this was done, and it is steeped into old Appalachian superstition and lore – she figures that the people of the time believed that if you hacked off the body's legs, it would keep them down in their grave. I don't think it was meant in a *literal* sense, like with zombies or vampires – but it was a thing done in a figurative sense to keep their spirits tied down.

I asked about that, and Jaime assured me – there were several ghosts recognized throughout Brushy's tenure of operation. One happened to be one of her own kin. You see, Jaime Brock's family had once owned the land that Brushy sits on, and it was promised, at one point, to be returned to her family line – something that, of course, never happened. Still, she says she is grateful that her family line is still very much involved in the goings-on at Brushy. Her son, one of the youngest legal master distillers of moonshine in the state, runs the distillery on-site.

The irony of how many men were incarcerated within Brushy's walls and behind its bars for that very thing, only for it to come full circle after its closure to become a distillery of fine spirits today.

I digress.

Her ancestor is the only known *female* ghost at Brushy, and she was a young woman by the name of Bonnie. Barely seventeen when she died in the 1800s before Brushy Mountain Penitentiary was even thought of – she apparently, according to family lore, died of appendicitis.

Her apparition is sometimes seen in the yard, mostly, and has pretty much been *the* prison ghost for its entire tenure.

She isn't the only member of Jaime Brock's line to perish here. One of Jaime's uncles was decapitated by an inmate with a shovel and, to date, is the only prison guard interred here on Brushy's land.

He's not the only one, either – decapitations, that is.

It seemed to be a violent theme within Brushy's walls as there are *several* decapitations on the prison's records. Everything from violent altercations like the ones mentioned above about Jack Jett and being stabbed in the neck, or the other inmate whose throat was slashed in the auditorium on movie night.

Jaime let me know the inmate whose throat was slashed in the auditorium didn't make it. He collapsed, asked for one last cigarette before he died, but perished before it could be brought to him. She says that his spirit still lingers and that he is fairly active in and around the auditorium.

That led me to ask about Jack, and she *did* confirm that Jack was indeed murdered on the property in the manner that was described – except it happened in the yard, not outside D Block as it was said on the show – no, Jack Jett's *killer* was shanked to death in the same manner as Jack, two weeks after Jack's murder and *his* death was the one to occur outside D Block.

I blinked and said, 'holy shit' – so the estimation of one to two bodies dropping per week from violence sounded like it was true!

Jaime confirmed this and said it wasn't just violence, either.

In 1918, the flu pandemic took its toll, and in the 1930s, there was an outbreak of tuberculosis, otherwise known as *the consumption* or *the white death*. Not only did these men go untreated for these diseases, but she also said that at one point, 95 percent of the Black inmate population at Brushy were left to suffer from untreated syphilis.

If you've never looked up how syphilis affects a person in the later stages of the disease, I invite you to pause in your reading and do a Google on that right now – spoiler alert – it's a really fucking bad way to go.

There are more than a couple of mass graves on Brushy's property from these epidemics that swept through the prison population. Some of them just now being uncovered through ongoing renovations and construction on the property.

I had to sit back and soak it all in for a minute. Suddenly, the description of *the Gates to Hell opened in 1896*, didn't seem like such a touristy and kitschy tagline anymore.

I asked about the broader list of things to go on supernaturally here at Brushy, what she might think caused this place to be so exponentially supercharged above and beyond just the absolute horror show that went on here day in and day out. Jaime nodded and said something along the lines of "funny you should say that…"

The distillery is fed by natural spring water that comes up through the mountain and has all but flooded a few of the old coal mines in the prison's hillsides. Brushy sits on an underground lake, she explained. Not as large or grand as the Lost Sea Adventure underground cavern and lake further to the south in Sweetwater, TN, but an underground lake, nonetheless. There's also a lot of limestone around and in the hillsides rising around Brushy. She also said if that wasn't enough, that a major fault line ran somewhere through the region the prison was built on, and that might have something to do with it too.

Again, it's wild and a lot to take in. I said that was a lot of energy being stored up and spit out around here and she agreed.

"That's why there's always something going on around this place," she said.

From doors slamming – or at least the sound of them – even when the door that *supposedly* slammed has been frozen open for years, to knocking, rapping, voices, screaming, whistling, singing – *oh, the singing!*

Jaime lit up about that one and said there are times that you can hear old work songs being sung by what she is sure to have been Black inmates. Hymns almost melodic and sweet to the ear. Snatches of recordings of this singing have been caught on tape, but other times, you can hear it with your naked ear, drifting on a summer's breeze.

It's one of the nicer sounds you can hear, and it isn't the only thing heard, either. There's Indigenous chanting that can sometimes be heard from an era long before the prison was ever conceived of. Long before white settlers ever came to this area.

Then there is the ringing. Loud, insistent, and droning on and on – as though a rotary phone was ringing damn near off the hook with no one present to answer – except there hasn't been any type of phone except for cell phones on the property since the closure of the prison in 2009. Even then, the only way a cell phone works on the property is by connecting to the Wi-Fi on-site. There is literally *no* signal in these hills in and around Petros.

I asked what else went on, and she said, "Oh, ghosts got jokes – my boys are pranksters."

She told me about a time that her shoes were stolen and how they went missing for over *two months,* only to reappear out of the blue one day, exactly where she had last left them.

She also had a funny story about a night she had used chocolate as a trigger object.

I asked what she meant.

She said they had great success luring entities out to interact with things such as whiskey, cigars, cigarettes, and especially *chocolate* – some things the inmates especially missed.

She said that one night, she was at the prison and happened to have a chocolate bar. She was recording an EVP session and enjoying her chocolate bar, saying out loud to any entities nearby, "Mmm, don't you wish you had some chocolate?" trying to engage a response.

She fully admits it was a bit of a dick move – *but* it would end up being one of the more profound paranormal experiences she would have with the prison, but not until the next morning at home.

She said that the next morning, she and her sister needed to head to the prison, and it was a super nice day, but by golly – she woke up *starving* that morning.

It was too nice of a day to pass up driving in with her side-by-side all-terrain vehicle, and so she and her sister hopped in. She was buckling up, telling her sister, "Man, I'm fucking *starving*," and upon starting the vehicle up, her own voice boomed out of the speaker system via Bluetooth connection, *"Mmm, don't you wish you had some chocolate?"*

Her sister demanded, "How did you just do that?" and Jaime, startled, declared, "I didn't!"

She was firmly convinced one of 'her boys' had followed her home and couldn't pass up the chance to rag her back for her little stunt of the night before.

She spoke with fondness over some of the spirits that still remained at Brushy, like the one she said she liked to call 'Pa-paw.' He's been seen quite a few times as a full-bodied apparition in and around the prison and has a penchant for whistling. She said he looks like an older gentleman who could honestly be anybody's pa-paw, hence the name.

She looked a bit wistful and said, "There's a ten-year-old boy who was incarcerated here for stealing a loaf of bread. In fact, there were more children than just him. They were known as the 'children of Brushy' and were all thirteen and under."

I couldn't imagine – can you? Children. In that type of environment.

To say that Brushy Mountain is a rollercoaster of emotions when going through its history and stories is an understatement, my little strangelings – and I could wax eloquent for hours upon hours about its history and the stories told to me. We sat in the breezy shade of that tent, just inside the yard's sully port, for *four hours...* but honestly, there are a shit ton of other haunted locations I need to get to in this book, and if I told you everything, it would deprive you of the wonder of experiencing some of these things yourself.

Brushy Mountain is a fully operational living history museum and offers both historical and paranormal tours – both private and public. You can book your own, or visit during its opening hours by visiting its website at https://tourbrushy.com/

Tell them your paranormal auntie A.J. sent you – and hopefully, when you get there, you'll see copies of this book somewhere in their gift shop.

CENTRAL EAST TENNESSEE

I consider my move from the Pacific Northwest to Knoxville my midlife crisis. No joke, I did little better than throw a dart at a map in initially making my decision to start looking at houses here. The more I looked into it, the more I thought about it, the more pros started racking up in the pro column than cons in the con column. Mostly, I was just excited to not live under the threat of a volcano burying my ass in a lahar – which if you don't know what that is, it would essentially be a fun-filled adventure in dying by both drowning *and* burning to death – *because why dread one, when you can dread both?*

Anyway – when I moved here, I really didn't know much about Knoxville other than it was a college town, home of the University of Tennessee, and the Volunteers (whatever that meant – and yes, I have since figured that out!) I also learned that it hadn't been hit by a tornado in a minute – and by a minute, I mean like twenty-plus years. That was another big thing for me – it was in a valley, and the tornadoes tended to keep their shenanigans on the plateau. I really like living in places that aren't inclined toward crazy natural disasters. I'm really not that much of an adventurist or thrill seeker in weather-related madness. I did the whole struck-by-lightning thing when I was eleven. That was more than enough for me…

What I didn't know when I moved here, which turned out to be a most pleasant surprise, is just how much weird shit happens around these parts.

No, really.

Knoxville's history is wild. Its ghost stories even wilder. They say truth can be stranger than fiction, and I swear to God, when it comes to Knoxville and its history, the people who lived here heard that and said, "here, hold my beer and watch this."

Seriously, without much further ado, let's go down that rabbit hole, shall we? Hang on to your sensibilities. Things are about to get progressively more violent and weird as we move along here.

-A.J. Mason

OLD HISTORIC HARRIMAN HOSPITAL, HARRIMAN

The Old Historic Harriman Hospital really is only just a wee bit south of Brushy Mountain, straddling that line between North and Central East Tennessee to the point it could really be in either, much like Brushy. So, to that end, since Brushy was the 'end of the line' for our section of the northern part of the region covered in this book, I decided a hospital, being a birthplace just as much as a death place for so many, it made sense to put it at the front of the line for this section.

It's the circle of life, death, and hauntings, my little strangelings. It almost feels criminal having three very cool, very haunted, and very investigable locations (should you have the coin) so close together in the same book, but that's just how the dice rolled, and here we are.

Old Historic Harriman Hospital was built in 1938 but opened in 1939 and sits where the Tennessee, Clinch, and Emory rivers all converge – which is a whole fuck of a lot of moving water and where there's a lot of a life force like that, there's bound to be hauntings. It doesn't hurt that the hospital sits on the land formerly occupied by the Cumberland Hotel, which burned and, yes, sadly, had casualties as a result of that fire.

It wasn't long after the hospital opened, just a few short years, before it was quickly at capacity and ground was broken for the first of many expansions. By the 1990s, a final four-story expansion was built, giving the hospital a new lease on life, but alas – it just wasn't capable of keeping up with the times and technology, and in 2013, it closed for good.

In 2022, it was purchased by the same folks who saved the Old South Pittsburg Hospital from destruction – which will be talked about further into this book, as it's one of our haunted locations in the southern portion of the East Tennessee region.

Today, it serves as a Paranormal Investigator's wet dream, as does its big sister hospital in South Pittsburg, Tennessee – having been preserved as a Paranormal Research Facility, inviting investigators from around the world to conduct their own investigations for a fee – which I think is fantastic.

I'll have more on that at the end of this entry, but first, let's get into the ghosts.

First up, we have Nurse Joanna of the legendary A3. The A3 at Old Historic Harriman Hospital served as the ICU and Cardiac Care Unit of the hospital, and Joanna was one of its dedicated nurses. So much so that she told her coworkers that when she died, she'd be back to make her rounds. She loved her job and the hospital and called it her home away from home.

Unfortunately, one of the only sure things in life is death, and Joanna passed away suddenly from cardiac arrest at entirely too young of an age herself, but she was as good as her word. There have been multiple reports from when the hospital was operational of Joanna being seen in the A3, making her rounds, and caring for patients as though she'd never left. Her spirit endures to this day, so it would seem, even though the hospital has long since closed down.

Not all of the spirits or entities at Old Historic Harriman are sugar and spice and everything nice like Joanna, however.

One entity seen on the grounds while the hospital was still in operation seemed innocuous enough. He was said to be a man in black, with a wide-brimmed hat and a ribbon tied like a tie around his neck. One of the hospital workers saw him as he waited for one of the elevators on the ground floor. She said that he gave her an eerie feeling and that she still politely acknowledged him with a polite nod of her head.

She said he nodded back, the elevator doors opened, and he got on. She continued down the hallway, and about the time the elevator reached the second floor, there was a code blue called there. The patient did not survive, and to this day, the woman maintains that she saw death that day, coming to collect the soul of the patient who had been about to die under the hospital's care.

Between its closure in 2013 and its purchase in 2022, few dared to venture inside the old building, but that didn't stop the paranormal activity from being recognized from the outside. People would sometimes report that they could see people inside the hospital through the windows during its time lying fallow.

One of the most active areas of the hospital post-closure is in the ICU, located on the fourth floor. Here, there is a nurse who, to put it both politely and bluntly, is more than a little territorial and protective of her patients. This entity is *not* Joanna but rather another nurse who worked in Harriman Hospital for most of her life before passing away at a ripe old age.

Still, in her afterlife, she is a staunch rule follower, and if you don't belong in the ICU, she will let you know in no uncertain terms that it's not visiting hours, and it's time for you to leave.

The only other floor considered more active is the second floor of the hospital, where the psychiatric ward was located.

Full-bodied apparitions and shadow figures have been seen here. Shadow figures that are so incredibly lifelike that people have been afraid there's been a living intruder in the hospital hallways and rooms on this floor, and it's been so far from disconcerting it's gone into full-blown terrifying. Especially considering those same shadow figures appear to like to *follow* you.

Figures that are so lifelike have been seen on this floor loitering around the nurses' station that the living have chased after them, only for the figure to duck into one of the many rooms along the hallways with only one way in or out of them to vanish into thin air.

THERE ARE reports from inside that there is some fierce poltergeist activity, with objects being violently thrown or strewn about. Worse yet are the reports from people who have been physically pushed against walls or out of rooms.

It's a lot, my little strangelings. Like, a lot, a lot. That's what we're all here for though, no?

I've saved the best part for last, though.

This historic hospital is paranormal-investigative friendly, and should you have enough coin or can pull together enough coin to purchase a ticket, you and your friends can investigate this place between the hours of six p.m. and four a.m. For booking information, please go to https://oldhistoricharrimanhospital.com/ and if you do go, and you happen to experience something? Don't forget to hit me up through the contact information I've left for you at the back of this book. I would love to read or hear your story.

COCKE COUNTY MEMORIAL BUILDING, NEWPORT

The Cocke County Memorial Building in Newport, Tennessee, is one of the town's more storied buildings. Built in 1931, it began life as a traveling stop for US military troops and has mostly served some militaristic purpose ever since. From a traveling stop to an Army National Guard Armory, to a VFW Hall in much later years.

It doesn't look like much after sustaining some serious storm damage from a hopping tornado, with little to no money in the town's coffers for repair. These days, it's been closed to the public for a *while*. That being said, it's got a bright future ahead of it as renovations have begun to turn it into a combination living and event space.

I had no idea about this place. Not that it existed, not that it was haunted, and never even would have known about it if I hadn't met a local man, born and raised in Newport, Tennessee, to tell me about it.

So, to that end, a big thank you to Cassidy! You're the real MVP for this one!

When Cassidy told me about the Memorial Building, I shrugged and immediately asked, "Why's it haunted?"

I expected a lot of things, my little strangelings, but a plane crash wasn't at all on the list.

We're going to take it way, way, back to July 9th, 1964, when United Airlines passenger Flight #823 crash-landed in the woods in nearby Parrottsville, TN.

Parrottsville is an even smaller town than Newport, which was the next biggest – and didn't have anything by way of a hospital or large enough building to process the crash – read, store the bodies.

There was evidence that there had been some kind of an explosion on board the plane, which had brought it down. The biggest piece of evidence to back up the theory was an eye witness who reported seeing a passenger fall from the plane – no one believed the man, until he led them into the woods, up the hillside from the bulk of the crash, about a mile away to where they did, indeed, find the body of one of the passengers that had fallen, by medical examination's best estimate, some 300 feet; only to have his fall broken by the trees.

His body was burned and charred, which led investigators to the conclusion that some kind of fiery cataclysmic event had happened on board the plane while it was still in the sky – a fire or an explosion of some kind in the passenger compartment, precipitating the crash.

In the end, thirty-nine people lost their lives on Delta Flight 823. Thirty-five passengers and four crew.

That's a lot of bodies in one event, my little strangelings, and Parrotsville, recovering from a devastating fire *and* tornado damage at the time, was not equipped to deal with that many – no facilities nearby honestly were...

Enter the Cocke County Memorial Building in nearby Newport, TN.

It was the armory for the Army National Guard at the time of the crash, and the mangled bodies and pieces of the passengers and crew were brought there as it'd been set up as an emergency makeshift morgue and investigation headquarters.

My little strangelings, I warn you, there's a lot of yuck about to come – not necessarily of the blood, gore, and rot variety but of the lowest of the low when it comes to greed and the callous behavior of mankind.

For one, it is a widely believed and accepted theory that Flight 823 was brought down on *purpose*. That the passengers and crew that died were collateral damage in a wider conspiracy to stop two or three whistleblowers on board from spilling the tea about how military facilities in Oak Ridge, Tennessee, were supposedly, knowingly, doing nefarious things that were resulting in locals living in and around Oak Ridge becoming sick and dying.

Supposedly, there were scientists and engineers on board the flight, as well as scads of documentation about testing or some other such super-secret squirrel bullshit going on in the military installation at Oak Ridge. Documentation and testimony outbound from Knoxville telling all about really fucking awful environmental impact going on and being ignored and allowed to continue by higher-ups running or a part of Secret City.

Adding to the grossness of this even being conjured up as a conspiracy was the fact that two of the passengers on board were a little boy and a little girl. The girl, aged only twelve, and an unaccompanied minor on the flight. The boy, not only just five years old but also fighting for his life in a battle with leukemia.

After the crash, the FAA needed to do something with the bodies and quick. It was July in East Tennessee – things weren't exactly going to stay fresh for long.

Enter Cocke County Coroner, Everett Roberts. Being both the County Coroner *and* a local undertaker, he saw a lucrative opportunity in the crash – *the fucking ghoul!* He was a local undertaker as well as the County Coroner, and his decision to bring the crash victims to Cocke County and Newport was a purely financially driven one with a heaping tablespoon of bitter official corruption to add to the wicked brew. You see, as the County Coroner, he made some kind of official bullshit rubberstamped ruling that the bodies couldn't be removed from Cocke County for their embalming or whatever. Making it so the families of the victims *had* to use local undertaker resources for their loved ones before they could be transported home for burial.

Guess who was all too glad to step out of his official coroner role and into his humble undertaker's skin to be of service to said families at considerable financial gain to himself?

Gross, right?

To that end, when Everett Roberts arrived at the crash site, which bordered the edge of Cocke County and the next county over, he sweet talked the FAA into using the Memorial Building as their makeshift morgue. Temporary air conditioning was installed, and the bodies were moved quickly – a team of pathologists and coroners at the ready to autopsy the passengers and crew and to piece together the parts of the victims as best they could.

Identifying each person and matching them to the passenger manifest became of paramount importance in the wake of the tragedy and this diligent team of rock stars worked around the clock to get those people to their loved ones and their bodies back home.

The plane went down on July 9th, and they had every last victim identified by the 15th. That's dedication, but I'm also getting ahead of myself a little bit.

One eyewitness to the macabre scene was a fresh recruit, having just graduated mortuary school and taken to helping his father with the family funeral home out of Newport. He arrived at the crash scene in an ambulance to help transport remains back to the Memorial Building and said that he personally witnessed a man putting out fires with a fire extinguisher while simultaneously groping through crash victims' pockets for loose money or change.

The thing that makes this exceptionally horrifying is that of the thirty-nine souls on board, only the one man's body was found intact. The man who had fallen only to be caught up by the trees. Everyone else was in pieces and burned – so badly, that identification was *shockingly* achieved in only just six days. Like I said, the pathologists and investigators working around the clock were absolute rock stars in an era that was well before DNA was even a known thing.

When I say these people were dedicated, I meant it – but that didn't stop the fact that they had enough unidentifiable pieces left to fill a casket that was interred in nearby Union Cemetery there in Newport. A mass grave of sorts that would go unmarked until sometime in 2014.

With this event as shockingly awful and bad as it's been described in various articles, it's honestly no wonder at all to me that the Memorial Building is haunted.

I went to check it out for myself a few weeks past the anniversary of the tragedy itself. It was July 31st when I went – the building long closed down, again, due to severe storm damage to the roof.

I found two caretakers hard at work on-site, mowing and weed-eating the grass surrounding the building, and I asked about the building.

All the two gentlemen would say was that it was haunted, but they wouldn't share their personal stories, and for good reason – the building is in the midst of being renovated now to serve as a combination private residence – being divided into apartments to serve women and children looking to start over after certain trials and tribulations. The other portion of the building, specifically the gymnasium portion with all of its original wood, is being restored for use as a meeting and event space.

You can see why they might look unkindly at anyone poking around about any hauntings. One of the two gentlemen in particular fully admitted to having experienced *something* in the building but he wouldn't give me specifics without getting the okay from his boss's boss – which I completely understand and am on board with.

It's not worth their jobs if talking to me would have brought the ire of the people who sign their paychecks.

Again, all they would say was "yup, it's haunted alright," and the one gentleman in particular said to me, "I would tell you all about it, but everyone I work with knows my stories about this place, and it wouldn't take long for any of 'em to figure out I was the one who talked by reading your book. I don't want any trouble."

Perfectly understood, my man – but I will share what I observed, and that was, simply put, *this guy was hella uncomfortable.*

I wish like hell he could share what it is he encountered in the building, because he *definitely, without a doubt,* without a single *shadow* of a doubt in my mind, encountered *something* in that building.

I asked if he could narrow down what kind of activity for me. Something seen, something heard, something smelled, something felt?

He looked me dead in the eye and, with the grimmest expression that was thoroughly spooked, said to me, "Yes. You think it, you imagine it, it's happened here – but that's all I'm gonna say."

I didn't press further – I just vowed to dig deeper and harder to find out just what had gone on in there.

This is what you've all waited for – the ghosts of the Old Memorial Building and Flight #823.

Surface findings on the hauntings say that it is predominantly a child's ghost that haunts the premises. That a child's apparition has been seen in the gym area on the stage. That a ball or balls had been introduced to the interior of the building and that the balls would move or relocate from room to room, from the upstairs to the downstairs and every which way in between when the building was locked up and deserted.

Someone would come to do work one day, and the ball would be upstairs. They'd lock up and leave, return the next morning, unlock the doors, and go in to find the ball in the gymnasium.

That sort of thing.

In 2017, the show Ghost Brothers investigated the Cocke County Memorial Building. I found out about it from one of the firefighters located in the firehouse behind the building. I saw the hose boy sitting outside and wandered up to ask if he or any of the other hose boys in residence had ever seen or heard anything in or around the building.

That's when he told me that several years prior, he had been one of the individuals to accommodate the Ghost Brother's investigation of the space, and while he wouldn't admit to seeing or hearing anything personally, he did tell me he did *not* like going into the building at night – that it had thoroughly given him the creeps and he didn't like it.

I thanked him, gave him my card, and he said he would pass it along to all the other hose boys and that if they had any stories, they might reach out. They did not, and it is the first time I ever remember in the history of ever thinking disappointedly, "fuck the fire department." An honorary distinction usually held for the police. (Oh, come on. I couldn't resist making the joke. That was funny.)

Anyway, I went home and started writing this up – and, of course, I cued up my streaming services and hunted down the Ghost Brothers episode in question. It's Season 2, Episode 5 for anyone wondering.

I was curious if they encountered anything or not, and as I was struggling to find any actual stories other than "Yup, it's haunted alright, now please fuck off before I get in some kind of trouble," I figured it was worth watching – at least to see if I could find some meatier stories of anything happening *after* the grisly events of the plane crash.

Supposedly, a lot of shit has gone down inside the old building. Apparitions, disembodied voices, and people have even reported being touched.

Jackpot.

Stories include EVs, or Electronic Voice Phenomenon, being captured in the hallway that runs parallel to the gymnasium portion of the building. The gymnasium is the specific portion of the Cocke County Memorial Building that acted as the makeshift morgue in the weeks after the crash of Flight #823.

For those of you not in the know or new to paranormal investigation, Electronic Voice Phenomenon is a tactic employed by paranormal investigators in which they begin an audio recording in a reportedly haunted location, asking questions, leaving pauses, or just recording in the background during normal operations of an investigation. Upon playback, if you're lucky, you can sometimes capture disembodied voices within the recording that weren't heard when the investigator was physically present on the premises.

This is known as Electronic Voice Phenomenon – now if the investigator *did* hear the voices while physically present in the space or on the property, then it is just known as a disembodied voice.

In this particular instance, the EVP captured in the hallway said clearly in a female voice "I was fucking murdered!"

Within the gym, doors have slammed of their own accord, and laymen and investigators alike have reported hearing knocking sounds and noises emanating from sources that can't be humanly replicated. It's also where they have had BINGO balls thrown at them by unseen forces. I did mention the building has been a VFW and a social hub for Newport throughout its varied history, right?

Okay, cool.

The basement is considered extremely active, with people reportedly being pushed and physically assaulted by unseen hands. The words touched and chased being used as descriptors down there. Whatever is down there is considered a dark energy or entity. Disembodied voices have also been heard down there, but the strangest tale is that of an apparition of a two-foot-tall man seen in one of the defunct lockers down there.

From the bottom to the top, there's something present in every aspect of this building. The apparition of a child, specifically a little girl, being spotted in the building's attic space.

Of course, there isn't any way to discern if all or just some of these spirits are attributed to the plane crash. The building had quite a bit of life energy flowing in and around it with the hustle of military activity and all the social functions before and since the two-week period that the building was used as a makeshift morgue.

The Ghost Brothers employed many tactics during their overnight investigation of the old Memorial Building. From bringing out the old BINGO machine to see if any spirits were feeling froggy in tossing BINGO balls around to bringing in medical equipment, specifically, gurneys and body bags to potentially re-create some of the conditions during the plane crash investigation that was held there.

Some of the equipment they employed was a REM Pod, which, after almost 18 years out of the field, I confess I need to do some homework on. I'm not up on what one of those things is supposed to do.

They also had, obviously, audio and visual equipment running such as infrared night vision cameras and microphones.

At one point, while in the gymnasium, messing with the old-fashioned BINGO equipment and peppering pointed questions between drawing numbers, one of the Ghost Brothers asked, "Is anyone from the plane crash here with us?" and he got some kind of a response by way of a rather loud, rather sharp knock.

Now, obviously, I take these shows with more than just a grain of salt. I take them with an entire factory load – because what's to say they don't have a crew member off camera fucking with shit and making noises to make good television? Ratings are King, after all – and not everything is a thing.

By that, I mean, that legends and historical events aside, not every place is prone to activity, and even the most haunted locations I've visited – things might happen one night, but on others? There's nothing… to that end, I'm not saying everything about this show is manufactured to make great television – but one *does* have to wonder because, again, not everything is a thing – some things do have logical, non-paranormal explanations.

It's when you've ruled everything out that could possibly be a mundane explanation and you're left with something unexplainable that, well, you've more than likely hit paranormal pay dirt.

There I go on another soapbox digression, but hey – these things and observations are important.

Anyway, a loud knock can be heard, coming from off camera and it does seem to genuinely startle our intrepid trio of investigators.

Say that five times fast.

…you totally did, didn't you?

The investigators moved to chase down the sound and reported that it sounded like a door had slammed in another part of the building adjacent to the gymnasium – a phenomenon that was reported at the beginning of the show.

More knocking and one of the investigators swore that for a split second, he saw a shadow person standing on the stairs. He said that it was just for a split second, out of the corner of his eye – and *that*, my little strangelings, I am entirely inclined to believe, as I have seen and encountered that my very self on investigations.

Only *once* have I ever seen something straight on, but that is a story for another day.

The investigation continued with the investigators moving back through the gym, reportedly feeling nauseated and ill on their way to the attic.

I would be curious to see what, if any, EMF readings were present during that time, as consistent exposure to elevated Electromagnetic Fields has consistently yielded reports of feeling nauseated, imbalanced, and has also been known to cause riproaring headaches in more sensitive persons in the path of exposure.

Cut to the pair of investigators in the basement reporting an uneasy feeling. Like someone was staring intently at them. They ran an EVP session in the basement, the results of which were, of course, held to the very end of the show. Spoiler alert – they didn't get anything that they later talked about. Not that this entire story hasn't been some kind of a spoiler for this episode already and will continue to be to the very end.

Cut back to the other pair of investigators as they finished up in the gym and headed for the attic, where they likewise attempted to contact the children's apparitions that have been reportedly seen there. They brought with them a trigger object of a teddy bear that contained some sort of EMF detector that would cause the bear itself to light up with any fluctuations should a spirit approach.

The investigators began asking questions, when, clear as day, a child's disembodied voice called out to them from the bear, "Did you make it warm in here?"

My little strangelings, regardless of if this was real and not some farce deployed behind the scenes of the show – this one gave me chills.

If you'll recall, the plane suffered some sort of fire or explosion, causing it to crash and yeah – you see right where I'm going with this.

The yikes are off the bikes and running freely!

They asked the bear several more questions, and while the bear spit out a bunch of answers, none of them were as clearly or concisely relevant to the situation of the plane crash as that first one.

Back in the basement, the investigators running the EVP session were asking their questions when as an aside, Marcus was lamenting how he wished he had brought – both of them stuttered to a stop when they both heard, and the camera clearly picked up, a child's voice calling or screaming out either 'Marcus!' or what I think was a child calling out in the same sing-song voice "Marco!" as in Marco-Polo.

It was clearly a little girl's voice.

They investigators leaned into it, trying like hell to communicate.

Thumping and bumping, a door possibly closing stopped them mid-conversation again in the next spot in the basement.

The guest paranormal investigator local to Newport made the observation that some definite poltergeist activity was taking place and that the haunting they were dealing with was intelligent in nature – and by this point, I was definitely inclined to agree that this was intelligent over residual.

Rapping and knocking can be heard in the basement locker room with no discernible source, and everyone reported a heavy feeling down there. Movement across the floor, in another portion of the basement away from where the investigators were gathered.

A special camera was employed, and two anomalies in the form of stick figures were detected, smaller than man-sized, like the size of a child or a man with the condition of dwarfism.

Just as suddenly as the activity began in the basement, it ceased, and the investigation moved back to the main floor. A local Spiritualist was brought in and the use of a pendulum was employed.

I'll let you guys watch the show and judge that session for yourself.

Overall, I'm pretty convinced that yes, the Cocke County Memorial Building *is* haunted – but that has a whole lot less to do with a television show, and the very real discomfort and fear I saw on the building's caretaker's face, and in his eyes.

I would love to know what he saw, heard, and felt to cause that reaction. Maybe, someday, well after this book is published, I'll go back and ask.

If I'm lucky, maybe I'll get my answers.

For now, it's best to leave the Cocke County Memorial Building be. After all, its new life may be enough to lay the dead within it to final rest – and even if it isn't, it's slated for a noble purpose in becoming a private residence and the women and children it will house deserve that privacy. After all, with the plans in place for the building, they've clearly already been through enough. Perhaps their healing journey will heal the fractured psyche of the building itself and the activity will stop.

I hope so.

Ramsey House & Plantation Grounds, Knoxville

Out of all the history and ghost stories attributed to Knoxville itself, the ones surrounding the Ramsey House and Plantation grounds are probably the most straightforward and tame. Likewise, the deaths precipitating the hauntings aren't nearly as violent and wild as some of the stories further along in this book, but I digress... and I do that a lot by the way, I'm telling you to get used to it now.

Located on Thorngrove Pike, on the "Forks of the River" where the Holston & French Broad Rivers converge to form the headwaters of the Tennessee River, lies the old Ramsey House and Plantation grounds.

Built for Francis Alexander Ramsey in 1797, its commission was first made to London-trained cabinet maker, Thomas Hope, who liked to dabble in architecture as a hobby.

I'm not going to get too far up into the history of the Ramsey House, as we're all here for the ghosts, but to sum it all up the house first passed from Francis to his son, B.A. Ramsey, who then sold it to his brother, Dr. J.G.M. Ramsey, who then gifted his childhood home to *his* son as a wedding present when he had a mansion of his own built nearby.

By all accounts, the years leading up to the American Civil War were prosperous ones for the Ramsey family, but when the war came around, the Ramsey family immediately aligned themselves with the losing side of the Confederacy. It was a *fuck-around-and-find-out* moment for the Ramsey clan. One that proved disastrous for them financially and then some when the Union came to town and ended up taking over their house and the plantation grounds during their occupation of Knoxville and the surrounding area.

Dr. J.G.M. Ramsey would not only lose his two sons to the war effort, but also his own mansion containing his vast library and what can only be described as a sort of museum that was filled with Indigenous people's artifacts, which is the real tragedy here. All of it was razed and ruined during the course of the looting and burning of the home he'd had built for himself. That vast library of his turned to ashes, the artifacts he'd collected stolen, never to be seen again.

Thankfully, his childhood home of Ramsey House was spared; but as J.G.M. and his family were forced to flee the area to North Carolina, his hope of ever seeing his childhood home returned to its former glory, or to live in it ever again, seemed like it would never come to pass.

The house lay empty for some time and in the early 1870s, Dr. J.G.M. Ramsey *did* make it back to the Knoxville area, however, he would die in 1886 with the old Ramsey House still destitute and falling further into disrepair. In fact, the closest he would come to returning to his childhood was to be laid to rest alongside his parents at the nearby Lebanon in the Forks Presbyterian Church graveyard... *or was it?*

Stories have been told of a figure that looks much like J.G.M. Ramsey in life, glowering down out of the upper floor windows in either the front or the back of the house on occasion. Giving rise to the rumors that he had finally made it home, and that he dared any vandals or vagrants to come and try anything at the old house.

Indeed, Ramsey House continued to lie fallow for many years, but strangely, remained intact. Sure, windows were broken from thrown rocks and the ornately carved wooden cornices and consoles of the old homes roof had rotted away, but it was the early 1900s when the whispers and murmurs began that someone or some*thing* had been keeping worse vandals at bay – that something was in the house and should you go there, you would *not* want to meet it. Was this J.G. M. protecting his former home in death as he couldn't in life? Or was this something darker, with more malevolent intentions? We'll circle back to this, so just you hang on.

In 1927, the old Ramsey place would get its first real break since the Civil War, when the local chapter of the American Daughters of the Revolution had a stone marker placed, honoring Dr. J.G.M. Ramsey's contributions to the city of Knoxville, and noting the historical significance of the Ramsey House, which was by now over 100 years old. They had this marker placed proudly out front of the place and this marked the turning of the tide for the old Ramsey place.

It was the 1930s when the old home began changing hands between tenants and as a storage space, all the way up until in 1952, it was purchased by the Association for the Preservation of Tennessee Antiquities and thus began the long road to the home's restoration... and the ghosts of the house were finally formally met.

There are several ghosts spoken about when it comes to the Ramsey House Plantation, other than J.G.M. There is 8-year-old Billy, who is the mischievous spirit of William Bane Alexander Ramsey (the first) who I so call him the first, because the Ramsey family had a rather odd penchant, (by today's standards) of naming subsequent children in their line after older siblings to have died before they were born. Indeed, all four of Francis Ramsey's surviving children from his three wives, all bear names of older siblings that died before they were even a sparkle in their daddy's eye.

Interestingly, Billy Ramsey died of what was then known as "The Bloody Flux" or what we refer to in modern-day terms as Dysentery. Although Dysentery is quite communicable and no others in the family surrounding young Billy ever came down with the disease, so it is supposed that he may have died of something with similar symptoms such as Giardia from the nearby beaver pond that once resided on the Ramsey property.

Billy is said to visit all around the house and grounds. He's a friendly if slightly mischievous spirit, who seems to like the attention of the tour guides and museum docents. In fact, there is a gameboard of checkers in the upstairs bedroom that was once occupied by Billy and his siblings, and the tour guides when making their rounds, will move a piece, and when they return will find another piece moved in counterpoint to theirs.

They say, that if they get to winning over young Billy, too much or too often, that they will sometimes come upstairs to the checker pieces swept off the board and rolled up under the beds which they then have to retrieve. It seems Billy, like most small children, really doesn't like losing.

There are three rooms in the upstairs to the Ramsey House. As you reach the top of the stairs, Billy's room is on the left, then a room straight forward in the center of the landing, and then Billy's parent's room is on the right. On the tour that I was on, I was standing in the doorway of the parents' room, the tour guide, and two other tourists inside the eldest Ramsey's room – while my friend that had gone with me that day had gone back downstairs.

I saw a shadow out of the corner of my eye cross from the right side of the children's room go across the open doorway, and dart to the left side of the room where the checkerboard lay. There were no sounds accompanying, preceding, or proceeding the movement – just that quicker than light flicker of a boy-shaped shadow moving swiftly from one side of the room to the other so fast, I almost didn't believe my own eyes and that I'd seen it at all – but I know that I did.

I'm sure of it.

Another spirit associated with the Ramsey House resides *outside* the back door leading into the home's kitchen. He is a man in Revolutionary War era attire and is sometimes accompanied by a little white dog.

The tour guide named this ghost as Reynolds Ramsey, the father of the original owner, Francis, and grandfather to young Billy. Reynolds and his wife lived at Ramsay House in their later years with Reynolds' son Francis and his family; and today it is said that he has been asked about multiple times by tourists, volunteers, and other guides alike. Reynolds has never been seen inside the house, but always outside by the back door. Some tourists will enter the giftshop and ask about the man in costume. Other times, guide will be giving their tour and either will glimpse him or one of the tourists will, through the wavy panes of glass in the kitchen windows.

When guides step out to gather the straggling tourist – he's simply gone.

Of interest to note; our guide said that when he is glimpsed like this

– through the window from the *inside* of the house, he is sometimes seen in something *other* than his Revolutionary War era attire – and in something a touch more modern.

I've never heard of a ghost making wardrobe changes, but apparently Reynolds Ramsey does!

I asked about the little dog, and why the tour guides thought that this particular spirit was that of Reynolds, of all people, and the tour guide laughed and said something to the effect of: 'You see, Reynolds was the first pet licenser of Knox County and would walk from place to place to gather the yearly pet licensing fee for dogs from local farmers and populace. Farmers were sometimes unwilling to part with their coin, and would lie to Reynolds and say that wasn't their dog, that it was a stray and that they just kept feeding it since it came around... and if they didn't want to pay and since they refused to admit that the dog was theirs, that Reynold's Ramsey was often seen with more than a few dogs and that the Ramsey property could sometimes be quite the menagerie of local 'strays' that had been gathered by the older gentleman.'

Thus, the little white dog appearing with the older Ramsey patriarch completely tracks, not to mention it's an adorable added dimension to the Ramsey House ghostly tales.

Just inside the back door that Reynolds and his small furry companion are regularly spotted near, lies the kitchen itself. In it is the ghostly presence of an unknown woman. Perhaps the residual energy of one of the Ramsey House slaves or servants? No one really knows and there wasn't a great deal of information on this spirit.

There is, however, plenty of information on the presence of one of the former ladies of the house, Margaret Ramsey. She has been seen in the upstairs windows and on the stairs leading up to the second floor. So strong has her visage been, several times local police have been called to the house because someone believed an intruder inside! It got to the point that one of the museums managers, who lived all the way across town in West Knoxville would be called and they would check the cameras within the mansion and let the police know – "Nah, it was just Margaret – everything's fine. No need to respond or go inside."

In addition to being seen, Margaret has been *heard*. Sometimes stopping tours in their tracks so that the guide can go upstairs to investigate the sound of a woman's footsteps across the floor up there – which can be exceedingly off-putting, our tour guide claimed, adamantly assuring us that there have been entire tour groups upstairs while a tour is simultaneously being conducted downstairs and that you can hear nary a tread from the living when they're up there – but for some reason, Margaret's footsteps, when she is active, can always be heard sharp and crisp.

Then there's the story from a woman who happened to be born in the parlor of the house sometime before the home's purchase in 1952. She said that her own mother had seen a Confederate soldier in the house, usually on the stairs. The tour guide made mention that this spirit was very unfriendly and had quite the rough vocabulary. She called him Seth, and I snorted and said Seth and I would get along fucking *great*. It got a laugh, as intended, but her smile quickly faded when her thoughts went back to Seth. She went on to say that Seth was very clearly *angry* and no one knew why. I asked her why she called him Seth and she said that *several* paranormal investigations utilizing the spirit box method of communication, spread out over many years, when speaking about or trying to attempt to contact the spirit of the Confederate, would repeatedly have the name 'Seth' come up. It'd happened too many times by now, she said, for it to be merely coincidence and so that was the name they'd stuck with when it came to him.

Seth doesn't seem to be the only malevolent or unhappy spirit at the Ramsey House Plantation. You ready? Because we've officially circled back around from where we started with this one.

There is another shadow person that has been seen in the home's kitchen, and by the back cellar doors, that the docents and tour guides of Ramsey House coined the name of Mr. Big for. Mr. Big *looms*, and *menaces* to the point that in one experience, a group of archaeologists who were on the plantation's grounds and had occasion to be in the home's basement found themselves momentarily trapped there when Mr. Big manifested threateningly between them and the door.

Our tour guide didn't say how the situation resolved itself or how the archeologists managed to extricate themselves from the basement and the situation – but she did say that all of them refused to ever set foot in the home's basement ever again, and that a few even refused to return to the property altogether.

I asked if she thought if Mr. Big could be a guardian of the house or property and she said no, that she didn't think so… and then I asked if she thought that Mr. Big and the Confederate soldier known as Seth could be one and the same? To that she said it could be a possibility and that she didn't know – but that as far as Mr. Big went, I should return on a Saturday and speak with the assistant working then, as she'd had the most encounters with this entity.

So, I did.

The assistant was adamant that Seth and Mr. Big could in no way be the same entity. That Mr. Big was almost exclusively seen in the cellar and the kitchen, while Seth was *always* on the stair leading up to the second floor outside the narrow door leading to the even narrower stair that led to the cramped third-floor attic rooms. She said, that after encountering one, or the other, or *both* – you could tell, their energy was distinctly *different* from each other and there was no way they could be one and the same.

At the beginning of this story, it was strongly hinted at that it was theorized that J.G.M. Ramsey was the guardian of the old house, scaring off vandals to the point no one wanted to venture inside the mansion. Could *he* be Mr. Big?

I don't think that Mr. Big and J.G.M. Ramsey are one and the same, but I also am not one hundred percent that J.G.M. haunts the premises at all. I feel like Mr. Big has always been at Ramsey House, and that he is indeed the one responsible for frightening off the vandals and vagrants that tried to use Ramsey House in the past, but I think that people versed in the history of the home tried attributing that phenomenon to J.G.M. and the benevolence he felt toward his childhood home in wanting to return and to protect it.

By the same token, I don't believe Mr. Big's intentions are as pure. Not with how just about *everyone* who has seen the malevolent and looming shadow has described how they *felt* upon seeing him. None of them described the feeling like Mr. Big was trying to protect anything – they all used words like 'menacing,' 'looming,' and 'threatening.'

Which doesn't track for the culprit being J.G.M. I mean, why would he threaten anybody for doing what he so badly wanted to do before he died? Which was to restore his childhood home to its former livable comfort. Why threaten to do harm to the people trying to do exactly what *he* wanted to do? Which was to restore Ramsey House. I can't see him being angry at the people trying to preserve the home, study it, and who valiantly protect it for future generations to learn from it and enjoy it, not just for its age and place in history, but for the beauty of its simplistic yet sturdy construction and the materials and eye for detail that was used in its erection.

To that end, Ramsey House holds a few enigmas within its walls. Things like *who is Mr. Big?* And *who is the woman in the kitchen?* Does J.G.M. Ramsey haunt the premises at all? Who is the Confederate soldier known as Seth? Why is he in the house? What skin does he have in this afterlife game?

So yeah, there are plenty of unanswered questions about Ramsey House to fuel historians and paranormal investigators for years to come, and I highly encourage you to visit this location and to pay the nominal fee for a tour of the inside.

Who knows, you might glimpse Billy yourself, like I did – you might hear Margaret upstairs, or, if you're really lucky, you might have a paranormal experience all of your own to write your own tale about or to tell all of your friends, cementing your own place in the legends and lore surrounding this fantastic historical location and one of the first homes in Knoxville ever built.

Wouldn't that be wild?

The Bijou Theatre, Knoxville

Here's where shit starts to get wild, my little strangelings. The marquee outside the Bijou proudly proclaims the old theater to be "Knoxville's Cultural Jewel for the last 115 years" but if you know the history of the Bijou from start to finish or were a local Knoxvillian here between the 1960s and the 1980s or so – you know that's a bit, shall we say, tongue in cheek.

I'm getting ahead of myself, here.

Before the Bijou Theatre was even a theater, the building that housed it started its existence as a tavern and hotel – it's longest stint as The Lamar House Hotel for a good number of years. Still, long before that, it began life in 1817 when it was first built and introduced to the city as a hotel and tavern known as the Thomas Humes House after the man who'd built it. Humes actually died before the completion of the building, and soon after it opened, it was rented to another man who renamed it 'Archie Ray's Tavern' before taking his name off of it and simply renaming it 'Knoxville House.'

The Knoxville House had an original thirteen rooms available for rent, a bar, a ballroom, and a dining room and it quickly became something of a social mecca for the city up to and including hosting such notable guests as General Andrew Jackson himself, *before* he became the United States' seventh president but most assuredly after his amazing feats as a general during the War of 1812.

(Don't think for a minute I stan that genocidal douchebag – I just find him a fascinating historical figure for a lot of reasons. Kind of the same way I'm fascinated by serial killers – I digress… see, I told you. I'm going to do that a lot.)

The lease to Archie Ray came up in 1821 and for whatever reason, he didn't renew. Things get hazy concerning the building from then until a couple years later in 1823. We're not sure if it stayed open and operating or if it closed down, but in 1823 the hotel became managed by a man by the name of Joeseph Jackson, who also happened to be an American military general – but I don't know if he was a genocidal douchebag like Andrew or not.

Jackson would stay on and manage The Knoxville House for the next thirteen years until, in 1836, he sold it to a man by the name of James Pickett who renamed it simply to The City Hotel.

Bankrupt by 1842, Pickett sold the building and it entered a sort of limbo where it passed from one set of hands to another all the way up until 1852 when Northerner named Coleman bought it and renamed the establishment after himself. Coleman House underwent a significant expansion at this time nearly doubling its original capacity as a hotel with an all-new kitchen, several parlors, a new dining room, an added courtyard, a new ballroom, a new ladies' entrance, and the addition of a brand-new, and at the time, state-of-the-art elevator.

Fancy.

By 1857, the new and improved Coleman House Hotel was purchased by local Knoxvillian businessman William Sneed, who cunningly renamed it after wealthy New York investment banker Gazaway Bugg Lamar and The Lamar House Hotel was born.

This would become the longest running iteration of the name and the point where this hotel above any others became absolutely central to Knoxville's social scene.

Until the Civil War came along and fucked that up.

You see, surprisingly, Knoxville has just about always been a little blue dot in a sea of red politically. Even back during the days of the Civil War, most of Knoxville and the surrounding area of East Tennessee was pro-Union. (Shocked the hell out of this Pacific Northwest girl to learn that, but I guess it was mostly West and Central Tennessee that voted to peace out from the Union and secede, and it was only by one vote that they did it – one that was bought with a bribe no less... but here I go digressing again. I would say I was sorry, but this is my book and I do what I want.)

Sneed, who was staunchly Confederate, tucked tail and ran like a little bitch when the Union captured Knoxville, (which didn't take much, honestly. Most of the locals either pitched in with them or just didn't help their Confederate neighbors when the Union hit town. Still, there were a few bloody battles around these parts – we'll get into that in a minute with this story and in future ones.)

Anyway, when the Union hit Knoxville, they took a look at Lamar House and said, "Bet, that's our HQ and will work as a hospital." Okay, I'm sure they didn't say it *exactly* like that, but close enough, because that's what they did with it. Lamar House became Lamar Hospital, and Union General's Sherman and Sheridan (yes, *that* Sherman) actually used the big dining room as their war room to plot their next moves against the Confederacy.

On November 17th, 1863, there was some battle or other nearby. How do I know? Well, history books for one, but for two, it's the one that Brigadier General Sanders was mortally wounded at before being carried off to Lamar Hospital.

He was a tenacious man, and hung on, but ultimately died that night or in the wee hours of the next morning in what'd been room 11, or the bridal suite of the hotel – and he's going to be the first notable haunting of what would later become the Bijou Theatre – but we still have some history to slog our way through. I'm trying to Cliff's Notes this as much as possible without losing too much context so bear with me...

So, Sanders kicks the bucket, dying in agony on something like the second or third floor of the building, when it was a hotel. I'm sure a bunch of other soldiers didn't make it either, but we for sure know that Sanders didn't and that he died a slow, agonizing, and thus traumatic death.

It was a whole thing, okay? Not as much as a big deal as what's to come here, though, so buckle up.

Okay, war's over, right? Right. Sneed, the owner of Lamar House, slinks back to Knoxville as one of the losers and ultimately has to *sue* the US government to get his hotel back, which he does, and then, well, he does... get his hotel back, I mean; and I'm not like, one hundred percent sure it immediately went back to business as usual or whatever, but it sure seems like it.

In 1877 Rutheford B. Hayes gave a rousing speech from one of the hotel's balconies, and by all accounts, a good time was pretty much had by all right on up through the 1890s... except for that one time in the 1870s that Tom Sneed, the son of William Sneed who owned Lamar House, shot the son of a rival hotelier in the face after a drunken altercation in one of the Lamar House hallways...

Oh, yeah. Shit got real that night... Here's what happened.

It was a Tuesday, and apparently some kind of a holiday or grand ball was going on where *everyone* was pretty much toasted all to hell and drunk off their asses with no expectation of having to be in to work the next day. So, the people of Knoxville were partying *hard* at, where else, but The Lamar House Hotel.

This included Thomas Atkins, the son of a rival hotelier family who owned a hotel across and up the street from Lamar House. Thomas Atkins and Tom Sneed weren't exactly what you would call buddies, but due to their similar social standing they *did* run in some of the same circles including this weird parade dress marching corps thing that honestly gave off the vibe in its description of kind of being an ROTC thing before ROTC's were a thing.

That little footnote will be important later in that it potentially is the explanation for one of the auditory hauntings at the Bijou as it stands today, but once again, yeah, yeah, yeah – I digress; and we've already covered quite a bit that I do that a lot and that I don't care.

Anyway, Thomas Atkins was drunk, and I do mean liberally drunk, just like everyone else at this party was drunk except that Thomas Atkins was ahead of his time in that he realized, *hey, I'm thirsty, and I probably should surprise my liver with a glass of water or three tonight.* So, he's staggering through the Lamar House hallways, bumping off of walls, and his mouth is running sort of disparagingly about not being able to find a glass of water up in this joint because apparently, they legit weren't serving any that night. Only booze. Seriously.

So, Atkins is bitching about it, and rightfully so, because who *doesn't* serve water with alcohol? Apparently, the Sneed's who own The Lamar House Hotel, but of course, who should happen down the hall and hear Atkins uttering his distasteful remarks about the Lamar House? Yup. Tom Sneed, son of the Lamar House owner who basically proceeds to call Atkins a pussy for wanting water instead of a 'man's drink' like more whiskey.

I imagine Atkins said something along the lines of 'Hey, fuck you, buddy!' and a shoving match ensued, escalating to throwing hands, which ultimately led to Sneed drawing a pistol and shooting Atkins point blank in the face.

Oops.

Horrified guests ran screaming, Atkins slumped to the floor dead, and it was at that point, Sneed realized that he'd fucked up. To his credit, though, he didn't run like a little bitch like his daddy. He stood there, probably sobered up by a hell of a lot in that one instant and waited for the law to arrive.

He ended up acquitted in a court of law, but his social standing was ruined and he ended up leaving Knoxville altogether after his undeniable conviction in the court of public opinion.

Skipping back ahead to the 1890s when so many celebs, and past and present presidents had come through Lamar House, that by 1895 it was decided it needed another re-branding and was subsequently renamed The White House.

It, predictably, didn't stick and went bust by 1900 when it was auctioned off for a mere $25.00 – of course, in today's money that's still pretty much a pittance coming in at just $923.59 in 2024 money. For a whole-ass hotel building. Keep that in mind.

They tried to keep it going as a hotel from 1903 to 1904 calling it the *New* Lamar House Hotel, but it just didn't happen – but, that new owner that'd scooped it up turned that $25.00 investment into a $50,000 profit by selling the building to The Auditorium Company. (In case you're wondering, 50k in 1903 money is worth $1,763,215.91 in 2024 money. So yeah, he basically turned a thousand bucks into $1.7 million in the span of a little under four years. Good on yah, buddy. Must be nice.)

This is where things took a massive turn for the building, though.

They gutted the place and renovated what'd been a standing hotel for ninety-two years into the Jake Well's Bijou Theatre that when opened to the public in 1909 was proclaimed to be "one of the south's finest."

Now they didn't *completely* take out the hotel. They just renovated the front half into the theater. The back half remained a hotel for years to come – but that's a different story and yet remains inextricably linked to the ghosts and hauntings within the theater today so it's totally worth mentioning so as to avoid any confusion.

The history of this place gets a little rapid fire after this point so I'll spare you the bullshit and just get to the bullet points.

- 1926 the Tennessee Theater up and across the street bought the Bijou for the sole purpose of knocking it out as their competition.
- 1932 the theater portion of the Bijou became the LaConte Hotel.
- 1935 Paramount Pictures leased the building to run second string pictures that had already had their first series run at the Tennessee Theater.
- 1965 the lease by Paramount was up, and the theater became 'The Bijou Art Theater' which mainly showed porn flicks. At this time the area was seedy as fuck and the hotel behind the Bijou was rife with prostitution and vagrants. Most guys went to the porn theater, then went to the hotel in back to get a taste of the real thing. (Super gross, I know.)
- 1971 – 1973 it became a burlesque and exotic dance and novelty act venue.
- 1973 it was closed down for non-payment of rent.

It was at this point that the hotel had been shut down by court order by a judge with how bad things had gotten and due to public outcry. When the woman who actually owned the Bijou found out what it was being utilized for, she promptly donated it to a local church (as if that somehow made things better) and the church turned around and sold it off.

Thankfully, the good people of Knoxville recognized the value in the old theater building's history, among other things, and fundraising efforts began and donations started pouring in to save the venue from the wrecking ball.

And now what you've probably all skipped ahead for, the ghosts.

Today, the Bijou Theatre is a prominent performance venue for everything from bands and intimate performances to art house film festivals, to the occasional musical or play and has been fully restored as a working theater with more than a fair few ghost...

Obviously, there's Union Brigadier General William P. Sanders. Sanders reportedly haunted the hotel right up until 1908 when the portion of the hotel he haunted was demolished inside to make way for the theater. Still, his tenacious spirit supposedly prevails and has become one of the most prominent figures in the Bijou's ghost lore.

Often times, General Sanders is depicted or spoken about as a glowing white light with no earthly source that tends to appear in the theater's upper balcony just about the place where the bridal suite of the old hotel used to be. In another source, musicians playing at the Bijou have asked Bijou staff "who the guy in the uniform with the brass buttons on the 3rd floor balcony" is.

It's said that phantom sounds are the prevailing phenomenon here. Everything from echoing laughter, to applause, to footsteps running up and down stairs and even marching... Remember how I said Atkins and Sneed belonged to something like an ROTC marching parade dress crew that would participate in local parades? Awww yeah, here we are back at that. I guess they used Lamar House's courtyard and a section of stairs as their practice grounds – which accounts for the sounds of marching feet.

There's also thumping, bumping, and knocking sounds that emanate from the ceilings, floors, and walls when the theater is empty, and from time-to-time ghostly conversation as though heard from another room, quiet and indistinct can be heard.

In the second-floor ladies' room, a woman can be heard weeping, but upon investigation, no one is ever found, however this spirit manifests in a physical sense by tugging on clothing as though desperate to garner someone's, *anyone's*, attention. She's not the only one, either.

One of the ghosts of the Bijou is considered an 'unidentified male' and given the description of *his* activity – I can hazard a guess as to where he might have come from, but alas, it puts any would-be investigator no closer to garnering his identity.

Female paranormal investigators who have investigated the Bijou in the past have reported the touch of icy fingers as well as the clatter of coins on the stairs even though no dropped coins were found. One of those intrepid female investigators spent the night alone in the theater, making up a pallet to sleep on the floor. She said she settled down and felt a weight on the blankets over her and when she turned and looked behind her, she could swear there was an indentation of a head on the pillow beside hers!

I don't think this is Thomas Atkins, nor do I think it to be Brigadier General Sanders, but given that long tract of history of the theater's seedier days and the even seedier hotel attached to it, could it possibly be one of the lost or lonely souls from the theater and adjoined hotel during its less than stellar stint as a porn, prostitution, and drug riddled fleabag?

There's a certain plausibility there – but I'm afraid no way to really tell.

What I can tell you is that I finally had the occasion to head to the Bijou myself. I like to mark as many tasks as possible with as few stones as possible, and so when I finally arrived on Saturday, June 15th, 2024 for the Old Gods of Appalachia live show, I went with the intent to poke around as much as possible, to take as many photos and videos as I could get away with, and to talk to as many employees as I could without getting in the way of their duties.

I managed to talk to several ushers, and actually had the best luck with the one to show us to our seats.

I asked about the known location of Brigadier General Sanders and his appearances and he told me point blank, that it was the third level balcony area, which was currently closed for safety reasons with plans to restore it, and that any time anyone was up there, that the Brigadier General was known to tap them on the shoulder, and when they turned around, it was to see his full-bodied apparition of Sanders telling them, "You don't belong here."

Chills... for sure, but not as many chills as when I went upstairs, skipped past the merch line, and slipped through the gallery on the second floor to the oft mentioned women's restroom.

The feeling I felt up there was nothing short of *charged*. Like those plasma ball things with the pink and blue lights and when you touch the glass, the hair stands up all over – it was very much so like that. Goose flesh rising on my skin and the air feeling almost... not electric but *magnetic*.

There was something up there, my little strangelings, a definite presence – although I saw and heard nothing out of the ordinary while I was there.

I went back down, sat through the performance, which was most excellent, and at the end of the night *returned* to the same area upstairs – and even in the crowded hallway, while waiting in the long line outside the restrooms for my turn to go past the merch table for the show, it *still* had that almost magnetic charge to the air.

It was *fascinating...*

I got my merch, managed to get a photo with one of Old Gods' creators, and then myself and my companions following the directions of security and theater staff, headed for the exit. Before leaving, I paused and asked for a brief audience with the manager of the theater on staff, and murdered my final bird with that same stone and got her information to contact her later for this book.

I think she was relieved that's all I wanted and that I wasn't some wild Karen.

Who could blame her?

I contacted her the following Monday to ask about any other first-hand accounts or stories that any of the Bijou's staff might be willing to share with me.

Unfortunately, while I heard back from her, it was just to say she would pass it along to her staff to see if anyone was interested and apparently there were no takers, because I never heard anything more. Still, as far as haunted locations go, the Bijou is one of my local-to-me favorites.

BLOUNT MANSION, KNOXVILLE

This one's going to be fairly short, my little strangelings, but that's okay. Consider it a bit of a palate cleanser between the last story and the next. Something a little less heavy… anyway, let's get into it, shall we?

Sitting at the end of Gay Street on top of a bluff overlooking the Tennessee River is the oldest house in Knoxville. No, really. It's the first frame house ever built in the entire territory before Tennessee was even considered for statehood.

Built in 1792 it was intended to be the territory's governor's mansion by order of William Blount, the man for which the house still bears its name. Blount, at the time, was the governor of the territory, a position that he held for around five years. In fact, he was instrumental in Tennessee achieving statehood in 1796 and then went on to be her very first state senator…

Of course, he was also the very first state senator to ever be expelled from the assembly – but that part is neither here nor there. It is one of the reasons he was home to die in the house in 1800, though before he could ever be formally charged or tried for his alleged crimes – not that they didn't try. It's just that Blount was an affable fellow, and well liked in Knoxville by her citizens, and so when they dispatched a man to apprehend him and bring him back to the capital, he basically said 'no, not gonna fly, there's more of us than there is of you, but hey – I can appreciate you were just trying to do your job. Come on by for some supper and meet the missus.' Which is pretty much exactly what happened. He had the dude that was sent to capture him by for dinner and sent him on his way back to the capital empty handed.

Only in East Tennessee, I tell you what – and I say that with a big grin on my face. The more I read history like this, the more I feel like I belong here.

Anyway, it was too bad for Blount, but the whole kerfuffle in the capital with him pissing in their Cheerios made it so he was home on one of the many occasions that mosquito borne illnesses were sweeping through the south and in 1800, he died in the house – but interestingly, he's not the ghost that I've read about haunting the place.

The Blount Mansion is two-hundred-and-thirty-two years old as I write this, which means one thing and one thing only when you're that old – you been through some shit. So it is for any historical building, I think. In the case of the mansion, she fell into disrepair, was pulled out of it, fell back in it, and finally somewhere along the way somebody was like – *hey, we should, you know, actually preserve this damn thing. It's the oldest and very first frame house in Knoxville, if not the entirety of East Tennessee, and that should mean something!*

To that person, I say, good on yah!

Probably not so much for one of the poor bastards tasked with fixing up and maintaining the joint, though.

The story goes that it was a blustery day. The wind was kicking up and the clouds were thick and leaden, pregnant with rain and threatening a deluge any minute when a painter was finishing up one of the second-floor window sashes on the outside. He was contemplating whether to risk doing another one, or if he should call it quits for the day when a flicker of movement inside the house caught his attention. He turned, just in time to see the *top half* of a little boy exit a bedroom, float across the hall, and take himself down the stairs.

He wrapped it up right then and there, and supposedly called it a week.

I would say I couldn't blame him, but I'm the crazy bitch that would have gone in the house looking for the kid and seeing if I could make contact.

…this is a two different kinds of people moment, isn't it?

Yeah. I thought so.

CRAIGHEAD-JACKSON HOUSE, KNOXVILLE

Just right next door to Blount Mansion lies a brick house that according to local legend is ten times as haunted as Blount Mansion will ever be.

In fact, just about any time I tried to bring up Blount Mansion and get a further accounting of its ghosts I was always shot down immediately and told that Craighead-Jackson House, on the other hand, was *nuts* with activity.

Undaunted, I still covered Blount Mansion in this book, but for as active and as wild as Craighead-Jackson House is supposed to be, I haven't found much more than I did about Blount Mansion.

Built next door to Blount Mansion in 1818 by John Craighead, its tenure within the Craighead family was long lived, as far as the age of the building goes… too bad we can't say the same about the Craighead family – they all died out sometime in the late 1850s, at which point the house passed in ownership to Dr. George Jackson, who purchased the place.

I bet you're thinking that when Jackson took possession of the house, and moved his family in, is when they started noticing activity – but you'd be wrong. It was actually pretty chill. None of the Craighead clan feeling the need to hang around, apparently.

No, it was *during* Dr. Jackson's tenure of ownership that our ghost story begins, and most definitely in one of the most tragic and horrifying ways possible.

Like most rich white dudes at the time, Jackson was no stranger to owning slaves and he had at least one in a woman who ran his kitchen and did his housekeeping. Sadly, her name is lost to history and as much as I would love to give her name back, I assure you there is no listing in any historical record of what it could be.

At any rate, one of the features of the Craighead-Jackson House is that it had an indoor kitchen that was part of the main house, albeit a basement kitchen. Like earlier homes and mansions of the region, it had a large, wide kitchen hearth and fireplace. One that wasn't raised and wasn't exactly cordoned off with safety features or under regulations like many modern fireplaces today.

The story goes that somehow, some way, the cook's long skirts caught on fire. In her frantic efforts to beat out the flames, the poor woman somehow struck her head, knocking herself unconscious. Horrifyingly, she then fell more completely into the fire where she proceeded to burn to death.

It wasn't long after the woman's tragic and untimely death that strange activity began in the house, starting with the grandfather clock in the hallway on the main level functioning without any earthly means to start it. Soon, disembodied footfalls were heard on the empty basement's stairs; and finally, the inability to keep any of the home's doors locked entered the fray. Before long, the Jackson family was remarking on these activities and how unnerving they were to friends and neighbors on the Knoxville social scene.

Jackson's daughter was especially fit to be tied, and as the paranormal activity ramped up, the more unnerved the Jackson family became, until it wasn't long before they noped right the fuck out of there with all of the haste.

While the home remained forever branded with the Craghead and Jackson names, the modest brick house would transfer hands many more times over before its acquisition by the Blount Mansion Association right next door.

With plans to restore the historic home, funds were raised and a phone line was put in… and it wasn't long before both workers and members of the historical society began to notice the peculiar happenings in and around the old house themselves.

They too noticed that the doors they certainly remembered

securing would be found standing open only moments to hours later. Likewise, their conversations would be suspended, staring at one another in disbelief, as the echo of phantom footsteps reverberated through the home, centering around that lonely basement stair…

Just as soon as the phone line went in, another phenomenon was added to the home's repertoire, in that the phone would suddenly just start ringing, but when the handset was picked up, there was no one on the other end, just empty static or silence… a phantom caller.

Today the Craighead-Jackson House is sort of a part of the Blount Mansion's little historical complex and acts as an event space on the main floor. The basement is primarily used as a staging area for those events and was partially in use as a storage area and garden shed when I visited; several flowering fruit trees having been acquired and sitting before the old fireplace where the slave cook supposedly lost her life.

The second floor I was asked politely not to film, though I was allowed to go up and see it. It is under renovation and I was told its final intent was to be archive and archive office space in addition to careful museum item storage for some of Knoxville's history. It is a work in progress as of the writing of this book, and with a grand vision, which of course requires funding; so, if you find yourself in downtown Knoxville, and you stop in at the Blount Mansion and Craighead-Jackson House visitor's center, in addition to dropping the nominal fee to take the historical tour of the property, maybe leave a few extra bones in the donation bin and as always, tip your tour guide!

Even if you aren't in it for the spooky, the history is well worth it for both Blount Mansion and Craighead-Jackson House.

BAKER-PETERS HOUSE, KNOXVILLE

The batshittery continues, my little strangelings. For this one, we go back to 1840 when this two-story brick house was built by Physician Harvey Baker out near Baker's Creek when Kingston Pike was but a muddy dirt tract cut in by the passage of wagon wheels over time.

Once again, I remind you, East Tennessee was staunchly Union in the lead up to the Civil War, and that when Tennessee as a whole seceded from the Union it was pretty much by virtue of Central and West Tennessee fucking things up and outvoting the eastern third of the state... well, that and there was some bribery involved that changed a single vote and yeah, it was a whole thing – and stupid – but it happened and Knoxville and the eastern portion of the state up in the Appalachian Mountains and hills up into West Virginia were less than thrilled about it remaining pro-Union throughout the war.

Not Harvey Baker, though. Or his son Abner. They cast their lot with the losing side of the Confederacy, Baker even turning his house into a makeshift Confederate hospital where he treated the boys in gray in secret.

In short, yah boy fucked up and when the Union took Knoxville and the surrounding area in 1863, it wasn't even a day into the official occupation before he found out.

It took no time at all for pro-Union citizens of Knoxville to dime Harvey out. Not that it was honestly a big secret. Of course, Generals Sherman and Sheridan were like, 'go get 'em boys, I want him arrested' and to that end a posse of Union soldiers headed on out to Baker's house.

Let me tell you, my little strangelings, how this shit went down is *nuts*. You couldn't script it better for a damn movie.

Picture this: It's morning, Dr. Harvey Baker and his wife are making morning rounds within their house, going from pallet to pallet, cot to cot, tended wounded Confederates who are too sick or too injured to be moved.

Dr. Baker straightens up from one of the bedsides and *oh, shit*. There's a posse of Union soldiers riding into his front yard.

He tells his wife to carry on tending to the sick and he bolts out the back door, swiftly mounting his horse.

The Union soldiers sight him but they're too far to apprehend him and as Dr. Baker takes off, they do they only thing they can do to stop him – they shoot his horse out from under him.

Now somehow, some way, they bungle catching up to Dr. Baker in time, and he manages to bolt back into his house through the back door and goes running upstairs, barricading himself in one of the second-floor bedrooms.

In every account that I've read about this, the Union detachment or whatever, rushed the front porch, kicked down the front door, and stormed upstairs, pausing outside the bedroom door, and demanding loudly for Baker to surrender.

Baker, predictably, shouted a hearty refusal to surrender through the locked bedroom door he'd taken refuge behind, and me being me, I imagine it sounded a lot like "Fuck you, you Yankee bastards!" At which point the Yankee bastards dispatched to apprehend Dr. Baker decided nothing in their orders to do so said they had to bring him back *alive* and so they fired through the closed bedroom door.

One of those shots found its way right into Dr. Baker's chest, killing him instantly, if not pretty close to it.

You would think that would be it; that Dr. Baker's violent death in the house, on the property, would be more than enough cause for the place to be haunted; but no – the intrigue and this cinematic retelling doesn't stop here, my little strangelings. In my best Billie Mayes impression: *But wait, there's more!*

You see, the apple didn't fall far from the tree and fast forward to sometime after the Civil War in the midst of the Reconstruction era, and Abner Baker has returned to Knoxville just as Confederate as when he'd left and with one thing on his mind: *vengeance*.

(Seriously, why hasn't there been a movie made about this?)

There are three different accounts of how Abner Baker met his demise, and all three are more violent and gruesome than the one before it. All three of them, however, follow the same basic formula. Abner Baker started shit with a man named Hall over his father's death, either believing or knowing that Hall had either, A. been the man to dime Harvey Baker out to the Union as a Confederate doctor that was helping Confederates, or B. as one of the men who made up the posse who'd gone out to the Baker's house to make the arrest that'd subsequently ended in Abner Baker's father's death.

Whether it was option A or option B is pretty immaterial at this point in the story – either one of them get the point across. Abner believed Hall had a direct or indirect hand in his father's death and he was pissed about it.

So, on one fine September Day in 1865, Abner Baker marched his happy ass into Knoxville and one of these three scenarios went down:

#1. Abner Baker verbally started shit with Hall, a courthouse clerk, when he was at the courthouse on an unrelated matter. Words turned to Hall smacking Baker across the face with his cane, fisticuffs ensued, and Baker pulled out his gun and shot Hall in the head at which point, an angry mob scooped Baker up, dragged him to a nearby tree, and lynched him immediately without benefit of a trial.

#2. Hall was in a nearby bar, having a drink, when he spotted Baker outside the courthouse and it was *Hall* that started shit with Baker, drunk off his as and talking a big game, going out there and just started wailing on Baker with his cane, at which point Baker shot Hall in self-defense and a Unionist mob strung him up from a nearby tree in their ire.

#3 and the worst of them all, was that the man Baker went after wasn't Hall the court clerk at all, but rather was Knoxville's Postmaster General. That Abner Baker marched down to the post office with nothing but vengeance on the brain, walked in, and shot the man at point-blank range. Following this, the postmaster's friends ganged up on Abner, beat the hell out of him, tied him to a team of horses, and dragged him through Knoxville's streets until he was dead.

So yeah. Fun times in Old-Timey Knoxville, I guess.

In the grand scheme of things, it doesn't really matter which of the three stories of Abner's demise is true; they're all pretty much more violent and screwed up than the last, and definitely tick the box of *traumatic death* on the *is it haunted* checklist of criteria for any potential haunting.

I mean, you can't have a haunting without a ghost, and you can't have a ghost without someone dying, after all. It's generally accepted that the more violent and traumatic the death, that the better chance you have of getting a haunting afterward. It's just a sad fact of life, and in this case, a sad fact behind the haunting of the Bakers-Peters House because it's widely believed that both Dr. Harvey Baker *and* his son Abner remain on the premises to this day.

Let's get into it:

By all accounts past and present, the ghosts of the old home are mischievous rather than malevolent, responsible for poltergeist type activity. Objects move on their own, lights flickering, and kitchen appliances inexplicably turning themselves on or off of their own accord are just some of the things listed that I've read.

People outside the old brick house sometimes report seeing golden flickers of a kerosene or oil lamp passing behind the panes of glass from window to window and room to room. Perhaps it's Dr. Baker making nightly rounds among his wounded Confederate patients...

As for visible specters or full bodies apparitions, I ran across two written accounts. One little more than a footnote, of how there is supposedly a photograph of a male specter somewhere in the building, but it's the other one that I like best.

Back when the building was derelict, Knoxville police had been called for a supposed break in. An officer said he swept the building and apprehended a suspect somewhere on the second floor; one of the four-legged variety. There was no mention of what particular flavor of varmint it was that the officer encountered, but it was said that after shooing the perfectly normal critter out from the access point it'd come in through – a broken second floor window, the officer decided to take the time to rummage through some of the things laying around the house to put a temporary fix into place to keep the critters from returning and Knoxville PD from being called in again. A little manual labor now to spare a whole lot more paperwork later kind of a thing.

The officer said he finished blocking off the access point, and that when he turned around, there was a 'transparent gray lady' standing in the room with him with the saddest expression on her face. He said that they stood there looking at each other for a moment and that she faded away before his very eyes.

Historians think that she might be Mrs. Sherrill, the wife of the farmer who took possession of the house and surrounding fields in 1953. After Mr. Sherrill died, Mrs. Sherrill discovered that he'd set it up in his will that she be allowed to live in the house until her death, but that she wasn't to inherit it. Instead, either upon her death or her choice to vacate the home, it went to his children from a previous marriage. So, she could use it, but didn't technically own it, and thus things got sticky when it came to the upkeep of the place – and as such, it began to or continued to fall further and further into disrepair over the remainder of Mrs. Sherrill's life.

It is theorized that she appeared to the officer to possibly thank him for his repair of her home, but judging by the sad look on her face and knowing how her generation could be, I rather think she was appearing to him because she was *apologizing* for the state of the place as well as to give thanks.

CARMICHAEL INN, LOUDON

I found this one by happy accident, my little strangelings. I had to go down to the Loudon County Clerk's office to transfer the title to my trusty Jeep Patriot, Ruby, over to a friend of mine who needed her much more than I did now that I have my Nissan Rogue, Eliza.

I was lamenting the fact that I still needed a few more stories for Southeast Tennessee for this book, and my friend looked past my shoulder, pointed, and said, "Look that place up. It looks old and haunted."

I turned around to look and what I saw was a *very* old, *very* original to the town's building that now was serving as a restaurant – The Carmichael Inn, built in 1810.

With its split log cabin construction, it looked a hell of a lot older than that.

"Son of a bitch!" I cried and looked back at my friend. He grinned at me and me being the smartass I am, I said something along the lines of, "I swear to God, if this motherfucker is haunted…" as I punched it into Google on my phone.

"Oh, what? You'll thank me?" he asked laughing at me.

"Or fucking hate you," I shot back. He grinned bigger and got me then.

"Or you could just hate fuck me."

Ah, the life of being a full-time romance and erotica author. Never ever will any type of sexual innuendo go unspoken around me.

I muttered something about him threatening me with a good time when the results populated and *BINGO*.

"This motherfucker *is* haunted!" I cried.

He laughed at me, and we got into my car, but I made him drive so I could research further.

This is what I found out on the fly on our drive back home to Knoxville:

The Carmichael Inn was built in 1810 and was initially used as a stop for travelers to take the ferry to Loudon's sister city, Lenoir City before the bridge was built over the river to connect the two.

It also served as a battle post, Civil War hospital, a restaurant, a coffee house, and in its initial and much darker days before the emancipation proclamation, held salves within its basement.

Honestly, it's been a lot more shit than that in its 214-year history but those are just the bullet points.

With a history that long and far reaching as 214 years and standing tall and serving throughout the Civil War – it's not just one or two spirits housed within the old building – according to eyewitnesses and those who have both worked and lived here, there are *several*.

The main activity reported here are the quintessential classic signs of a haunting.

Disembodies voices, drawers and doors opening and closing on their own, phantom children's laughter, and cold spots are all evident here said a woman who lived in the apartment that is on the top floor.

Down in the restaurant, staff has, in the past, have complained of items disappearing and reappearing at random; a phenomenon known as apporting. One manager reported coming in to open up one morning to find all of the pictures hanging on the walls had been mysteriously re-arranged. She then walked into the dining room to find all of the chairs had been removed from the table tops where she had stacked them the night before and were now neatly pushed up under the tables – so at least the ghost or ghosts had spared her the drama of some of her opening routine.

When the building held a coffee shop, one barista who was a non-believer had an experience they would never forget. The barista in question was sent down to the basement for something and went willingly. No sweat, right? After about five or more minutes, when they didn't return, the manager sent another barista to find out what the holdup was.

When the second barista opened the door, the first came barreling out accusing the second barista of locking or holding the door closed, trapping the first barista inside and shutting off the lights for them.

The second barista had no idea what the first was talking about, and the manager had to get involved, telling the first barista that the basement door only locked with an old skeleton key – something that they didn't have access to. That no one had access to it for years and they didn't know where it was.

The first barista never said a word about it again, although they refused, from that day on, to ever go into the basement again.

Did they encounter the angry ghost or spirit of one of the slaves that had been chambered there? We'll never know.

Another day, another barista. This one came in to open up the coffee shop. She was going about her morning routine when the radio behind the counter kicked on by itself. She turned and switched it off, and it kicked on again a moment later. When she turned to switch it off again, a disembodied voice called out, "Leave it alone."

The same employee that reported this encounter also swore that she had been pushed or pinched on occasion, and that the ghostly activity was most prominent in the wee hours of the morning, just before or as the coffee shop was opening.

If I've said it before, I'll say it again, my little strangelings. I don't believe any place is more active at night than any other time during the day. I just think that any activity that is want to occur during the day is masked or missed by the hustle and bustle of daily activity and the living moving about.

One of the other reports coming from the building happens after hours when everything is closed up tight. There are reports of lights being on in the windows – but not electric lights. Something more akin to candle or lantern light.

Today, the Carmichael Inn is a restaurant known as the Carmichael

Restaurant & Tavern and has a wide fare of southern cuisine that honestly looks like it's to die for. You just might have to wait in line behind some spectral patrons that came well ahead of you.

SOUTHEAST TENNESSEE

Not gonna lie, I've absolutely had to *scrape* for haunted shit in Chattanooga – which surprises the fuck out of me, with how the river snakes and bends right on through it. Where there's water, there's usually spirits and ghosts abound. I don't make these rules, but they *are* the unspoken rules of the paranormal.

Where energy and life forces such as water flow, pool, and connect – there's a lot of spiritual activity. It's just a thing, and one more aspect of the paranormal and ghost hunting that I think should be paid attention to.

Anywho – while I didn't find *a lot* of hauntings and ghost stories in the southern part of East Tennessee, at least not half so many as I found in Central East Tennessee, I did find some good ones for you, my little strangelings. So, if you aren't already, make yourself comfy, have your favorite snack and drink on hand, and cozy up under a comfy blankie or in your favorite spot – because you're going to want to read this section, and once you're through it, you might not want to stop.

At least I hope that's the way this is working for you.

Anyway, let's get into it, shall we?

Welcome to Southeast Tennessee and it's major city with a fun, fun, name – Chattanooga.

There's a lot in Chatt to see, and it's an exciting overall place, just not as haunted as some of the others we've covered in this book.

Still, it's got enough thrills and chills to make you pleasantly tingle – at least it did for me.

Donna's Old Town Café, Madisonville

I walked into this one after covering some of the rougher locations in this book. Meaning, I took this one on after a string of prisons, jails, and hospital entries – which are some heavy, heavy, places to deal with when it comes to the paranormal.

To say walking into this café was a breath of fresh air after so many places steeped in fear, pain, and a myriad of other really deep emotions that can weigh on the soul like wearing a boat anchor around your neck is an understatement, my little strangelings.

From the moment you walk in, you feel it in this homey and cozy little, small town breakfast spot. It's full of light, the atmosphere bright and welcoming, and it's something a little more than just the super tight-knit and friendly staff.

I spoke to Melissa Graves, the owner and lead caterer of this family-owned restaurant and I awkwardly stammered out how I couldn't remember for the life of me how I had heard that the Caff was haunted, just that it was, and she cheerfully said to me; *"Oh, yeah it is!"*

I'm telling you, after some of my experiences around these parts, her cheerful demeanor in affirming her business' status on the rolls of *haunted buildings in East Tennessee,* was *everything*.

I asked what was up and sat down to take notes and order breakfast. I wasn't hungry when I set foot into Donna's Old Town Café but the delicious smells coming from the breakfast buffet quickly changed my mind.

"First of all," she said, "I want to make it clear there's nothing negative here."

I had to laugh as I said, "For sure! I could have told you that!"

She laughed with me and started to tell me how there was a woman here, who mostly kept to the second-floor offices and the like. That no one knew who she was or why she was here, but that she really protected the place.

I asked how, and she told me how no one could seem to leave or go far if something wasn't right. How more times than a few, someone has closed up, gotten halfway up the block and stopped without any real reason to go back only to find something that needed attention in the Caff. Something that could have been catastrophic.

Like what? I know you're asking, and I asked too.

Like the pilot light going out on the gas stove, or that the person was on the phone or chit-chatting with someone else with them and got a bit up the block before second guessing themselves on *did I lock all the doors?* Or that the doors had been left unlocked, but upon return, they would be found secured. She told me of an incident that had just happened the week before where they had some plumbing issue in the building that a plumber had come out for. She said she was closing, and actually in a hurry to get out to where she was going when she had the strongest, most out of place urge to look *up*.

There, where the wall met the celling, something had gone down, something bad, because water was pouring silently down the wall. She called the plumber back with the quickness and he got there and fixed it, telling her if she hadn't called him back, that the water leak would have easily shut them down for a lot longer than the couple of hours that it took to clean up what ended up amounting to a superficial mess it was caught so early.

She attributes this protective sixth sense that she and almost all of her employees have had at one time or another, to the benevolent female spirit upstairs.

"One time," she started, "I had a cook who was out for a time..." she said the cook had had a pretty invasive and heavy-duty medical procedure that took her out of Donna's kitchen for a while. She was a morning cook, and a pretty steadfast, dependable, and loyal employee

– one who rarely if ever missed work, so it was pretty significant her being absent.

Melissa said that her cook started calling the restaurant and asking what they needed, and Melissa having made no call, of course said she had no idea what the cook was talking about and what do you mean?

The cook said she was getting a call from the restaurant every morning of her absence at her start time of around 5 a.m., and that when she picked up the phone it was just dead air, she couldn't hear anyone.

Melissa said something like *'no way'* as no one had been calling the cook, the cook needed her rest!

Insistent and undaunted, the cook came into work as soon as she was feeling able and showed Melissa her cell phone's call record and sure enough, every morning at around 5 a.m. there was either a missed call from the restaurants land line number *or* a call lasting only a few seconds as the cook had picked up but couldn't get anyone to hear her or answer her on the other end of the line!

"I really believe it was the woman upstairs calling to check on her and make sure she was alright," Melissa said.

I asked about her, the woman upstairs, if she had ever been seen, or what she looked like, and was told she was seen usually in the hall, walking into one of the back offices and that she wore an old-timey black dress. Usually, if anyone went down the hall to look after her or see who she was, they would peer into an empty office or room – she would be gone, just vanished.

One of the waitresses said that she'd heard one time that people on the outside of the café had tried the door after closing one night, claiming they thought the café was open because of the woman in the white dress coming down the stairs at the front, but looking into the café she had disappeared.

I asked what other kinds of activity took place here and I was told there was another, male entity here that was somewhat of a practical joker.

I asked how, and the waitress that had told me about the woman descending the stairs in the white dress said that the only experience she personally had was at the invisible hands of this male jokester entity, when he made a pair of plastic salad bar tongs fly across the kitchen.

He's mostly responsible for making objects move, and hiding things, making them reappear at random later.

I asked how they knew this entity was a male and separate from the woman upstairs and was told because he had been personally seen by Melissa.

She said she was taking a box of paperwork into the basement through the old-fashioned access hatch set into the floor behind the register wrap. She said that she didn't like going down there, that it was dank and dark, and the stairs were at a freaky steep pitch, but this stack of paperwork had to go down, and so she took it.

She said that she was watching her step, and that when she got to the bottom of the steps, she went to move forward into the next room through a doorway down there and ran *smack* into the hulking form of a man in an old-fashioned leather type apron near where the old coal furnace for the building had once operated.

She said her papers went flying and she startled something awful, but in the split second between running into the dude and looking up – he was gone, there was no one there.

Still, she said she high tailed it out of there, back up the steps and tries not to go back down there if she can help it.

I asked if he scared her so bad, how she didn't think he was a negative spirit?

She said that she got the impression that he wasn't harmful at all, that she literally just happened to step down there when he was out and doing his thing. If anything, she got the impression he was possibly some kind of developmentally delayed and that she'd perhaps startled him just as much as he'd scared the crap out of her!

She also said that the types of things to fly, or disappear, were all harmless items. Maybe a little annoying, but nothing overtly malicious or damaging to getting things done in the course of doing business. Just a sort of 'ha ha! I got your thing!' before it would come back or scuttling something she's reaching for just out of reach – a teasing sort of presence.

One last story she relayed was something I'm certain was a residual haunting of some sort.

It happened upstairs. She said she was down in the café working and a friend of the family came in and headed upstairs for something. She said he came down and asked who was up there, that he'd gone down the hall, stopped outside one of the closed office doors, and that he'd clearly heard a lawyer of some kind talking about a real estate deal with another man.

Melissa was dumbfounded, no one was upstairs. She said they went up to look together, and nope – no one was there, but the man swore up, down, and side to side that he'd heard two men, a lawyer or maybe even a pair of lawyers speaking about some kind of real estate deal or contract through the closed door!

Melissa reassured him that she didn't doubt him for one minute, and that weird things like that happened around here all of the time.

I nodded and scribbled furiously, and she told me one final story about the café and a strange incident that had happened concerning one of the myriads of black and white photographs decorating the walls. She took me to a corner and pointed out a set of tables saying they were pushed together for a large party consisting of a family.

Among them was a little girl, no more than toddler age, and she was just beaming and obsessing over one of the photos on the wall to the point she asked if she could have it.

Her parents were just as baffled as Melissa over the girl's behavior and her all out obsession with the photo until one of the older family members pointed out that it was the little girl's great or great-great-grandmother in the picture!

Melissa and I both were on the same page, chalking that one up to the great or great-great-grandmother's spirit being present and communicating with the little girl in ways the adults around her couldn't even begin to fathom or understand.

If you're looking for someplace with a wholesome atmosphere, filled with love and light that you can taste in the French Toast, and you happen to be near Madisonville, TN – I 10/10, do recommend, Donna's Old Town Café.

HALES BAR DAM, GUILD

Of all the haunted places in East Tennessee, I was surprised to find one of the ones considered one of the most haunted was a dam on the Tennessee River. It stands to reason it would be, though. One, the project was one of those things that was considered doomed from the start. Mostly from all of the freaking mishaps and deaths. Two, where there's water, specifically pooling water or running water – for whatever reason, there seems to be an increase in paranormal activity. Three, and most importantly – the land was cursed by one seriously pissed off Indigenous chieftain – but more on that part later.

Hales Bar Dam has so much going for it in the *'reasons it should be haunted'* column that it should come as way more of a shock if it *wasn't* haunted at all.

I first encountered the mention of this place as simply *Haunted Hale's Bar* in *Haunted Chattanooga* by Jessica Penot and Amy Petulla, but I hadn't dug into the book to realize that it was a Dam. I honestly figured it was a *bar* as in Beverages and Restaurant. (Which I bet you didn't know that's where 'bar' came from, that it was an acronym: B.A.R. so for those of you that didn't know, today you learned something new. Yay!) In my defense, I was both born a dishwater blond, and it was an easy enough mistake to make. I mean, who names a dam a bar?

Anyway, another digression on my part – you should be fairly used to them by now.

It wasn't until I was indulging in one of my guilty pleasures, *Paranormal Caught on Camera*, that I found out what was going on surrounding this place and then went back to my books for more information.

According to the show, it was 1905 when construction was started on the hydroelectric Hales Bar Dam just outside Chattanooga, Tennessee, and from the start during its eight years of construction, it was one thing after another. The shit just seemed to rain down when it came to mishaps, accidents, and general bad juju fuckery.

It wasn't *just* during the eight-year construction period that shit went sideways either – but also in the decade *after* its construction. If it's anything this dam was known for, other than stopping up the mighty Tennessee River – it's for killing people. Accidents resulting in death racked up to the tune of over one hundred during the tenure of the dam's construction. Which is easy to believe when you had over five hundred men per shift working around the clock to git 'er done.

The show claimed that, today, the ghosts of workers trapped in the concrete, and the spirits of lost children wander the halls and tunnels of Hales Bar Dam. It even went on to say that some folks said there was a demonic presence in and surrounding the dam.

May of 2020: Enter Justin Soto, and his paranormal investigative homie; Frank. (No last name given. Sorry, Frank. Still, big ups.)

They were led into the dam's old hydroelectric powerhouse building – all that remains of the dam today, by an employee named Steven. Their cameras at the ready, the power immediately went out. No. It wasn't a supernatural power outage – I wish, but you could see in the footage that blue light was flickering through darkened windows – so an electrical storm was going on outside.

Kind of ironic they were investigating a haunted hydroelectric dam's superstructure while a power outage ensued, don't you think?

Of course, from my perspective as an investigative veteran of the paranormal going on twenty years now, (shut up, I know I'm old and I sound pretentious AF, but it's nonetheless true) I've long held theories about ghosts and electricity – that the reason batteries drain, or lights flicker, is that they draw on those energy sources to manifest in other ways; be it visually, audibly, or by moving objects – AKA psychokinetically.

So, for them to be investigating during an electrical storm? You best believe I paused the television and went and popped some popcorn. Shit was about to get real. *Real good.* I wasn't disappointed, either.

Steven took Justin and Frank on a basic tour, then, camera rolling, they left Justin alone by himself in one of the dam's supposedly subterranean tunnels his camera rolling on its battery backup.

Sounds can be heard. From echoing footsteps and the shuffling sound of feet to the indistinct voices of a distant conversation. Justin can be seen frantically looking up and down the tunnel, calling out into the dark, "Hello?"

The distinct sound of a coin dropping, more noises, and then it happens; clear as day, a child's voice, feminine, asks, *"Where are you going?"*

Justin turns white as a sheet, and of course, the footage cuts back to him talking about the dam, safe and sound, sometime later via an internet FaceTime meeting – it was the pandemic of it all, after all when this was filmed.

He said that the tunnel he was in once ran the width of the Tennessee River, below the water's surface. That during construction, children would traverse this tunnel crossing *under* the river, to go back and forth between school and home.

It was the very early 1900s, my little strangelings. I don't think OSHA had been invented yet; and what could go wrong sending little Johnny and little Suzy through a construction zone that'd already taken a number of adult lives?

Well, I'll tell you what happened according to Justin's research: One day, the dam breeched, and the tunnel flooded with two little girls trapped inside. They drowned. It was one explanation put forward for the presence of the child ghosts within the dam, although I wasn't able to find any corroborating evidence on the internet to back this claim up, I did have a couple of books that made this assertion, too.

Another explanation put forth on the show was that of the supposed demonic presence reported here. It was broken down, that demonic presences oftentimes mimic children's voices. A way to emotionally manipulate the investigator or target into luring them closer via their good natures. Truthfully, I'm much more on board with this as a plausible explanation, I just honestly can't believe that with the dam claiming so many lives during its construction, that any parent would send their kids through it to go to school.

Actually, I *can* believe there were people that stupid; I just don't *want* to believe children died here. Child ghosts are the most heartbreaking and kind of creepy there is, and I don't like them.

While I admit, I love *Paranormal Caught on Camera,* I also admit that I take a lot of these spots with more than a grain of salt. More like a damn truckload, because *damn,* do some of them leave me *salty...* usually by their lack of deep diving any actual history of any given place, making wild conjecture over what's in the footage – unnecessarily, I might add, as oftentimes their more believable footage is sensational enough in and of itself.

I'll tell you what I did take from this spot, however – this dam, or what's left of it, is indeed some kind of haunted. Haunted enough I was ready to start looking it up for myself in preparation of going there if I could.

I started with a few faint internet queries, which did seem to back up the assertion that the damn was haunted by *"hundreds of workers that died during its construction."* That seems to be a truth that is unilateral throughout *all* of my research. That hundreds of workers fell, drowned, or were smothered and forever encased in the concrete used to construct the old dam.

(Which is no longer there, by the way. The only thing that remains of Hale's Bar Dam is the old hydroelectric powerhouse and a few other outbuildings. The dam itself is gone, demolished in 1968.)

Remember the pissed off Indigenous chieftain I mentioned in the first paragraph of this story? Well, there's nothing stronger to point to the dam being cursed than an Indigenous tribal chieftain by the name of Dragging Canoe telling the colonizers that 'bought' the land and I quote: *"You have bought a dark and bloody land, and it is cursed."*

If ever there is a reason to kick off a haunting of the magnitude described here, with scores of deaths on-site from working men to children, I'm pretty sure that clinches it... but it could just be me.

As for the hauntings, there's a lot of wild stuff here I haven't covered, so buckle up.

In addition to the sounds heard within the remnants of Hale's Bar, cold spots have been felt, clothing has been tugged, hair has been pulled, (and yes, if it ever happens to me, I'll probably do something wildly inappropriate like say *'Augh! Daddy!'* just to see what the ghost would do. You wanna make me uncomfortable, Caspar? Well, game, set, match!)

Part of the reason the dam was demolished was because of a huge design flaw in utilizing what the engineers of the time thought was solid bedrock on either side, to build on and into – it wasn't. It was limestone, and as such, the Hale's Bar Dam leaked like a drunk at a bar on nickel night – the foundations of both the damn and the powerhouse sinking slowly into the river.

Indeed, three of the floors of the powerhouse have sunk so completely, they're completely submerged under water.

In one particular part of the building, there's a place known as the whirlpool, the above an explanation as to how there's a damn whirlpool inside the place – I honestly don't have a clue how a powerhouse or hydroelectric dam works as I write this. I'm a ghost hunter and an author who loves history and writing smutty romance novels. I'm smart, just not in this particular arena.

Anyway, the mists that rise up from 'the whirlpool' tend to follow people and patrons around the area and into other parts of the building as though it's more than mere water vapor.

Paranormal investigators have seen full-bodied apparitions within Hale's Bar's old powerhouse and caught numerous EVPs on recordings. They've also, reportedly, caught things on both night vision and thermal imaging cameras.

Some of the lore about the ghosts that haunt the powerhouse are the aforementioned workers who have died here, the supposed school children who drowned here, and unfortunately, at least one spirit the paranormal investigation team in charge of the property contacted by what they think is the name of Rachel. She identified herself as a woman who was raped and murdered in the powerhouse at one point in its over 100-year history. While I didn't go chasing down any news articles or whatever – it's so within the realm of believability for me as a woman, that I don't doubt it.

As to how the paranormal investigative team arrived at the name Rachel, one of their team members, a woman, had it whispered in her ear when no one else was standing anywhere near her – so that's what they went with.

Pretty solid, if you ask me.

Guests and investigators at the old powerhouse describe awful feelings of dread, fear, sadness, and a pervasive melancholy around a particular window in the building's upper floors. Many have gotten the distinct and overwhelming impression of a woman struggling, fighting for her life, and that she went out the window, falling to a horrible and painful death below. Many attribute this narration to the story of Rachel, and too many have felt it or said something about it without knowing any prior information about others' impressions about it or Rachel for their personal experiences to be easily dismissed or ignored as being made up or a fairy tale.

Likewise, the apparition of a man has been seen in upper floor windows when the facility is known to be empty and locked up tight – upon investigation, he is never found, and investigative teams do wonder if his appearance is linked to Rachel's ghost in some way.

In my experience, a heavy limestone presence plus a heavy water presence, is a prime recipe for a residual haunting – or a recording on time and space itself. With a death as traumatic as the entities of Rachel's, I wouldn't at all be surprised if this was a residual haunting of, perhaps, her killer taking a peek out the window to make sure the job was done.

Of course, he could also be the residual haunting of one of the power house's workers, checking on things during the tenure of the dam's working days.

Or maybe he's not residual at all, and just one of the resident ghosts poking his head out for some fresh air.

There're so many explanations for who he is and what he could be doing, and so little time, my little strangelings – but this is a fun book about ghosts, hauntings, and other weird shit spotted and going on in

East Tennessee; so, I'll indulge in more than a little wild conjecture here and there in the interest of keeping things fun.

On the professional investigative side of things, I try like hell to avoid that. It doesn't serve in the interest of the scientific approach that which we cannot prove or back with solid, historical, empirical data.

I'm fascinated by Hale's Bar for this reason, as there *has* to be a historical record somewhere of the men who died during its construction, or about the leaky tunnel that ran the length of it for children to cross the river to school.

I would love to investigate here, or to even cross reference findings from prior investigations to see if there is anything that we can match up with the historical records.

At any rate, other than being featured on *Paranormal Caught on Camera*, Hales Bar Dam has also been featured on *Ghost Adventures*. While I'm not a fan of Zack Baggins or his methods – some of you reading this might be, and if you want to do a deep dive of your own on Hale's Bar, there's a starting point for you.

As much as I would love to go deep and deeper still into this one, I'm going to halt my writing about it here. Hopefully, I'll have some personal experiences to add to this entry before this goes to publication.

The Read House, Chattanooga

Oh, my little strangelings. I had already written this entry into this book once before but then my dear friend Cassidy surprised me by booking us a night in this hotel along with a tour of the haunted room and I realized that *so much* was wrong with my initial entry on the Read House that I might as well scrap it, and do it all again – only right this time. Which is what I'm doing, and I am so excited because on our specific tour of the haunted room of the Read House, something paranormal happened!

Before we go there, let's get into some of the history of the Read House Hotel, shall we?

First established in 1872, it wasn't known as the Read House then. It was an Inn by another name, The Crutchfield, which was built in 1847 and spent a while as the political epicenter of Chattanooga. It was also primarily a wooden structure. During the American Civil War, it spent time as both a Confederate and later a Union hospital, accepting wounded and dying men from the nearby Chickamauga Battlefield.

At one point, it burned to the ground. The lot sat full of wreckage and/or empty for a year or two but then, the current brick ten-story iteration of the Read House Hotel began construction in 1925 and opened its doors during a 4-day long celebration in 1926.

With me? Cool, cool.

This quick round up of its history is important, my little strangelings, for a few reasons. One, the land is haunted. Why do I say that? Because Civil War era apparitions have been seen in parts of the hotel – and if the previous burning of the building didn't release those spirits, then obviously, it's the land and wasn't the building that was haunted. Stands to reason, though, because this building is just blocks from the Tennessee Aquarium that, you guessed it, sits right on the banks of the Tennessee River.

So, we have water kids! Not only do we have water, but we also have a lot of limestone in the area, and if you've been paying attention, you'll know that limestone is a *great* conductor of paranormal activity.

It was also shortly after the brand-new Read House Hotel, boasting ten floors and four hundred rooms, opened its doors that she acquired her most famous ghost: Annalisa Netherly.

This is where this gets good.

Back in the days of the rip-roaring 1920s, it wasn't uncommon for rich people to rent out a room in a hotel like the Read House long term. This is where young and beautiful Annalisa Netherly comes into play.

You see, her husband was some kind of big business tycoon type with more money than sense, and so he booked his young wife Annalisa a room at the Read House – Room 311 – and then fucked off by train to do whatever it is that big business tycoon type of the day did.

Annalisa got bored with this shit *real* quick, and the combination of her ennui, solitude, and well, just plain loneliness led her to take a lover, which then turned into a *string* of lovers – which eventually would give rise to the popular myth that she was a "Lady of the Evening" from San Francisco – but no, what she really was, apparently, was a bored housewife without an actual house of her own to keep. Just dropped at the hotel for days and weeks at a time while her husband fucked off to do big money things leaving her to her own devices.

As I understand it, that does not a hooker make – it makes a cheater, for sure, but not a hooker.

Here's where the story gets a little murky, my little strangelings.

What we know for sure:

Housekeeping found young Annalisa Netherly's nearly decapitated body in her room's clawfoot bathtub *days* after she was murdered.

There are several theories as to how she got dead in the first place, with no real answer as her murder remains unsolved to this day. Still, we gonna speculate and have a ball doing it, so buckle up True Crime and Old-Time Crime siblings in whatever higher power you believe in.

Rumor has it, Annalisa was a girl after my own heart. Which is to say, she was a carefree hedonist type that enjoyed pleasure and would indulge in it as often as possible.

Unfortunately, if you're a woman who likes sex, even today, that makes you a slut, while dudes typically get the free pass of being called a stud. Fair? Fuck no, but them's the breaks. You know it, and I know it.

It was especially damning for her being that it was the 1920s and she was *married*.

Honestly, Annalisa, sweetie, cheating is *bad*. I know it was a different time, and women were pretty much nothing without a man, but honey, baby, sweetie pie – cheating is just gross. There's good fuckery and bad fuckery, and that was just bad fuckery.

I don't know if she had more than one lover, but that's how this was squared up.

So Suspect A is a lover who was jealous of her other lovers, and/or the fact she wouldn't leave her husband for him, and in a fit of rage he picked up the straight razor off the bathroom sink and slit Annalisa's throat from ear to ear so savagely, that she was nearly decapitated.

The yikes are off the bikes and running freely, kids.

Suspect B is who *everyone* first suspects anytime a woman is murdered, and that's none other than Mr. Netherly – and I'm inclined, after hearing this story from our tour guide, to believe this is what happened.

The prevailing story is the generally accepted chain of events that led up to Annalisa's murder. It starts with Mr. Netherly on the train, either heading back to or just leaving Chattanooga. That part is immaterial.

It's as he is sitting on the train, he overhears another gentleman – if you could call him that – talking about how he just can't wait to get back into Chattanooga and essentially, back into Annalisa Netherly.

Her husband, incensed, disembarks the train, goes back to the Read House, dispatches his wife, and fucks off into the sunset.

Now, there are two theories and stories as to how this went down:

1. He barged back into the room, a dude in there with his wife, grabs the straight razor and kills her in a fit of passion.

Which absolutely doesn't track, because again, this is an unsolved murder. I'm pretty sure if he violently barged in with a dude there, that dude would have sounded some kind of alarm, and as you'll remember, her body wasn't found until *days* after she died.

Which I'm going to pause here and remind you, while the building had these really cool double bladed and sort of curved ceiling fans in the 1920s – what it did *not* have was modern air conditioning. While these fans did move a considerable amount of air, what they didn't do was sufficiently cool things off to the degree that they are today, so a human body, decomposing, in a bathtub full of water and blood for a few days... yeah, that human soup was *not* good soup if you catch my drift.

Pretty sure that housekeeping bypassed the Do Not Disturb sign hung on the door because things were getting, ah, *ripe* in there to the point you could start to smell unpleasant things permeating out into the hall.

This brings me to theory number 2, and the one I find most plausible.

Mr. Netherly returned to the room and didn't find his wife – *at first*. I think she and one of her suitors came in and fooled around and Mr. Netherly hid in the closet; waiting them out.

After his wife's flavor of the day, week, whatever, fucked off, he waited some more and listened as she drew herself a bath, then he slipped out of the closet, slit her throat, and casually hung the *Do Not Disturb* door hanger out on the knob.

He then made it onto the next train and off to wherever he was heading and poor Annalisa wasn't found for several more days.

Or, similarly, but quite a bit less dramatic, when he got in from wherever, Annalisa was alone, was casually having a bath, he came in, called out to her, she called back something like 'in here, darling!' and he went in and did the deed.

All I know, is that without access to crime scene photos or sketches, or whatever they did back then, I can't paint a fuller picture on if there was a struggle or not – if she fought back or was taken by surprise, or what... but then again, I suppose, if I really wanted to, I could just try to ask her.

You see, Annalisa Netherly is the Read House Hotel's most famous ghost. It's Lady in White, sometimes seen wandering the hotel's halls, but most of the time? Spotted as a haunting specter in the room in which she died: Room 311.

Seriously, though. Not only has her phantom been seen in the room by guests who have paid to stay in it, she's been photographed on numerous occasions in the suite as well.

One photo taken in 2023 that was shared on the tour, shows her standing blurry and in a dark rather than light dress, at the foot of the bed. Her hands resting on what looks very much like a rounded, pregnant belly.

The tour guide told us that many a time she's appeared to people in the room she has appeared pregnant – which makes me wonder if this is another facet of the story that we are unawares of. Could it be, the reason her husband or a lover killed her, was because of an unplanned pregnancy?

It was the 1920s of it all, after all – and her being knocked up by someone who wasn't her husband is a pretty good motive for murder by either her husband or one of her lovers. After all, could it be she was pregnant and a lover, wanting her to leave her husband and have his child, killed her in a fit of rage for her refusal?

Again, I'm wildly speculating here, but having a damn good time doing it – but while speculation isn't exactly a scientific method of doing things, I had to go buck wild with at least one of these stories and this one, for whatever reason, was the one that demanded I go full ham.

Anyway, another photo the tour guide shared was one that gave me absolute *chills* and that is really hard to do anymore.

It was a picture taken back in 2019 of the room's bathroom. It's pretty unassuming at first, until you turn your attention to the tryptic mirror set atop the vanity just inside and set against the left wall as you go into the bathroom's door.

Reflected in the mirror in the far right third, is a woman. A woman in a black dress, her hair in a bun, her pallor gray, and her entire countenance set apart from ours. She is in a different era, a different dimension or time from ours. Her expression somber and melancholy – she isn't in the room but she *is* in that mirror. The photo is one of the clearest and most insane full body apparition photographs that's ever been put in front of my face.

It wasn't, however, the coolest thing to happen on my visit to room 311.

You read that right. Buckle up, my little strangelings, I had a paranormal experience of my very own in room 311 and I'm going to tell you all about it before getting to some of the other tales I heard.

The tour consisted of five people when we went up to Annalisa's room. Myself, my partner in spooky for this trip, Mr. Cassidy Jones, the tour guide, and a husband and wife. The wife was some kind of travel agent and was studying the Read House for her business. Taking photos and getting the building's history. She made it a point to say that she worked with exclusively high-end clientele and seemed nice enough in a professional sort of way, but also was pretty down to earth.

Room 311 isn't a single room like most hotel rooms you're used to, with a smaller bathroom in it.

It's more a three-room suite that consists of a sitting room, the bedroom beyond that, and the bathroom to the left of the bedroom that you could only access through the bedroom.

As you enter from the outer hallway, the sitting room is right in front of you with a line of two chairs, and a table between them, just inside the door. The husband of the other couple on tour asked if it was alright to sit on the old furniture and was given permission by the guide and he took a seat in one of the chairs as the tour guide spoke about Annalisa and how she has quite the reputation for not liking men. Particularly, men who smoke.

Now part of the table between the two chairs was a phone. Something I've never seen before, the phone being literally made of marble, carved right out of the same chunk of stone the smooth, round, tabletop was made of.

The husband picked up the phone and gave it a listen and of course, this phone was non-functioning, and the tour guide, with a chuckle, said as much.

His wife joked dryly something to the effect of, "Yeah, you better quit fucking with her phone, you're going to piss her off!"

We shared a laugh and all of us moved from the sitting room to the bedroom.

No sooner did the tour guide take up position and resume talking, than he was cut off by the sound of the real phone to the room ringing. This phone was located on the wooden buffet or sideboard piece of furniture in the sitting room, behind the table and chairs with the defunct phone. He went to answer it and I went with him.

He picked it up with a confused look and said, "Hello?" and I asked, "May I?" and held my hand out for the phone. I put it to my ear and nothing – just a dial tone – waiting for us to dial out.

He *swore* up and down, that phone never rang.

I swear up and down that the only reason it did was the travel agent's comment poking fun at her husband over his handling of the other phone.

I whole-heartedly believe that Annalisa Netherly was present in the room with us and was letting us know.

After the incident, we talked about the bars on the room's windows. How they were once on all three bottom floors of the hotel to prevent folks from climbing out and skipping out on their stay's bills, until the fire marshal declared them a really bad idea in case of a fire.

All of the bars were removed, save for room 311's, which, for a time, held Al Capone as he was transported from Atlanta to his trial for tax evasion in Chicago, IL. He stayed one night in room 311, with guards posted on the roof outside the barred windows and outside room 311's door leading into the hallway.

Capone came through the Read House in the 1930s, well after Annalisa's murder, and is reputed to have smoked.

We all wonder how he fared that night, and if his sleep was a restful one.

Today, room 311 is mostly kept vacant to facilitate tours for guests staying at the hotel. However, for a pretty penny, the room can be rented on weekend nights in the months leading up to and through Halloween.

It's said that very few visitors make it through the night, despite paying up to almost a thousand dollars to stay in Annalisa's room.

On Halloween of 2020, a husband and wife paid $999 to spend the night in Annalisa Netherly's room. They didn't even make it past the witching hour according to our tour guide. The wife calling down to the front desk for help, and to get her and her husband moved out of there and to a different room.

Two of the hotel's managers from different departments went up to the room in the late hours of the evening to find out what was going on and to maybe assist. The scene they found in the room was the furthest thing they could have conceived of when riding up the elevator.

The wife was practically in hysterics, saying she had never seen her husband this way, while her husband was in quite the state.

He was lying face down, on the floor, clawing at the area rugs and flooring between the bathroom and the sitting room screaming incoherently, as though possessed. The managers thought him intoxicated, but the wife insisted that drunk though he may be – he had *never ever* acted like this!

The managers, with the help of the wife, got the man flipped off his stomach and onto his back, while the woman manager went to the bathroom and fetched a cool glass of water.

The male guest still wasn't making sense, his eyes closed, and appearing delirious and quite out of sorts. The female manager dipped her fingers in the water she brought and flicked the droplets on his face in a bid to make him come to.

The man shouted and immediately began to moan, saying "I feel her tears! I feel her tears!" repeating this phrase over and over.

I guess they got the couple moved to another room that night, and there was no further incident – the man fully recovering after sleeping through the rest of the evening.

Still, it's one of the more notable and bizarre encounters in the room.

Another couple, also paying handsomely, also around Halloween, also didn't make it through the entire night in the haunted room – requesting to be moved when the lady half of the couple woke to the apparition of Annalisa in a long, 1920s style white dress, standing by the windows of the room staring intently and unsettlingly at the sleeping couple on her bed.

The woman woke, stared at the scene before her, decided *nope!* She didn't like that! Called the front desk and had her and her husband moved with the quickness.

Other activities reported in the room include intense cold spots out of nowhere, lights flickering off and on, footsteps across the floor, and the intense feeling of being not only watched but of not feeling welcome in the slightest in the space.

Some people report feeling a ghostly touch, like fingers brushing along the back of their neck, or down their back, giving them another type of chill that has nothing to do with the temperature or how a thermostat might be set.

Annalisa doesn't just haunt room 311, nor is she the only ghost on the property.

She is frequently seen out in the hallways on multiple floors of the building. Almost always wearing 1920s attire, almost always in a white dress, except for the times she appears in her former room in something decidedly darker clothing wise.

She is often times seen turning a corner in one of the halls and when someone rounds the corner going after her, finding they are utterly alone at the junction of the two hallways and with no woman in sight. Likewise, the floor ringing in silence. No door shutting, no other sounds to indicate she slipped into a room or that she was really there at all.

Other times, guests report an overabundance of sounds in the hallways. People laughing, old-time music drifting out of rooms as though a phonograph plays, conversation and party going – though when they open their door to their room to politely ask the people making the ruckus to stop, the sounds cease and there's not a single living soul in either direction up the hallway.

When the silver ballroom was added onto the building much later, in either the nineteen sixties or seventies, Civil War soldiers were reportedly appearing and disappearing in front of staff and patrons' eyes.

Finally, there is the ghost of a little girl in a red coat that has been seen in the lobby and outside the elevator's doors. The rumor surrounding her that she fell from the mezzanine level of the hotel, suffering a fatality. A tragic accident.

There are so many more stories than these at the Read House Hotel in Chattanooga. In fact, I have no trouble in pronouncing the Read House the jewel in Chattanooga's haunted crown.

If you ever find yourself in Chattanooga, Tennessee I strongly encourage you to try the Read House for your lodging. Failing that, I urge you to at least try to get in on one of the tours of room 311.

Who knows, maybe you'll have an experience like mine to haunt you for the rest of your days.

As always… happy hauntings. I hope you get the opportunity to check this one out like I did.

The Hunter Museum, Chattanooga

Once run by the family that began the Coca-Cola empire, the Hunter Museum now a museum of American art, sits atop the highest bluff in Chattanooga, overlooking the Tennessee River.

This piece of land has a storied past, my little strangelings. Once believed to be the home the legendary giant hawk of Cherokee legend, in the years before the American Civil War, what is now the northwest corner of the mansion's property was dedicated to a metal furnace and smelting factory. During the war, this smelter was destroyed and this bluff served as a lookout for both Union and Confederate soldiers, with skirmishes happening here, and a tide of bloody battle happening down below and on the nearby Chickamauga Battlefield which spans over both the Tennessee and Georgia state lines. (We'll get to Chickamauga in a bit, there's plenty to go over there.)

After the war destroyed the smelter and the land lay pretty much fallow throughout the Reconstruction era post-Civil War, the land was eventually bought and construction began in the early 20th Century on a mansion which still stands today, many of its details still original to the home and perfectly preserved as a mark of the architecture of its time.

It was a private home for many years, before transforming into the Hunter Museum of American Art, and it was during these intervening years between construction and becoming a museum that we find ourselves in the midst of a mystery – one that is, for all intents and purposes, responsible for the main ghost story behind this beautiful and historic turn of the 20th Century building.

The original mansion portion of what is the museum today is haunted. It's an undisputed fact by this point – and while the mansion itself is haunted by no less than five ghosts, only one of them is identified by name, and that is poor murdered, Ms. Augusta Hoffman.

Ms. Hoffman never lived directly in the mansion, but rather, in the years 1914 and 1915, she was a boarder in the home next door.

Augusta Hoffman was in her sixties and while she owned a bit of property up in Knoxville, she didn't make enough money on her own to remain self-sufficient, and thus she lived with her sister and her nephew, the three of them renting from the Hunts. Described as a "pathetic old woman," by the newspapers of the time, she rather strangely up and disappeared one day in 1915 – vanishing without a trace.

No authorities were called, her sister Nancy Bennett and nephew William Bennett and his wife, claiming that Augusta had married a man up in Knoxville and had quietly moved up that way. They said this was Augusta's way – that she had ever been a private woman and that she wasn't prone to gushing or sharing her private affairs, even with her sister and her family.

While the family never did hear from Augusta again, they *did* receive letters regularly for a time from Mr. Brown, the man Augusta had purportedly married, and those letters mentioned Augusta's welfare with enough regularity that her family didn't think much of it.

That is, until Augusta's sister Nancy passed away sometime in 1916, and the letters, that had been coming from far and wide – New York, Ohio, and the Washington DC area some of the more notable locations, just suddenly stopped.

The remaining Bennetts, Augusta's nephew William, and his wife genuinely thought nothing of it; chalking it up to *you know how Aunt Augusta can be*, and eventually, they too moved on with their lives. First, they moved up to Knoxville for a time, before permanently relocating and settling in Roma, Georgia.

It wasn't until 1924, when Mrs. Hunt decided to have the basement floor of the rental property re-done, that anyone would know there was something amiss.

Upon beginning their work, carpenters noticed that pieces of the floor in the basement were rotten through. One of them struck the floorboards with a hammer, to start tearing them up, and while the hammer went through alright, and into the dirt below the floor, it came up with more than just chunks of rotting wood and dirt – it came up with a chunk of material that would later be discovered as *bone*.

The worker, thinking that this material was odd, started digging in the earth beneath the rotting floor where he discovered an intact skeleton, the clothing rotted completely away but for the shoes, a pair of spectacles, and the false teeth still ginning eerily from the mouth of the skull.

Authorities were quickly summoned to the crime scene, and an investigation was begun.

Witnesses came forward with a multitude of reasons why this was, in fact, Augusta Hoffman. Mrs. Hunt, at the time, recalled the sudden disappearance of Augusta Hoffman from next door, and told the authorities that while she had thought it odd, she disappeared so suddenly, that her family had assured her that she'd just gotten married and had left to be with her new husband.

However, the dressmaker that Augusta had worked for, doing her fine needlepoint, said that not only had Augusta left suddenly – which she'd found odd – she had never claimed her last paycheck, which she had found to be not only odd but alarming.

The dentures were taken from the corpses' mouths, and were dispatched to Knoxville, and to the dentist in Knoxville who had crafted Ms. Hoffman's dentures. He positively identified them as the ones he had made Augusta Hoffman nine years and some change prior – before her disappearance.

Forensics of the time, which it was the 1920s of it all, my little strangelings – and forensic science was still in its infancy. It was only 1892 that fingerprinting was first used to solve a crime, and here it was, only 32 years later – so things were still being figured out, for sure.

At any rate, the investigators at the time deduced that the body had to have been doused in some kind of acidic – due to the fact that the hair and clothing of the corpse was so thoroughly rotted away, and that it was entirely too soon for it to have done so after only nine years without some sort of catalyst to help it along.

Suspicion quickly fell on the surviving Bennetts – William and his wife, down there in Roma, Georgia. The citizens of Chattanooga were outraged at the condition that Ms. Hoffman was found in, and the excuses that she had suddenly married off with a man that the Bennetts had never met and that she was neither seen nor heard from again while her family just accepted that? It wasn't flying with the general public, nor did it fly with the Attorney General in charge of the Augusta Hoffman investigation.

The final piece of circumstantial evidence that was enough for the authorities to issue a warrant for the Bennett's arrests was the fact that detectives had scraped and scoured every marriage license registry from Chattanooga to Washington DC looking for Augusta Hoffman's name, only to come up empty.

The authorities in Chattanooga lured the Bennetts back to Tennessee under the pretense of just a simple interview, and no sooner did they cross the boundary line into the city, placed them under arrest for the Murder of Augusta Hoffman.

To wit, the public and authorities alike were outraged that the Bennetts had gotten away with this for so long. That they were made to believe that a woman in her 60's and a veritable recluse by nature would spontaneously abscond and marry a man that her family nor anyone else close to her had heard one word about from Augusta, let alone met. That she herself never wrote a letter, or came to visit, nor did anyone in her family bother to look for her in all the time she was away or disappeared. Of course, why would they look if they already knew she was dead?

While Augusta Hoffman was murdered and her remains disposed of next door to the Hunter Museum at No. 15 Bluff View Drive, her spirit has been, for the most part, spotted next door at the mansion that now contains the American Museum of Art.

Her haunting brings with it the phantom smells of something acidic with an underlay of rot – an unpleasant odor that no one can trace to any source within the museum. Likewise, her shadowy figure has been spotted inside the window of the area of the museum that she is known to haunt, with many ghost tour groups claiming to spot her or even capture her apparition with their cameras as they photograph the outside of the building.

While time has worn away the willingness of anyone at the museum to admit to the haunting, some of the stories surrounding the ghost of Augusta "Aunt Gussie" Hoffman are pretty gruesome.

After the residence where Augusta Hoffman was murdered, and where her body was subsequently found underneath the floorboards was torn down – her shade didn't really start to appear right away. It was only after the addition to the museum was completed where her home once stood, that the reports started of a woman appearing within the mansion portion next door to where she resided.

It was almost always after closing, the woman looking real enough as she wandered through the rooms perusing the art, that museum staff would panic, thinking one of the patrons had been missed and locked inside. Except, horrifyingly, when they approached the woman, they would quickly realize that she wasn't whole, or even alive, as they noted that her head was catastrophically bashed in, before she faded before their very eyes.

That's one encounter that I would like to call a whole lotta NOPE.

I don't know why she would appear this way, but for one reason... perhaps she feels as though justice wasn't served in her case.

You see, while her nephew and his wife were arrested for Augusta Hoffman's murder, and they were both tried and convicted of the crime – their conviction was later overturned on appeal and they were let go.

I guess that's to say that I believe Ms. Hoffman's spirit is an intelligent haunting, rather that a residual... what clues me in on that?

None other than she's been spotted, wandering through the same part of the museum, closest to where her residence once stood *looking at the artwork on the walls*. Stopping and pondering the paintings that exist in the here and now – that tells me she is interacting with the current reality and space versus some past iteration of the mansion.

Some food for thought, my little strangelings, some food for thought.

So, if you happen to be outside the Hunter Museum after closing, or dark – be sure to keep an eye on the old mansion's windows. If you happen to see a dark shadow going by, or an old woman peering out one of the windows; spare a thought for old Augusta Hoffman – as she's likely bound to this place, waiting for a justice that can now never be served.

CHICKAMAUGA BATTLEFIELD

We're not really sure what Old Green Eyes is. Somewhere between phantom and cryptid, sightings have been made of this peculiar and malevolent creature even before the Battle of Chickamauga took place, but he certainly rose to prominence when soldiers returned from the battlefield describing the spirit or creature as follows:

A tall figure or creature with straggly hair, sometimes human-esque but certainly not human. Some have even gone as far as to describe him as half man, half beast – sometimes he has been described as being nothing more than a floating disembodied head; but no matter who has seen him when, there is always one detail that stands out: the creatures malevolent and terrifying green eyes that glow sharply with a phosphorescent infernal light.

Located on the Tennessee/Georgia line just south of Chattanooga, the Cherokee Indigenous people named the Chickamauga region, which as I understand it means the River of Death. To be sure, the area was most notable as an old Indigenous burial ground but the name was eerily prophetic when in September of 1863 Union and Confederate forces clashed with enough losses sustained on both sides to amount to the loss of over 35,000 lives.

While Old Green Eyes has been spoken of in Cherokee legend predating the Battle of Chickamauga, it was sightings of this malevolent being, somewhere between a phantom and a cryptid, during the fighting among the mounting corpses of the Battle of Chickamauga that cemented its place among legend… so what is he?

That's a good question, and one, that I unfortunately can only present a theory rather than any significant answer.

Due to the many varying descriptions with only the one major detail outstanding, and the fact that several people have unequivocally stated that he was a strange sort of sprit or ghost, I would posit that Old Green Eyes may be some sort of ancient earth spirit or elemental.

Perhaps protective of the grounds due to its status as burial mounds for the Indigenous peoples who lived here, long before the white man and colonizers came.

One thing is for certain, my little strangelings – given the description of Old Green Eyes, I would rather not meet him alone like Denise Smith did in 1980.

She said she had been working a late-night shift at a local fast-food place in nearby Fort Oglethorpe, and decided to take a short cut through the National Battlefield Park of Chickamauga to go home. She was driving slowly, as it was late, and there was dense fog in the area from the river valley when she is quoted as saying "I saw something big in the road at eye level, and all I could see was these big green eyes. It was so foggy; I couldn't see a body. I got closer, and it just disappeared."

Denise Smith is not the only modern-day individual who has seen Old Green Eyes. A Civil War re-enactor who went unnamed claimed to have seen Old Green Eyes himself one night, after the reenactment was done for the day and he was headed back to his car. He said that he heard groaning or moaning coming from the nearby tree line or woods near his parked vehicle as he unlocked it to get in. He stated he immediately felt a heavy sense of foreboding as the sight of Old Green Eyes appeared in the twilight nearby him. He said and I quote: "This floating head with glowing green eyes burst out of the trees. This thing wasn't scary – it was terrifying! I just yelled and ran like hell."

Frustratingly, I recall one other tale of Old Green Eyes – an account from one of the soldiers on the battlefield itself, but I cannot for the life of me remember where I read it, my little strangelings. Whether it was on a plaque on the battlefield itself, or within the pages of a book that I errantly picked up but decided not to buy – whatever the case, this is what I remember:

The soldier was on the battlefield, the air choked with gun smoke, cannon fire, and the ground thick with bodies. He said he lay among them – whether he'd been wounded or not, I can't recall, but the account said that he looked up and Old Green Eyes stood before him, wading through the thick of the piled bodies around him and staring directly into the young soldier's eyes as though he knew he were alive and not dead. The soldier said he was utterly terrified at the sight of the ghastly and ghostly creature, and that after a moment, Old Green Eyes moved on, leaving him among the dead, confused and even more frightened than he'd been from just the fighting alone.

Old Green Eyes isn't the only ghostly figure of the Chickamauga Battlefield, my little strangelings, there is also legends and lore surrounding ghost lights, seen moving above the fields and through the trees. These lights are accompanied by the wailing and lamentation of female voices. It's widely known, that after all was said and done, as the sun set over the fields of battle, women from surrounding areas and homesteads would come out in small parties, with lamps and lanterns, looking for any wounded that might be saved, but also for their sons, brothers, husbands, and other kin that might be out there.

These ghost lights are attributed to these women, looking for their lost or fallen loved ones. A residual haunting, perhaps. A recording on time or the environment itself. At least I hope that is what this one is.

Park rangers, throughout the years, have spoken of strange encounters out within the park and the woods. From encounters with Old Green Eyes himself, to witnessing men approach and pass them on horseback, ignoring the Ranger's calls to stop, hold up, and talk with them. Horse and rider disappearing into thin air. On one such occasion, the Ranger noted that the phantom rider couldn't possibly hear him as the rider had no head.

There is a White Lady who wanders these hallowed grounds of battle and bloodshed. She has been sighted by a multitude of different people, in and around all areas of the park. No one really knows who she is, but it is widely assumed that she was the wife or lover of one of the soldiers fallen in battle. Just more of a full-bodied apparition, though she hasn't been recorded as carrying a light or lantern like the lamenting ghost lights of the searching women mentioned before.

Lastly, hundreds of people who visit the Chickamauga Battlefield Park every year report talking to soldiers as real as you or me out in the park, assuming that they're re-enactors, only to discover that no, they are just lost and confused spirits from a conflict of a bygone era who vanish right before their eyes. Some of them actually talking back to tourists, answering questions about the war before fading right before their eyes.

In every one of these cases, the tourists report that their camera batteries have suddenly drained or died before they could photograph the spirit. Other saying that while they snapped a photo, mostly during the era of film cameras where a development process was required, that when printed, the photo was empty, just a shot of underbrush or open field where they could have sworn that they had talked to a living breathing human being.

Sadly, nothing occurred of interest when I visited Chickamauga last summer, but I have had a few experiences at the Shiloh Battlefield, in Middle Tennessee – which is a topic for another book and another day.

OLD SOUTH PITTSBURG HOSPITAL, SOUTH PITTSBURG

J ust west of Chattanooga, and just barely within what I consider the south third of East Tennessee, this one could arguably also be in Middle Tennessee territory but given that the closest major city to it *is* Chattanooga, I'm letting it make the cut for this book. If I ever get to a book on Middle Tennessee, I might put it there, too – we'll just have to see if I ever get there.

South Pittsburg, Tennessee is a sleepy little town that only 3,018 people call home. At least according to the data available on it in 2022.

It doesn't have much by way of claims to fame other than it's the home of Lodge Cast Iron's main manufacturing plant.

However, this sleepy and unassuming little town has one big, bad, and bloody violent past – we'll just be starting with a massacre that occurred on Christmas Day of 1927. To this day, no one knows why an as yet unidentified assailant went through the town peppering it with blasts from his shotgun, leaving several men bloody and ravaged, their bodies in the town's streets. Most of those bodies dropped being the town's law enforcement officers – the majority of them left either dead or permanently disabled by the shooting spree.

As weird of an introduction to South Pittsburg as an unsolved Christmas Day murder spree from 1927 is – it doesn't even begin to stack next to the hauntings and spooky bull fuckery coming out of the 68,000 square foot old and now-defunct historic town hospital.

Going further back, the land that Old South Pittsburg Hospital sits on today, was former ground where the second bloodiest battle of the

American Civil War was fought – a portion of the Chickamauga Battlefield.

With the dark origins of this land, sitting on the river that the Cherokee once called *the river of blood* or *the river of death*, it's no wonder that the resulting buildings resting on this land are considered haunted... but what if there is another, more scientifically based reason for the activity here?

I'm not sure if I've said it before in this book, but I know for sure it's going to come up *many* more times – water is a great conductor of haunting activity. Where there is water, hauntings are usually somehow amplified and this location which sits on a riverbank is no exception. In addition to the river running nearby, the ground here is a limestone bedrock or base – and limestone, historically, is another great conductor of spiritual activity with its calcite crystalline structure.

Old South Pittsburg Hospital, founded by just four doctors, opened its doors in the year 1959 and was the main hospital and medical center for the small town right up until it permanently shut down in 1998. Serving for over forty years, this place has seen more than its fair share of life and death within its hallowed halls. Such is life in a hospital setting, no matter how big, or small, the facility.

Many believe the rumors that it was a fat stack of malpractice and wrongful death suits that led to the shuttering of this place, and with something like that as a potential fundamental part of a place's history, it's not exactly a stretch to believe it might be haunted by some outraged and upset former patients.

For real though, he main attribution of Old South Pittsburg's closure was the opening of a thirty-million-dollar, state-of-the-art, medical facility in the nearby town of Jasper, TN. Why go to this dinky, outdated, little rural medical center when only ten to twenty minutes up the road, you can get state-of-the-art and the newest medical and surgical technologies, treatments, and techniques?

Honestly, I don't think there's a hospital in existence that isn't haunted, I just think it's a question of is it an operational hospital, or not? If it is, there's far too many people and things moving and working in it. Even at night, hospitals are a place where no one ever seems to sleep and with that level of business and activity, a lot of smaller paranormal tells can be missed.

That nurse that walked across at the end of the hallway is just another nurse out of the corner of your eye and it might not register that instead of scrubs, she was wearing a long white skirt and white blouse. Was that an old nurses' hat or a pair of PPE glasses perched on her head? Ope! Alarm going off in room three! No time to stand around and dissect what you think you thought you just saw.

No, we don't really get to receive messages or see any paranormal in action in these kinds of places until wings are shut down, renovations have begun, or... in the case of this hospital and Old Harriman before it – when the building is completely shut down and mothballed when it comes to any further in-patient or out-patient care.

After Old South was shut down, it wasn't totally abandoned or forgotten. While it wasn't open, and no patients were present, there has always been a small team of people present. Typically, only by one or two, alone in the big old building, taking inventory or doing whatever it is you do with an old shutdown property like this.

One woman, who was at one point the hospital's director, related a story in which she was in the hospital and was supposed to be alone. She said that she saw an old woman, cross the hallway in one ward, from one room into one of the old surgical rooms. She said the lights were on, and that this woman was one hundred percent within her visual acuity and that she sincerely thought someone was playing some kind of a joke, or that someone had gotten into the hospital and onto that floor that wasn't supposed to be there.

She said she went tearing up the hall to have a talk with the woman, but that when she entered the surgical suite, the woman was simply gone, as though she'd never been – but still, the woman working there *swears* what she saw was a living breathing human being but only after finding no trace of her, had to admit to herself that what she had seen was clearly nothing or no one alive at all, but a ghost.

A maintenance worker for the building has said that he's seen everything from moving shadows to full-bodied apparitions. That he'd been spoken to, on more than one occasion by a disembodied voice, or that he had heard indistinct conversation up a hallway, or around a corner in a room, only to round the corner or move up the hall to find nothing, and no one. He even stated that some of his more disconcerting paranormal encounters included something unseen, growling malevolently at him in dark passageways and unlit rooms.

In addition to the black shadows and disembodied voices, full-bodied apparitions, and growling entities, other paranormal activity has been documented and observed by paranormal investigative teams allowed to conduct full scale investigations of the property.

EVP's have been recorded, shadow figures have been captured in still photos and on video, and objects have been witnessed moving under their own power. Things like doors slamming of their own accord by an unseen hand, defunct medication carts rolling down the hallway on their own, and chairs scraping across linoleum floors have been reported. Phantom phones will ring at nurses' stations where neither phones nor service exist anymore, and there are also electrical disturbances, such as flickering power or lights in some places. Even though the building is old – its electrical systems have been inspected and declared sound at the time of these disturbances, not long after the hospital closed its doors for good. At the time, and to date, no earthly cause has been attributed to these electrical disturbances.

Ghost lights have been seen in what the geriatric ward of the hospital was, bouncing and floating down the hallway, disappearing into rooms. Shadow people have also been reported on this ward, as well as disembodied voices and footsteps.

On an episode of *Destination Fear*, further history and activity within Old South Pittsburg Hospital were related.

One of the spirits of the hospital is that of an emergency surgeon. He died on the premises, supposedly horrifically and involving one of the hospital's elevators – although there wasn't a whole lot of detail given beyond that.

Supposedly, this surgeon can be heard in one of the surgical suites, still performing phantom surgeries. I wholeheartedly believe that this isn't the actual surgeon himself, but rather a residual haunting – a recording on time and space if you will. A phenomenon that has been recorded with greater frequency particularly where limestone is present – which is some food for thought when it comes to this particular location considering the geological makeup of the surrounding area and the land the building is set upon.

The second-floor nurses' station is said to have residual hauntings that include the elevator dinging or pinging audibly, even when the entirety of the building is without electricity. There are those who say that if you sit at this nurses' station long enough, that you can feel the swift breeze of former hospital staff walking briskly by in the performance of their duties.

Photographic evidence of apparitions and shadow figures were shown, as well as photographs of some very real, very angry looking red scratches along one female paranormal investigator's arm.

The biggest focus was on an entity on the third floor of the hospital. An entity that seems to be angry with or at women. An entity the hospital and investigators call *the creature*.

The creature is considered a particularly malevolent ghost or spirit and one eyewitness said that she was up on the third floor by herself, when the entity materialized out of a wall in front of her, fixating her with its *glowing green gaze.*

Are you with me here? Are you thinking what I'm thinking?

So, you mean to tell me, that this hospital sits on a portion of what is the Chickamauga Battlefield and there's an entity in the building with malevolent intent *with glowing green eyes* and no one has made the connection to the Old Green Eyes legend from the Chickamauga Battlefield haunting that I conveniently but accidentally put right before this entry?

Oh, okay... *okay...*

The woman went on to say the dark shadowy entity with the glowing green eyes materializing out of the wall scared the absolute hell out of her – which *duh*, and that she watched as he stared her down before going back into the wall and disappearing. She said startled but undaunted, she continued up the hall before the entity materialized out of the wall again, right beside her, eyes glowing red this time, and it physically attacked her, shoving her bodily into the wall on the opposite side of the hall before disappearing into thin air.

Another woman, on another occasion, said that she turned around and saw the creature come from a wall, crawling up it, to skitter across the ceiling, before climbing down the opposite wall and disappearing into it. She said that to her it looked like some kind of a janky dog, and that sometimes its eyes are red, and sometimes they're green – and she feels like the spirit is some kind of an overseer.

I still think it's Old Green Eyes myself – as it has been described as both humanoid and not on multiple occasions as well and like this *creature* entity isn't known to be human at all but rather some kind of elemental or something completely *other*.

The coincidences and similarities are too many for my tastes and that's my theory and I'm sticking to it.

There's also the spirit of a toddler on the third floor. One that the staff at the hospital calls Buddy. He likes to play, and even likes to ask for help – but some say the malevolent spirit of the creature likes to torment Buddy and tends to keep him away.

In room 304, there is a spirit known as Nellie, a former psychiatric patient of the hospital that is not overly fond of men. Nellie does *not* like her door to be shut and so the current caretakers of the hospital try to leave it open as much as possible.

Another story, when the hospital was fully operational, came from a local resident of South Pittsburg. She said that she was in the hospital after giving birth and she and her baby were in the room. It was late at night, and a doctor came in to check on her and the baby. She said she watched him touch her child and that her child even wrapped her little fingers around the doctor's thumb. She said the doctor told her to let the hospital staff know if there was anything she needed them to do and then left. The next morning she mentioned the encounter to hospital staff who insisted that there had been no doctor on duty the night before, let alone one making rounds.

Today, Old South Pittsburg Hospital has a new life as Old South Pittsburg Hospital Paranormal Research Center.

You read that right. You can book a four-hour daytime investigation, or an overnight ten-hour investigation with some of your closest friends, if you have the budget for it.

As far as I understand it, all proceeds go to keeping this place up and running for paranormal investigators to keep on keepin' on within this unique field of research. You can book your own tour or investigation direct with OSPHPRC at the following link:

https://osphprc.com/

And yes, if you've made it this far, Old South Pittsburg Hospital is the *second* haunted hospital in this book, but it is the flagship haunted hospital owned and operated by the OSPHPRC – in 2022, the same fine folks who purchased Old South Pittsburg Hospital, also went out on a limb, and purchased Old Historic Harriman Hospital in Harriman, Tennessee and they operate both as paranormal research facilities. So, if you're more Central to Northern East Tennessee than Southern East Tennessee, you might want to check out Old Harriman Hospital first.

Lookout Mountain, Tennessee Side

There are several ghost stories associated with Lookout Mountain. All fairly short in nature, so I've gone ahead and made it sort of its own little subsection much like I did with some of the Gateway to the Smokies stuff you have yet to get to. I'm not going to give this much preamble, but rather want to get right into it, so carry on my wayward little strangelings! There's ghostly fuckery ahead!

RUBY FALLS
&
RUBY FALLS CAVERNS

There's much more to Lookout Mountain than just the soaring vista of the mountain itself – although, if you're from the Cascade region, or the Rockies, you would take one look at Lookout Mountain and probably declare it just a very tall hill by comparison to the two aforementioned, much younger, mountain ranges.

Here's the thing about Appalachia, though, and something we'll get into further along in one of Matt's sections: The Appalachia mountains are *old*. Older than *bones*. So old, they run through other parts of the world because when they were young, towering spires, much like the Rockies – the entirety of the planet Earth looked much different than it does today.

That makes Lookout Mountain incredibly old. A sleeping giant, its veins and arteries calcified into tunnels and cave systems that we still don't have a full grasp of how deep or how far they range. How interconnected they are...

These mountains and hills are literally so old the perfect word to come to mind when trying to take in the full scope of what that means is *inconceivable*.

It was 1928. An elevator shaft was being drilled above what was known as Lookout Mountain Cave when the workers broke through into a natural shaft that was about eighteen inches high and a little around four feet wide. Further exploration showed that this narrow passageway opened up into several large chambers with all kinds of formations from stalactites and stalagmites, to flow stone, that make this area one of the biggest tourist traps there is today. The pièce de résistance, however, was the 145-foot natural waterfall found in one of these chambers, fed by natural spring sources and that after traveling through the underground fed into the Tennessee River snaking around the foot of Lookout Mountain.

The waterfall was quickly named Ruby Falls, and the caverns surrounding it Ruby Falls Caverns, dedicated to the wife of the man to initially discover these hidden natural wonders.

One of the men who initially discovered and took on the task of exploring and mapping out the cave systems discovered with Ruby Falls Caverns was a man by the name of Lomax. We'll visit him, and his story, in the Unexplained section further along in this book. It's a doozy of a story and one you're going to want to stick it out for – or pause here to skip ahead to read it, I don't care. It's your book now! Read it however you'd like.

I digress…

Whether you skipped ahead and read it, and now you're back, or whether you're still here and haven't gone anywhere, I'll refrain from spoilers either way – because there's other things to get into when it comes to Ruby Falls and Lookout Mountain's warren of cave systems.

Still, we're going to stick to the section of cave that Lomax discovered and drove him batshit for a minute.

It's said, after Lomax noped the fuck out of the Chattanooga area after his harrowing experience, the passageway was widened and the chambers he discovered were opened to the public and added to the tour.

It was in the small room sized chamber that Lomax was discovered in, that legend has it, ancient bones were discovered.

It was the 1920s and '30s of it all, my little strangelings, and who the hell knows what happened to these bones, but they were either buried deeper or taken someplace to be studied – you know how archeological sites were treated back then – and if you don't, well, not to put too fine a point on it, but archeological discoveries were basically plundered. For the most part, it was little better than grave robbing and why we have so many rules, regulations, and a whole scientific community dedicated to preservation and correctly logging and studying these kinds of things today.

Back then? They moved the bones swept things out and opened it up to take tourists through… and they used this room as a point on the tour where the tour guide would extinguish all of the lights to be able to say "See, this is how naturally dark it gets down here! Isn't that neat?"

Well, golly gee willikers – do you maybe think you could have picked a *different* chamber than the one that did what it did to Lomax for that?

It was a prevailing thing for the tour guide to douse the light and for one or two tourists to absolutely lose their minds, shrieking with terror into the dark.

Not because they were afraid of the dark, but they claimed because something was in it.

Too many tourists to count would recount, when the lights came back up, how something in the dark had reached out and trailed icy fingers in a very real, very physical touch, down varying parts of their bodies.

An arm here, a back there, along a shoulder or down a leg. Some even claimed an icy hand wrapped around a wrist, upper arm, or ankle.

It was definitely not something seen down there, but boy howdy, did they *feel* it.

The phenomenon became so problematic and so distressing, they sealed that part of the cavern up sometime in the 1940s and today, none of the tour guides even know where that section of cavern may even lie.

Could it be that the once inhabitant of that ancient pile of bones initially discovered in this particular cavern maybe has a whole lot to say about their final resting places disturbance?

It's pure speculation, but I'd take that bet.

Other phenomenon in the Ruby Falls tourist attraction includes shadowy figures moving around after hours and the apparition of an unknown woman in a red dress.

CIVIL WAR ERA GHOSTLY ACTIVITY

We're going from the inside to the outside, my little strangelings! There are a few ghost stories attributed to Lookout Mountain that hale from the Civil War era and the battles & skirmishes fought, won, lost, and something in between on her steeply pitched sides and top.

One story concerns a lost regiment of Union soldiers. They got separated from their division and it was not a good scene. In hostile territory, on the steep pitch of the side of Mount Lookout, with not just enemy soldiers to contend with, but also pissed off locals – in the driving rain, with pitfalls and caverns they couldn't see.

It wasn't long before the Confederates and civilian sympathizers to the Confederate cause whittled the regiment down. Thrashing through the brush, in the dead of night, in the driving rain whittled them down even further through slips, falls, and other such accidents until only seven men remained.

Seven men who wound up disappearing without a trace, never to be seen or heard from again. At least, not as far as the mortal coil was concerned.

Now, in the dead of night, when the weather conditions are just right with the rain driving from the clouds in a stinging deluge, it's said you can hear the lost regiment below the dull roar of the needling rain. Branches snapping, foliage crashing and men thrashing through the underbrush. Shouts of confusion, the men trying to stay together, and the odd crack of a rifle or roar of artillery – or is that just thunder now? It's hard to say, but for sure, something is out there in the dark, in the night. Perhaps not an intelligent ghost that would stop and ask you directions, but for sure, a residual *something* – replaying those last moments of the doomed Union regiment. Their fear, confusion, and desperation for survival and to stay together echoing out of the past, carried on the wind, and finding the ears of those of us who are around to listen.

Other sounds echo from the past when it comes to Lookout Mountain.

These sounds emanate from other parts of the mountain, closer to the summit. Shouts, screaming, single-load rifle shots, and cannon and old-time artillery fire sometimes come out of nowhere. Not surprising, at all, given the mountain is mostly formed from limestone, with springs and water running through the caverns and the Tennessee River winding below. As we all know, water heavy areas and limestone are great conductors of paranormal activity. Almost acting as a supernatural recording device, the stone itself seems to hold on to the events surrounding it, playing out within it and atop it. The wealth of water supercharging and acting as an almost battery, juicing the activity and making it prevalent in and around the area.

We don't yet know why this is, but after years of investigation and research, this is a generally accepted part of the unknown, specifically surrounding ghostly activity.

One of the most haunted locations on the mountain is pretty much unanimously called out as being the Craven's House.

The original structure that was used by both sides in the conflicts surrounding Lookout Mountain and its capture no longer stands, but the ghosts and activity remain strong in this area proving that it is, indeed, the land and not the structures that are haunted here.

There's one tale told of a woman that had gone up to what stands as the Craven House today. It's owned and run by the National Park Service and is only open a handful of days per year, shut to the public the majority of the time, however, she wasn't there to go inside. Just to take some pictures and to stand on the porch to take in the view of

Chattanooga and the sweeping vista beyond the city from the Craven House's vantage point.

As she approached the front of the house, she snapped photos, and felt an uneasy presence. She felt as though she was being watched, and felt a distinct kind of vibe of *what are you doing here?* She called out to relax, it was fine, she was just here to stand on the porch and look at the city, and the feeling abated – she stood for a time snapping more photos of the view and the city below and left, but when she went back through her photos of her approach to the front porch, there, on the side of the building, tucked half behind it was a tall, shadowy figure wearing what appeared to be an old-timey Civil War era duster coat or cloak.

Physical and tangible evidence that she hadn't been alone, despite the fact that no one had *physically* been there when she'd approached and stood on the porch all alone.

Moving on for the Civil War era ghosties that I have for you, specific to Lookout Mountain, I have the phantom sentry light.

Back during the contentions over Lookout as a vantage point for troop movements and a stronghold to secure those same supply lines, there were spots and tricky areas held by both sides. Particularly, there was one area that was well hidden that was perfect for a lone sentry to see quite a bit of the comings and goings of the enemy lines and he would communicate this fact to his own side using a variety of methods.

In the daylight, he would use a bit of mirror to reflect sunlight or light a campfire and send smoke signals. At night, he used a lantern and alternately blocked and let the light shine.

Typically, the sentry was set with a Confederate soldier who was already sick or wounded – allowing him to still participate in their doomed cause even though he wasn't able bodied enough to fight.

Unfortunately for him, with the arrival of Union reinforcements, though his position was well hidden, he found himself trapped well behind enemy lines and so while he remained hidden from the Union, he also had no way out or down from his position and thus, no way to replenish his supplies.

He wound up communicating things to the Confederacy to the bitter end, as he slowly succumbed to starvation.

Now, there are stories told of a flashing light up on the side of Lookout Mountain, visible from the bustling city of Chattanooga down below. The sentry spy of the Confederacy still desperately signaling his side of the war with no one left to listen.

This light has been seen both during the day, and at night; the sentry persisting in his duties long after his name, rank, and position was forgotten by history.

Kind of sad to think about it, eh?

Lastly, if you ever find yourself up on Lookout Mountain in the park up there, taking in the vantage points and views, you may just see a puzzling figure dressed in blue or gray. No, these aren't re-enactors, my little strangelings. People report seeing figures from either side all of the time, and that was their first thought too. Only when you approach these soldiers and get within a certain amount of distance to them, do they tend to disappear into thin air, right before your very eyes.

So, the next time you find yourself on this historic battlefield above the clouds, keep your camera at the ready, and remember – *control shot, control shot, control shot!* Take three of everything, that way if you catch something you know you got something rather than nothing. If you *do* happen to catch something on film, be sure to send it to us via the contact section at the end of this book.

We'd love to see it.

GATEWAY TO THE SMOKIES
&
GREATER APPALACHIA

When it comes to the Smokies, I can't think of any place more of a magnet for paranormal activity. Maybe it's because these mountains are older than bones, with roots traced back to Pangea and features in certain areas that look a whole hell of a lot like the ones in the Irish Dover Hills, and throughout parts of Great Britain. Maybe it's because there's scientific proof that they're so old they terminate somewhere up in Scandinavia…

Maybe it's because the Indigenous here, long before the colonizers came, recognized these mountains as a sacred space…

Or maybe, it's just because they really are just plain haunted as fuck!

For real, there is so much weird shit that happens in these mountains the folks around here have an entire set of rules on how to behave within them at night.

- Don't you dare whistle at night – it will attract unwanted attention.
- If you hear your name, or something call out to you after dark – no you didn't. Walk calmly, don't run, and take your ass inside.
- The further away it sounds, the closer it is. The closer it sounds, the further away it is. *Walk calmly, don't run, and take your ass inside.* Lock your doors. If you're in your car, don't stick around – drive away.
- The spirits can't cross running water, so paint your porch and porch ceiling a nice blue, and if you see blue bottles hanging from a tree, or a bottle tree, well you best just leave it alone.

It's those last rules that should grab your attention. A lot of people don't realize the rules don't just apply to the corporeal creepy crawlies and things that go bump in the night.

No, these rules apply to the *unseen* as much as the seen.

These woods and mountains are haunted, my little strangelings. There are more ghosts, haints, and spirits than you can shake a stick at in Appalachia – and you best follow the rules at night, not just to avoid the local bear, bobcat, and cryptid population, but to prevent the unseen horrors from the spirit realm from following you home…

WHEATLANDS PLANTATION, SEVIERVILLE

The legacy of this plantation, like most plantations, is one dipped in human suffering and soaked in blood.

Not only was it a slave holding plantation, as most if not all antebellum homes and farms were – it also saw bloody battles during the American Civil War, and even the American *Revolutionary* War take place on its grounds.

With over 70 documented deaths in the house itself, the majority of them natural causes, but even a murder or two sprinkled in there – is it any wonder this place is considered haunted?

I mean, you can still find bloodstains on the living room floor in the house; the result of a son murdering his father.

Let's get into it, shall we?

In 1780 John Sevier, the namesake of Sevier County and the city of Sevierville within it, led a contingent of men across the French Broad River into the Boyd's Creek area on what would wind up being the future site of the Wheatlands Plantation. He and his men got into a bloody battle with the local Cherokee Indigenous peoples on the future property and pretty much slaughtered them – because, you know, colonizers.

It wasn't long after those early colonizers, that more settlers moved into the area and started staking out property lines. Among these first early settlers was Revolutionary War veteran Timothy Chandler and his family.

Built in 1791 by Timothy Chandler, the Wheatlands Plantation started as a family farm. In 1819, when Timothy passed, his son John inherited the farm and under his oversight and direction, it grew to be the largest in Sevier County; in excess of 3,700 acres, and at one count, 4,600 acres, by 1850.

Wheatlands garnered its name after the abundant crop of wheat it produced yearly.

The daily operations of the plantation required that it harbor fifteen horses, ten mules, forty cattle, fifty sheep, and three hundred hogs.

Annually, Chandler had his fourteen slaves produce 3,000 bushels of corn, 400 bushels of oats, 200 bushels of sweet potatoes, 12 bushels of buckwheat, 10 tons of hay, 150 pounds of wool, 200 pounds of butter, and 200 gallons of honey. The plantation's distillery produced 6,000 gallons of whiskey, which if I were of those 14 slaves I would honestly need a drink after doing all of that work in a damn year on top of the absolute horse shit of being owned by another human being just because his skin color lacked the melanin.

I digress... it's my book, I can do that.

During the American Civil War, the Wheatlands Plantation was the Winter quarters for the Tenth Regiment Cavalry out of Michigan and the 8th division from Western Pennsylvania. These soldiers ran raids on Sevierville, and into Gatlinburg and Newport. They sent troops to the Brabson Plantation from Wheatlands and overtook the ferry there, going on to occupy nearby Bartley Chandler's home in Sevierville as a prison.

All things considered, when the American Civil War came to an end, John Chandler wasn't a major dick about it; opting to pay his slaves a living wage to stay on and continue to do the work they'd been doing up to that point. What's more, upon his death in 1875, Chandler actually left a strip of Wheatlands Plantation grounds at its south end to his former slaves who had stayed on. This area became known as 'Chandler's Gap' which remained a predominantly Black community well into the 20th Century.

Several of the plantation's original buildings endure today and are available to tour. Which is cool and all, but I should really get to the damn point:

Why's it haunted?

That, my little strangelings, is an interesting story with such a varied and storied past behind the old property.

Back to those bloodstains on one of the mansion's floors – one of the hauntings reported at Wheatlands is the echo from that terrible night. The father's screams rending the air and reverberating through time and off the mansion's walls as the trauma of his murder replays itself in a residual haunting when the precise conditions are met.

Another legend attributed to Wheatlands is the rumor of a mass grave filled with Cherokee Indigenous somewhere on the property – the result of that long-ago bloody battle between them and Sevier and his men.

Nothing like an old Indigenous burial ground to add to any spooky factor al la the *Poltergeist* franchise, am I right?

Indeed, Wheatlands *is* known for poltergeist activity, disembodied voices, full-bodied apparitions, and in at least one case – a possession.

The story on that last one goes that a boy visiting the plantation saw the apparition of a Black man, dripping wet with water on a day where there was no rain – only he said that the man 'rushed him,' jumping into his body, through the center of his chest, causing the boy to faint dead away as he and his mother were leaving what was supposed to be a learning experience for the day.

I would say he learned something, alright. That maybe it wasn't a good idea for him to go spooky places. Seems he was a little sensitive.

Speaking of children, indeed, there have been a multitude of children ghosts spotted on the Wheatlands grounds. Inside the house, there is the apparition of a girl in a blue dress seen on or around the staircase. She has been known to run upstairs, and when anyone that has seen her gives chase, they haven't been able to find a single living soul on the second floor where she tends to go – probably because she's not alive and a ghost, but yeah.

In addition to the little girl, slave children have been seen playing outside. Typically, a rousing game of hide and seek – of course you'll never find them if you go looking for them because they disappear. 10/10 ace trolling, if you ask me.

There have also been apparitions of several generations of the Chandler family seen on the grounds and within the house. Adults wandering the fields or in the house, doing their own thing as though no time has passed at all.

There are a couple of cemeteries on the property in addition to the mass grave of over twenty-eight Indigenous braves from that original fateful Battle of Boyd's Creek.

There is a family cemetery, of course, with several of the Chandler's interred, and there are also over fifty gravesites of slaves on the property in a slave's cemetery.

Both visible cemeteries are rife with activity, from disembodied voices, to wandering apparitions, so if you happen to visit you might want to bring a recording device. (Don't forget your phone counts! Just download an app to make voice recordings!)

So, there you have it, from the oldest farm in Sevierville, my little strangelings.

WILDERNESS AT THE SMOKIES, SEVIERVILLE

Pack your towels, sunscreen, and ghost hunting equipment – but do try to keep the latter out of the water.

These stories come from a former employee of this resort that worked there during the summer of 2017 and 2018 seasons.

It's no secret that a lot of shit goes down on cruise ships, in hotels, and at resorts that no one talks about. People die, it's a fact of life, and these places are home to some high stakes' drama and a breeding ground for interpersonal conflicts when lovers or married couples go on vacation to try and fix what's broken.

Not saying that's what caused any activity here, but it's certainly the underlying drama to a few hauntings we have coming up in other parts of this book and in other resort towns in and around the Gateway to the Smokies.

Let's get back to Wilderness at the Smokies here, though, shall we?

This booming water park and resort is fun for the whole family, with a five-star hotel and on-site dining as well as a fantastic water park for the kids and any adult who is still a kid at heart.

Indeed, book a weekend here, and you have no need to leave and do anything else… and apparently, there are those who chose never to leave at all even after their corporeal form shuffled off the mortal coil.

Back to the stories about this place.

When our intrepid new recruit joined the ranks back in the summer of 2017, the fellow employees of the resort were quick to warn her that shit got weird in the hotel and on surrounding grounds at night, and that it was a regular thing she'd best just prepare for now.

She filed this information away for later, but it wasn't until around three in the morning sometime mid-season that she had her first encounter of her very own.

She was sitting in her office, alone, doing whatever one does at a resort at three in the morning in an office.

In the summer, things get rather hot and humid in East Tennessee, for those of you who are reading this that may have never been around these parts it's a fair regularity for things to get hotter than Satan's hairy taint in the summer and just as grossly moist. Sometimes, in certain buildings or parts of any building it gets pretty warm, even despite the best efforts of that buildings' HVAC system.

So was the case on this particular night for this poor girl, who had a sizable fan running full tilt behind her, blowing cooler air into her stagnant office from out in the hallway.

She said she was working away, when suddenly, the airflow that had been stirring her hair and plastering her shirt to her back, had cut off. She said that she could still hear the fan running – so it hadn't shut off – but rather that it was like someone had stepped in front of it, blocking the wind.

She turned around, fully expecting to see one of her coworkers – but there was no one there at all, and just as suddenly as the airflow had stopped, it resumed again.

A short time later, she was in another building on the resort's grounds. The building that housed the restaurant and that is, reputably, the most active in terms of the paranormal.

She was sitting at some sort of a desk with either a mirror or glass in front of it, her back to the restaurant but the reflection laid out clearly in front of her. It was after hours, and no one was supposed to be in there, but she could clearly see the reflection of someone walking around the restaurant between the tables in front of her. The vision so real she immediately picked up the phone on the desk and rang hotel security without even turning around.

The resort security team dispatched someone who immediately came down and swept the restaurant floor – but of course, no one was there. Additionally, the security team reviewed the cameras to confirm; fully expecting that someone *had* been there based on the woman's adamant testimony that she had seen someone, but likewise there was no one present but her on any of the security footage.

She would later learn that at one point, one of the restaurant's chefs had unfortunately passed away in the parking structure on the property. Could she have seen *him* reflected in the glass? Inspecting the restaurant after closing, or before opening?

She also reported that it was very easy to see things out of the corner of your eye around the resort in the deep of night, when all was still and quiet. Things like shadows drifting across hallways or dipping around corners. Sometimes objects stirring in a wind or breeze that wasn't there, as if someone had swiftly passed, even though no one was there. Other times, objects would just *move* as though nudged or slid along a table or desk by an unseen hand.

While most of this activity seems to take place at night, I don't doubt that this place is just as active during the day – it's just easier to miss such activity with the active hustle, bustle, presence of people and ambient noise of daytime activities going on.

So, if you find yourself at Wilderness of the Smokies, enjoying some fun in the sun during daylight hours – maybe be sure to pack some equipment and set it up to record in the wee hours of the night.

You might just catch something you wouldn't expect out of this modern location.

The Titanic Museum, Pigeon Forge

Okay, I know what you're thinking – *the Titanic Museum, really?* Yes, I know it seems ridiculous, that it's a new building and it'd be stupid to think it's haunted but I don't think it's the *building* that's haunted at all.

This giant museum dedicated to the history of that fateful night of April 14th, 1912, when the Titanic hit an iceberg and slipped under the waves, was built, and opened sometime in 2010 – so no, I don't think it's haunted, unless it was haunted by something that resided on the land before it went up. Boy, do I believe that there's something in it now when some of the artifacts belonging to people who died on the ship were moved into place to make portions of the museum what it is today.

If you're new to the world of the paranormal, ghosts, and hauntings, I'm just dropping this here for you: A person, place, or *thing* can be haunted. You hear stories all the time about haunted dolls, such as Robert in Florida or even more famously, the Annabelle doll. Why can't a pocket watch, or a beloved necklace, or even a teacup hold a residual echo of a bygone era, or a spirit of someone that once owned or handled the object become imprinted upon it?

It's estimated that over 750,000 people visited the Titanic Museum in Pigeon Forge in its inaugural year – which doesn't surprise me, or shock me, as it's still going strong fourteen years later with almost every one of its days being sold out to visitors who come from all over the world.

With so many people filtering through this vacation destination, it's easy to miss the subtle noises and movements that can be attributed to a haunting in a place like this. But at night, when the attraction shuts down, the doors closing and locking after the last visitor of the day, things can become eerie just by virtue of what was a once bustling space becoming devoid of all human life.

It is said, that if you're present, and quiet, that you can possibly meet some of the passengers and the crew of the Titanic – that even her captain may walk these halls like the promenade of the deck of his ill-fated ship.

Footsteps, disembodies voices, and sometimes, yes, even full-bodied apparitions have been seen in the museum. Not just after dark, but while the museum is in full-thrall; but only to the very lucky few.

I've been to the Titanic Museum myself, with some out-of-town guests from the state of Georgia and their friends from Wales in the United Kingdom. By far it is a somber and eerie experience wandering through the halls and mounting the grand staircase that was built to scale.

The feeling, even crowded with people, is a heavy one within the walls as you bear witness to the terrible chain of events and life aboard the doomed ship.

10/10 if you find yourself in Pigeon Forge, I recommend you stop here and take the tour – and if you happen to catch any strange reflections in the display cases, or notice some suspicious shadows or strangely dressed and transparent individuals lurking in the backgrounds of your photos? By all means, email them to soundparanormal@gmail.com – I would like to have a look at that.

The Howard Johnson Inn, Gatlinburg

Just as you enter Gatlinburg's main strip, you may spot the familiar blue, white, and orange signage for the Howard Johnson Inn. I've found that just about every hotel in Gatlinburg has one story of tragedy or another associated with it – rarely does any ghost story begin with a happy ending to the life of the person who haunts these grounds… and so it is with the ghost of room 332 at the Howard Johnson Inn, so I think, because this entity is either angry, or so desperate to gain the attention of the living, it's done some very real physical harm.

Let's get into it, my little strangelings.

It all started when a woman, her husband, and her two kids checked into the Howard Johson for their vacation stay in Gatlinburg. They were given room 332, she remembers that, quite specifically, due to the traumatic events that unfolded during their stay.

They were *very* tired from the hustle and bustle of Gatlinburg and its main strip with its varied shopping experience and its many loud attractions all vying for one's attention along every inch of sidewalk which is wholly overcrowded with people any given day. Especially during the height of tourist season.

A fact that many locals lament with the oft uttered line of *"Remember kids, there are other places in the Smokies to vacation other than Gatlinburg."*

The small family was glad to be out of the sun and off the road and ready to unwind and start their vacation.

They bedded down that first night, and the father woke in the middle of the night to a dark, shadowy figure, standing at the foot of the bed. He sat up, rubbing his eyes, but it was gone.

He didn't say anything to his wife and kids, but they all three noted that they didn't like the room; that no, there was nothing physically *wrong* with it. It was clean, didn't smell bad, the linens were devoid of holes or stains… but something about the atmosphere in the room left both his wife and his children feeling deeply unsettled.

They dismissed it, determined to enjoy their week-long vacation, but the activity continued.

On one of the subsequent nights, it was the wife, rather than the husband who woke in the middle of the night – she was uncertain of *what* had woken her, but again that feeling of pervasive unease overtook her as she settled back down to sleep.

A couple of nights after *that* incident, the wife noticed a bruise on her leg… one she had no explanation for, and that was eerily in the distinct shape of a hand.

They experienced nothing else on their stay, at least nothing else they were willing to speak of, but if you happen to stay at the Howard Johnson directly on the Parkway in Gatlinburg, keep an eye out – and watch yourself.

Something supernatural is definitely at play here.

I happen to be a Wyndham girl – meaning I stay at Wyndham hotels more often than any other to take advantage of their rewards program. Lucky for me, Ho Jo's are within the Wyndham network of hotels, and I had enough points for a free night's stay.

I took advantage of it during the height of tourist season, and when I booked, I tried not to be an asshole and booked for a mid-week stay on a Wednesday to a Thursday night to run around town and do my research.

I also, upon booking, asked for the reportedly haunted room 332… and I *got it*, my little strangelings!

My two friends and I stayed in the two-queen bed spacious room and set up some equipment to record by way of my thermal imaging camera in the corner of the room.

The camera repeatedly shut off of its own accord, but at strange and staggered intervals. One video lasting 13 minutes and some change, the next lasting only 7, and the final one just a little over 10 minutes.

So it wasn't like the camera, which is honestly still relatively new-to-me equipment was naturally timing out at an even interval. That is most definitely not at play here.

Likewise, the television stopped working at one point in our room. To the point hotel staff had to come up and reset it.

Finally, while we were on the third floor, and there were floors above us, there came a point where we were talking and joking and two very loud, very sharp knocks came from not above, but beside us from the wall on the other side of the two beds that shared with our room's bathroom.

My friend, Nate, said that he was sure that someone had dropped something upstairs, but my other friend, Ellie and I traded a look – but neither of us were sure.

Finally, Ellie reported seeing a shadow pass by the foot of both beds at one point after I had fallen asleep. She said in was inky black and slunk low to the ground like a big cat or something.

I wish I had something more spectacular to write about this one – but I don't. Indeed, when I brought up any kind of prospective haunting to the staff here, they reacted with genuine surprise. None of them having ever experienced anything within the hotel or on its grounds nor hearing anything from any guests staying or who had stayed in the past.

Could this case be one of those cases where the hotel wasn't haunted at all? That perhaps the woman or her family were the ones haunted?

Only time will tell, I guess.

GREENBRIER RESTAURANT, GATLINBURG

I f you want great food and an amazing atmosphere, you have to visit this staple of the Gatlinburg community.

The Greenbrier Restaurant holds its beginnings in its prior iteration of the Greenbrier Lodge, which was first established all the way back in 1939.

According to local legend, one of the guests to stay at the lodge never left.

Her name is Lydia, and as the story goes, she was an excited bride to be who was staying at the Greenbrier on the eve of her wedding.

She got all dolled up on her wedding day, but alas, the groom had cold feet or changed his mind or something, because he never showed – leaving Lydia all alone at the altar to explain to their guests that they needed to go home. That no wedding was going to happen.

Lydia was *devastated* by this turn of events and returned to the Greenbriar inconsolable. She locked herself away in her room, and after finding some rope, tossed the line over one of the rafters, and made a very permanent solution to what amounted to a very temporary problem somewhere over the second floor's staircase when no one was around to stop her...

Or did she?

Sadly, Lydia's fiancé who had skipped out on their wedding, was found mauled to death by what many locals assumed was some kind of a big cat such as a mountain lion. I sort of wonder if it was a

Wampus Cat, myself – but that's Mattie's territory and can be found in the cryptid section later on down the line.

There I go, digressing all over the place, again…

Now this next bit, I hold no stock in whatsoever, but some say it was Lydia herself who's vengeful ghost turned into the creature to seek her revenge on her man – but again, that's way too much for me. Still, I thought it worth noting, otherwise I don't feel like I would be telling the whole story…

Anyway.

It wasn't long after Lydia's unfortunate suicide that ghostly activity began to make itself known around the Greenbrier – and truthfully, not just here, either. No, Lydia has become Gatlinburg's most famous ghost, and with good reason. While the Greenbrier holds the record for the frequency of both sightings and other paranormal activity related to Lydia's ghost – she has indeed been spotted other places around Gatlinburg, too.

Still, the Greenbrier has been and appears that it always will be the epicenter of Lydia's haunt, and those activities started with both the lodge's staff and patrons spotting her apparition on the same stairs that she hung herself above.

No, not her ghost swinging from the crude noose she'd made, but just Lydia, as though she were stepping out of the lodge she called home for a jaunt out on the town, or perhaps as though she was returning from one.

After her death, and her burial, it was unfortunately one of those situations that a headstone couldn't be afforded for her by her loved ones – who were, generally the people responsible for such details after an interment.

This apparently upset Lydia a great deal, because one of the caretakers or chefs of the Greenbrier, couldn't get a single night's rest without hearing Lydia's piteous moans of "Mark my grave! Mark my grave! Mark my grave!"

Her sobbing became too much for him, and he scrimped and saved and had a stone marker placed on her burial site with her name, birth, and death dates… and the pitiful sobbing moans of her ghost stopped and haven't been heard since.

For the longest time, while the Greenbrier still operated as a lodge, guests reported seeing her, and those that didn't, still said they felt an odd, cold, and unseen presence within the lodge. Particularly on the second-floor landing of the stairwell where young Lydia had taken her own life.

A travel review left on Yahoo in 2004 was a complaint from a man who had encountered Lydia's spirit in the men's room of all places. He stated that is was clearly a woman, she was transparent, and that she had reached for him! He then went on to complain that the establishment didn't have a warning sign up or something about their haunting.

As we all know, many businesses and establishments really would rather not advertise their status as haunted for a variety of reasons, but the Greenbrier, while not precisely leaning into Lydia's lore, doesn't exactly shy away from it, either. It just is what it is around there – and it's easy to understand why.

There have just been too many sightings, too many stories, and too much activity that can't be explained as anything other than ghostly for it to be credibly denied anymore.

While the Greenbrier is no longer a lodge or hotel, it is still one of Gatlinburg's most famous restaurants with fare that is reportedly just to die for – some diners go exclusively to see if they can't catch a glimpse of Lydia in one of the tall, floor to ceiling windows in the second-floor dining room.

Others just hope for just any sign of her presence, such as a flickering light, or something clearly moved by an unseen hand – honestly, I just wonder if it isn't happening at the Greenbrier at the time, does that just mean Lydia isn't home?

We'll get to her shenanigans in other parts of Gatlinburg in future stories, my little strangelings. Just you sit tight.

The Park Vista Hotel, Gatlinburg

Standing proud and regal on top of the bluff overlooking Gatlinburg, Tennessee is the Park Vista hotel. Which also happens to be one of the favored visiting spots of Gatlinburg's most famous ghost.

You remember Lydia from the Greenbriar, yeah? Of course, you do – if you're reading in order than you just came from the Greenbrier to the Park Vista.

Well, it seems that Lydia gets *around*, as she's been spotted on a multitude of occasions at not only the Greenbriar, but also the Park Vista as well as other places in and around Gatlinburg proper.

The Park Vista seems to be this elegant young woman's favorite haunt, other than her home at the Greenbrier, and mad props to my girl for having expensive tastes!

The cheapest rooms here go for about $200 a night, which for some reading this book, probably doesn't sound like much; but for a broke ass ho like me? I'll be fist fighting the ghost down at the Howard Johnson, thank you very much.

Part of the price tag of staying in the Park Vista is its absolutely *stunning* views of the entirety of Gatlinburg proper, as well as the Smoky Mountains all around it.

Definitely worth a look if you can afford it, but we're all here for the ghosts, so let's get into it, shall we?

It seems Lydia likes to cause quite the stir in the Park Vista's restaurant. She has been known to knock on tables, move things around, and in some cases, has even appeared to restaurant staff and diners alike.

While she has been seen in the occasional hallway of the hotel, she really primarily haunts the dining room – and no one knows why.

Perhaps even Lydia needs a night out on the town every now and again?

THE EDGEWATER HOTEL, GATLINBURG

This is another rough one involving a child murder, my little strangelings. So fair warning, if you want to skip it and move on.

Still here?

Okay, great.

On the banks off the Little Pigeon River, next door to Ripley's Aquarium, is the Edgewater Hotel of Gatlinburg with stunning balcony views of the Little Pigeon River.

Unfortunately, it was the last view one little girl saw before falling from one of those balconies to her death.

Police initially thought the whole thing was a tragic accident, but all too soon became increasingly suspicious that the girl's father had something to do with her death. It was to the point, so the account goes, that the father actively evaded police apprehension, took them on a high-speed chase, ended up wrecking his car by going over a cliff and plunging to *his* own death in the Little Pigeon River himself along with his wife, the girl's mother.

If that isn't instant karma, I don't know what is.

Today, it is reported that hotel guests sometimes wake to the ghost of this seven-year-old little girl standing at the foot of their bed, disappearing almost as soon as they wake – the guest unsure if they were truly awake or dreamed the whole thing. Additionally, it is said, that she can be spotted standing in the Little Pigeon River on the anniversary of her death, pointing up to the balcony she supposedly fell from – or was pushed from – or was thrown from by her father.

Here's the thing about this one, though, my little strangelings – there isn't a single piece of corroborating evidence that it ever happened.

I scoured the internet for '1972 death of 7-year-old, father responsible, Gatlinburg, TN' or other variations thereof for any sort of news articles or true crime documentaries, or *anything* pertaining to this particularly wild and fantastical tale and I came up with exactly bupkis.

Does that mean there is no haunting at the Edgewater?

shrugs

Meh!

There very well could be. Do I think that this really happened? Mmmm – I'm skeptical.

'But A.J., if this *didn't* happen, how can you say it's still haunted?' nobody asked, but I'm going to tell you anyway.

Two things.

One, the place is and always has been haunted by a little girl approximately seven years of age by all appearances, only her story has been forgotten, or lost to time.

Two, so many people believe the story of the 1972 murder of a seven-year-old, pitched off one of the Edgewater's balconies by her heartless father, that something called a 'thought form' has occurred, and now there's an apparition of a seven-year-old girl hanging out in the hotel, simply because enough people believe there is.

It's *Sound Paranormal*, not Sound-Ghosts-and-Cryptids, and this is one of those cases where, I think, a strong argument can be made for a thought-form entity. I mean, it wouldn't be the first time – but that's a story for another day, and an entirely different book.

For now, I want you to stick a quitter-strip (bookmark) into this spot, and really think about this one. It's something else, isn't it?

Don't be gone for too long, though. There's still a lot of good shit to come.

THE GATLINBURG INN, GATLINBURG (DUH)

This is one hotel that will take you into the way back when, my little strangelings. Built in 1937, it holds just about all of the nostalgia and charm of that bygone era that you could want in a place.

So, too does the Gatlinburg Inn have a named ghost, but no, it's not Lydia. Even more unfortunate than Lydia's tale is Wanda's story – because Wanda was no young woman of age, like Lydia. Wanda is but a little girl – and don't ask me why just about every ghost in Gatlinburg is a woman or girl – other than we're more murdered and tend to meet more traumatic deaths than the dudes around town, I guess.

Maybe it has to do with the Little Pigeon River flowing right through the center of town. As I've said it before, I'll say it again; where there's water there's hauntings. Perhaps this portion of the Smokies is tapped more into the divine feminine than other areas – whatever the reason, it seems there's an inordinate amount of both spirits and women and girls haunting the area. Far more than other areas in East Tennessee.

I, once again, digress…

If you're sick of it, I'm sorry – but also, I'm not sorry. You're still here, after all – which means I must be doing pretty good at keeping you entertained.

Anyway, back to Wanda.

The story goes that little Wanda passed away inside the Gatlinburg Inn, but like the little unnamed seven-year-old of the Edgewater Hotel, there has been no corroboration of that fact – doesn't mean it didn't happen, though. She could very well have passed away in the hotel, on the property, or nearby the property enough to stick around. This report may be unsubstantiated, but it's a hell of a lot more plausible than the fantastical tale out of the Edgewater.

Many people have reported seeing Wanda running up and down hallways and stairs, some have reported waking up to see her standing in their rooms or waking up to the feeling of the bedclothes being tugged off of them, only to see Wanda standing there – the little shit.

Additionally, there are points where Wanda is simply heard, but not seen. Phantom footsteps crossing the room as you're drifting off to sleep have been reported. Or the pitter-patter of little feet outside of the room, out in the hallway.

Alas, I kept digging, and I still haven't found anything about an origin story for Wanda, but I *did* find it interesting that on my visit, the front desk staff did say that it was widely known a little girl by that name had died in the Inn, supposedly of an illness – which would explain why I couldn't find any corroboration. People get sick and die in hotels and on cruise ships all of the time, it's not like a record is kept of it, especially in the event of natural causes such as an illness running its course. At any rate, that's not something you get with most ghost stories. The generally known and accepted fact that yes, a little girl with that unique name, did die on the premises.

One last point of interest about the Gatlinburg Inn, at least from a historical point of view, is that Room 388, known as the Rocky Top Suite, is where the famous song of the same name was actually first penned, sometime in the 1960s.

So, if you're looking for a place to say that checks all of the boxes of close to downtown Gatlinburg, haunted, and with a nostalgic, bygone, and noir-sy kind of vibe? Give the Gatlinburg Inn a try.

I know I was certainly eager to see it and I wasn't disappointed when I stepped into the lobby with its ranks of famous thirties through sixties signed celebrity headshots framed against one wall.

I was, however, a little let down when the front desk staff had a little chuckle and said 'no, we've never had any encounters here.' What's more, they said that a team for television had come to investigate, and that they didn't even call the ghost Wanda but Willemina or something of the like. The front desk staff were incredibly enthusiastic about the paranormal here and discussed all sorts of other places in the area with me, and even went so far as to print off a list!

Still, they were totally honest and disappointed themselves when they had to tell me that in their five years of working the Gatlinburg Inn, that they hadn't *personally* encountered anything, nor had they heard of anyone else having an encounter.

Makes me wonder if this little girl ghost, who again, the front desk staff *did* confirm that a little girl with a name that started with a 'W' though it wasn't Wanda, *did* die on the property at some point in the Gatlinburg Inn's past; but as we all know, not every death results in a haunting and they couldn't confirm any ghostly activity directly attributed to her.

That being said, there is one other ghost attributed to the Gatlinburg Inn that I didn't know about until *after* my visit there, and that is the 'dancing lady' or 'dancing woman' who apparently dances and spins, pirouetting in the lobby only to disappear before a visitor's very eyes.

Her ghost has no government name attached to her, but it is supposed she is a guest who felt happiest at the Gatlinburg Inn to the point that she just never left after passing.

At any rate, the Gatlinburg Inn was one of my favorites when visiting the tourist destination in the Smokies, and someday, I hope to join the ranks of the many guests to have stayed at the property – so a big thank you if you are reading this and have bought this book. I am grateful to you for making that dream a potential reality.

Manifestation, baby. Am I right?

GREYSTONE LODGE, GATLINBURG

It's at this point in the book that I think we can all agree, you can't throw a rock in Gatlinburg, TN without hitting something haunted.

So, it is with the Greystone Lodge, which I honestly wish was my last stop in Gatlinburg at this point – after all, there *are* other places in East Tennessee other than Gatlinburg to check out – but it's starting to feel like I'm trapped here after a week or more of working on it.

This one has a specific room number attached to its ghostly tale, and that room number is 213; in case you're a strangeling like me who specifically requests these kinds of rooms when you stay somewhere.

The story goes, a guest booked a stay here and was assigned room 213 one super warm summer evening. They went up to the room, and upon entry, immediately set the thermostat in it to sixty-nine degrees. (Giggity.)

They went to bed, and at some point, during the night they woke up, *freezing*, the temperature somewhere in the *fifties*.

Oh, yeah... and the covers were ten to fifteen feet off the end of the bed across the hotel room according to the story, which that would make for one seriously big-ass hotel room, I'm just saying. Do I buy the covers were off them and in such a way it was clear they hadn't been kicked off? Yes. Absolutely. Do I believe that distance was ten to fifteen feet? Not remotely.

Anyway, another thing that the guest reported was that while showering, the water turned a really creepy reddish-orange. Yeah, I'm sure if you could see my face, you would be laughing right now. I'm pretty sure it was rust in the pipes that busted loose too, at this point and the math ain't necessarily mathing to the sum of *it's haunted*... Although, to be fair, this person said it only happened once or twice, and that it didn't *seem* to be a pipeline issue – so while I'm not quite sure I'll give this one to them just yet, I'm hanging in there to see what comes next.

During the night, the wife-half of the couple staying in the room woke up to see the transparent glowing white figure of a little girl standing in the room with them – to which, I say, *jackpot!* Now it's haunted!

That's it, though. That's the story. Sadly, there is no more – but I would be curious to know if anyone else out there has had any experiences here. If you have, and you would like to share them, you can email me at soundparanormal@gmail.com and for your convenience, there's contact information at the end of this book. Who knows, your story may make it into a future iteration of Paranormal by Region, or one of my Paranormal by City books I have planned for the future.

I did stop into the Greystone in my travels through Gatlinburg in writing this book. The front desk person I spoke to and passed my card to was exceedingly professional and polite with a megawatt smile, and yet, her big beautiful brown eyes conveyed 'get the fuck out of my hotel with this nonsense' so loud and clear I will trouble them no more.

I'm not sure where the hostility came from, other than, could there be some truth to the legends and whispers? Did the couple in the above story really encounter something?

It's just speculation at this point, one could even speculate we *are* in the Bible-Belt and I just had some bad luck encountering the one person whose personal beliefs makes them staunchly anti-paranormal.

Still, this is not a case where persistence is welcome or warranted, there are so many other hotels and people working in and around Gatlinburg eager to tell their stories, as we'll see in the next one.

Holiday Inn Sunspree, Gatlinburg

Throughout this book I have *tried*, my little strangelings. I have really tried to stick to places that still exist and are visitable for you. I have also tried very hard to pick places that have little to no coverage in prior books or shows – and if they *do* have a lot of prior coverage, I have diligently attempted to find you firsthand accounts or stories that *haven't* been covered by anyone else.

To that end, this one breaks all the rules.

This one is confusing, my little strangelings. While I have it listed as the Holiday Inn Sunspree, that isn't just the hotel's former name, but it's *two* iterations before this current one. Most of the information I've found about it lists it as the Garden Plaza hotel – which in a tourist town as dynamic and ever re-branding as Gatlinburg is, has *also* since permanently closed. In fact, its buildings no longer even exist.

Searches on Google Maps are conflicting on the precise location of this one, and it's unknown if it is the same as the current iteration of the Holiday Inn resort that is open and functioning today, (spoiler alert – it is) but it's got several ghost stories between the two buildings to formerly stand here and while the two buildings that stand here today seem to have no activity, the stories about this place make it worth stopping to talk about for this book.

I was determined to find where these buildings are, or where they once rested to see if any of the following activity endures today – but let's talk about that activity, before we get into all of that, shall we?

First, there was a poltergeist in the kitchen by the name of Alvin.

That's right, the poltergeist has a name – and a pretty tragic tale that goes right along with it.

The story goes that Alvin was a cook at the original resort, and put in a stellar twenty-five or thirty years, working there since the day the place opened. This was a time when employees were rewarded with more than just a pithy pizza party for such achievements; and as such upper management, in recognition for Alvin's outstanding work ethic and attendance record, sprang for a *boat* for the man!

Unfortunately, the first time Alvin took the boat out onto one of the lakes in the area – it sank – and apparently Alvin missed the memo about wearing a life jacket and he didn't know how to swim; so, his reward sent him on to his *great* reward when he drowned.

Apparently, that great reward was to be stuck at work his entire afterlife; because it wasn't soon after Alvin ghosted on the mortal coil that his coworkers reported seeing his apparition in the hotel's kitchen in the wee hours as they were opening up and getting things started for the day.

What's more, during busy times, several people reported having their name whispered by their ear, the water taps would turn on by themselves, and if Alvin was feeling particularly salty, dishes would fly across the kitchen – yeeted by an unseen hand – to crash and shatter against cabinets, fridges, and floors.

I mean, I would be salty too if my great beyond was being stuck in a hotel kitchen for my afterlife, wouldn't you?

Or maybe it was Alvin's work ethic at play and he was pissed that corners were being cut and unsafe practices were going on in his kitchen... Maybe he was just letting his opinion be known on that?

I think I'll stick with that last one, as it certainly seemed like Alvin was happy to work there and liked the place after 25 to 30 years of service.

The other haunting attributed to the building of this hotel once known as the Holidome, is out of room 413 and the 1970s where it's said two women were brutally murdered by a strange-to-them man they'd picked up in one of Gatlinburg's many bars.

The stranger drowned one of the women in the bathtub while the second woman had gone outside to smoke a cigarette. He then hid the first woman's body under the bed, before going out and meeting up with the second woman. He strangled the other outside in the secluded smoking area, before dragging her body up and onto the roof where he dumped her to hide her while he made his getaway. Which, unfortunately, he did get away, scot-free – no one has ever reportedly been apprehended in their deaths, their murderer never found.

Ever since these murders, the cleaning staff have had a hell of a time in room 413 of this building of the hotel. Housekeeping staff claim they hear noises coming from the room's bathroom and objects tend to float or move around the room of their own volition.

My bet is the poor woman drowned in the bathtub is still here. I wonder if her friend is, too.

In the other building of the hotel known as The Tower, a suicide took place in the late 1990s. A businessman, disappointed by some personal let-downs or failings, left a $3.57 cent tip for the cleaning staff before suck-starting a .357 Magnum handgun.

What a dick...

People have reported encountering him in their room – which technically I guess is still *his* room, since he got there first – but dude, it's a hotel – you're supposed to move on. Especially after making that kind of a mess for the cleaning staff to deal with!

Other people report seeing his shadowy figure facing the pool at night – so in addition to being a royal dick, he's a creeper – which honestly, I guess that tracks.

Sorry, my little strangelings. Suicide makes me super uncomfy, and the uncomfier I am, the more my wildly black and sarcastic humor comes out as a coping mechanism. Not saying it's an excuse, but it certainly is a reason... I, say it with me now, *digress!*

Finally, our last story concerns a Boy Scout troop on the 7th floor of The Tower.

More murder and mayhem in this one, but sadly it involves the cold-blooded mass murder of children, which is an even touchier subject than suicide. So, if you're not down for that, maybe go ahead and skip to the next heading. If you're a sick freak like me, and not much fazes you, keep on keepin' on my sibling in strangeness!

Okay, so, the tea:

Apparently, the entire seventh floor was being rented out to a Boy Scout troop doing whatever Boy Scout troops do, when one of their scoutmasters lost his shit and fucking slaughtered a bunch of the boys under his command or whatever.

Years later, an employee of the hotel was scared shitless by the sounds of running children's feet and bloodcurdling screaming echoing down the hallway.

Nothing like the dulcet tones of phantom bloodcurdling Boy Scout screams in the middle of the night to ensure you don't need any more hits of caffeine to make it through your night shift, eh?

I'm not sure the employee *was* on the night shift, I just imagine they were, by the way. Call it a little creative license with that one. This is really the first time I've done it for this book, and if I'm making a hardcore supposition like that, I will universally call it out for what it is so there's no confusion should you go to retell the story.

I'm done digressing for this story.

So, here I am, after having gone to Gatlinburg to sus out this one's location, and settle in, my little strangelings, because this paranormal tea is piping hot.

I went to just about every haunted hotel in this book while I was there, and even stayed in one of them. I got a range of reactions from one to the next. Everything from a big, polite smile, with eyes that said, 'fuck you, get out of my hotel,' to 'I never heard about this place being haunted!' to 'Yeah, everyone says it's haunted, but it really isn't.'

It was in my search for the property that used to be the Holiday Inn Sunspree turned Garden Plaza turned mystery hotel that I accidentally wound up in a hotel up the road that wasn't at all the hotel I was looking for... but the employee at the desk was a treasure trove of information about it.

We'll call her Ms. Money, and Ms. Money had *a lot* to say about the former Sunspree. She said that she had started working there sometime in 1980 or 1981, and that she was in her late teens to early twenties at the time. She told me that before her first night was even over, that her coworkers warned her about the hauntings. Specifically, the ones tied to the two murdered women.

She said that had happened in the '70s, so before her time, and that the suicide of the businessman had been well after her tenure at the hotel, so she couldn't speak on that – but she did have some stories to tell…

She said one of the common things to have happen were guests calling the front desk, frantic, in the middle of the night, to let the front desk know there was a woman screaming in one of the rooms adjacent or across from theirs. That a fight was going on, and they needed to call the police!

The staff knew the routine by now and said they would send security right away – knowing that the sounds were coming from room 413 of the Holidome, and there wasn't anything, really to be done.

The room was empty – and hadn't been rented out. No one was in it, save for the ghost of the murdered woman, screaming and the sounds of her struggle to survive as her assailant brutally attacked her, and drowned her in the bathtub.

Still, security would dutifully go to the room, and as soon as they keyed open the door – the screaming would stop.

Another story she related was of a presence felt but unseen. She said this haunting was particular to the Tower portion of the hotel and centered all throughout the tower. She said, one of the cleaning staff, a man, was also a preacher for a local church or ministry who did work at the hotel on the side.

She said that one night he had told her that as he boarded the elevator in the Tower he had felt a presence in the elevator with him. He said that he got off the elevator and let it go; that whatever it was he wasn't riding with 'that thing' and that he waited for the next one before continuing on.

She also related a story of one of the security guards taking her through the lower basement levels of the Tower, late one night, in the wee hours of the morning. She said they were in an area like a banquet hall, and that there was something like floor lighting giving just enough ambient light to see by as the security guard left her at the door to walk across or down a hall to turn on the overhead lights.

She said she felt a tingle go down her spine, and that she felt a presence behind her, but when she turned around, there was nothing visible there. She said the feeling of being watched and that there was someone there got heavier with every step the security guard took away from her.

He reached the other end of the hall and flipped on the lights and looked at her. He grinned and asked, "Do you feel that?"

She asked, "Feel what?" trying to play things off and what have you.

She said the guard's smile got a little bigger and he said, "You do feel it, don't you? The whatever it is, it's in here with us right now."

She said that she felt that whatever it was, was decidedly a very masculine or make presence and that it tended to hang around the basement levels of the Tower, around the banquet kitchen, more than any other part of the hotel…

I personally think it was Alvin, who had also passed away before her tenure at the Holiday Inn Sunspree Resort.

Alas, she had nothing to say about the Boy Scout murders, and that she had actually never heard of that happening – but, Ms. Money had other stories, about other parts of Gatlinburg to tell me – both experiences she had herself, and that were told to her by close personal friends.

More on that later.

I spent the rest of the afternoon and evening that I encountered Ms. Penny, and did, in fact, finally sus out that the old Holidome building had been torn down and rebuilt into the Holiday Inn Club Vacations Smoky Mountain Resort while across the parking lot, the old building that had been the Tower had been torn down and rebuilt into a Holiday Inn Express.

I went to both, very curious if anything paranormal had been reported in either of the new buildings which were only eight and four years old, respectively.

You see, I wanted to know if it had been the *buildings* that were haunted, or if the tragic spirits of the Sunspree were tied to the land, instead.

In some ways I am happy, in some ways I am disappointed to say, no one at either of these new hotels had anything to report about the new buildings being haunted.

While one woman working in the Holiday Inn Club Vacations

Smoky Mountain Resort said she knew about the history of the Sunspree she hadn't been aware at all that this building had been erected where it once stood. That she had worked there for a while by then and no one had ever reported any sort of haunting or activity.

Likewise, the gentleman across the parking lot at the front desk of the Holiday Inn Express reported he had only been working there since February and he had no knowledge of anything paranormal happening in the building. In fact, he said, he and his coworkers were an affable bunch, and if anything of that nature had gone on he was sure they would have talked about it.

So, I'm happy to report that with the destruction of the old buildings that housed these hauntings, the spirits seemed finally capable of moving on. However, the investigator and lore keeper in me was mightily disappointed to hear that.

Still, if given a choice between these ghosts being laid to rest, versus having them still about for me to try and make contact, I will, almost universally, pick the former over the latter.

Maybe that makes me a good person? I don't know.

The Mysterious Mansion, Gatlinburg

We have finally gotten out of Hotel Hell, my little strangelings! Hooray! This story isn't about an *actual* Mysterious Mansion, even though East Tennessee is certainly littered with mansions both new moneys, and old... no, the star of this show is actually one of Gatlinburg's star attractions! A haunted house attraction, that's *actually haunted*.

Going strong since 1980, The Mysterious Mansion is an all-ages haunted house attraction that, once again, happens to be *actually haunted*.

How cool is that?

Okay, okay, I'm settling down, I promise. Here's how this goes:

Both employees and customers report seeing an eerie hooded figure on the grounds and inside the attraction that will follow people around – customers might just be under the impression that it's one of the haunt actors, which might be for the best, but the employees know the truth – *it's a ghost*, and thus when it follows *employees* around, rather than dishing out a fair helping of the heebie-jeebies, they tend to get a dose of what they're selling whether they like it or not!

I mean, one of the reports is that this hooded figure not only follows customers and employees through the halls of the haunted house, but has also been known to follow employees on their breaks and employees and customers alike to their cars at the end of their visit or shift – so it's definitely got the creep factor down and is performing for the venue at a solid 10/10 spooky rating.

In addition to the presence of the strange, hooded apparition, there is a lightbulb in the venue that flickers constantly and has been known to burn out repeatedly or regularly despite several electricians coming out to fix it, they can find no problem, and thus the fickle electrical fixture has found its way here into the land of Mysterious Mansion Ghost Lore.

That's all there is for this one, which honestly, with it being a haunted house, I'm all for it – I'm not a fan of the jump scare and so I don't frequent those places.

I'm strange, I know, just means I'm in good company here, doesn't it?

Haunted Cabins

With as haunted as Appalachia and the Smoky Mountains are, it's a roll of the dice and a sure gamble that just about any place you stay isn't bound to have a haint or two. Loads of people have come from all over for the scenery, hiking, and for attractions like Dollywood and the Museums and such all through Sevierville, Pigeon Forge, right on up to Gatlinburg and the Smoky Mountain National Park.

What none of them bargained for was that some of those cabins are already *occupied*.

The following are firsthand stories, legends, and lore from tourists both recent and past who have had paranormal encounters staying in cabins in the area – we'll start in Sevierville, move through Pigeon Forge, and end in the Gatlinburg region.

A lot of these stories don't have *specific* locations or addresses attached to them, but where they do, I'll try to include them.

Let's begin at the beginning, when you take that exit, 407, off I-40 and start heading on through Sevierville…

SEVIERVILLE

THERE'S SOMETHING IN THE WOODS

In October of 2022, a woman and her family rented an idyllic cabin located somewhere in Sevierville – it was anything but.

Things kicked off with a feeling of uneasiness or heaviness upon their arrival – but like so many before, and as we'll see in the coming stories after this one – she shook it off, ignoring her gut and determined to have a nice time.

I'm not judging… we do it all the time, not a one of us is immune to it. I know I'm certainly guilty of it; it's something I'm working on, though: *always trust your gut*, my little strangelings. It's so very rarely wrong and in the event that it is? You still kept yourself safe and there is *never* anything wrong with that.

I digress, likely by the millionth time in this book, but whatever…

The cabin was clean and well kept, cozy and as I said before, rather idyllic – so there was honestly no real *reason* for her unease.

She just chalked it up to watching one too many videos about Appalachia spooky time – as she was more than a bit of an enthusiast at the time.

The family brought in their belongings and established who would be staying in which rooms and kicked off their vacation.

By all accounts they had a blast, it was a fabulous week spent doing what you do when out and around in these parts.

By the end of the week, the misgivings she'd felt upon their arrival had totally evaporated, and she hadn't put a thought toward them since – but then, on their last night in the cabin, shit went south. *Way south.*

It was around midnight, and the family had just gotten out of the cabin's hot tub and gone in to watch some television before bed. As they were watching, they started to hear bloodcurdling screams emanating from the forest all around the cabin.

The family grabbed their flashlights and ran out into the night convinced that someone out there was in trouble and in desperate need of help – clearly they didn't know the rules about Appalachia – but I fully admit, I would have done the same… while I dialed 9-1-1 to get the calvary and the true professionals on the move.

I'd rather look stupid to a pack of first responders than have my face eaten off by a Wendi-boi or get whapped to death with a tree by Bigfoot.

Once outside on the huge wraparound deck, the family shining their lights into the woods in frantic search of whoever was screaming they started to pick out *other* sounds in addition to the wild and panicked shrieking. Scratching and rustling, crunching sounds like footsteps or possibly worse – but no matter where they shone their lights, they detected no movement. No branches shook, no trees swayed, there was nothing… nothing but those awful, awful, sounds.

Sounds of running, of grunting and groaning, and that awful, awful screaming.

This family wasn't some city slicking family from the urban jungle, either. These were kindhearted country folk from up there in rural Kentucky – so they were familiar with all kinds of your run-of-the-mill animal noises – and they swear up and down, this ain't it.

That they had heard nothing like this before.

Even their dog, who was typically super chill about stuff was on high alert beside them, hackles raised, growling and barking – and so it was obvious to them that the dog was hearing this too, and that it didn't like what it was hearing either – not one bit.

After several minutes of not being able to see a fucking thing, and wisely deciding to stay *on the porch*, the family decided there wasn't anything else to be done, and so they went back inside.

Things quieted down, everyone went to bed – albeit uneasily, and it was probably an hour and some change later when everyone was fast asleep except for the mom. She's lying in bed beside her sleeping husband, wide awake in the master bedroom when she hears knocking – but not at the front door, but rather the door from the master bedroom onto the wraparound porch, with some direct access to that hot tub they'd been in earlier that night.

She sat up in bed, her husband softly breathing in the deep and even intonation of deep sleep and listened, straining her ears, half convincing herself that she was imagining things. She was frozen with fear, staring at the (thankfully) sturdy wooden door to the outside. She said she was afraid for a couple of reasons, the least of which that it was after one in the morning, and rapidly sliding into the wee hours of darkest night. The main reason for her concern, however, was that if someone were to come knocking at any hour – shouldn't it be at the *front* door of the cabin? Not the bedroom door leading to the outside…

Even if someone wanted to knock on the bedroom door to get their attention, it wasn't exactly convenient. From the porch, it was a very narrow gap, to reach said door, and in the dark out there with no light? It wasn't exactly easy to find it.

The woman looked at her husband who was sitting up and wide awake by now, with his eyes glued to the door – letting her know without words that he'd heard it too and she wasn't crazy.

She said to her husband, "Now I know you heard that, too!" and he said, "Uh, yeah."

Now I did mention that these were folk from Kentucky – but I also mentioned they weren't no city slickers by any means. So, both husband and wife got out of bed and went for their firearms that they'd brought with them.

The husband told his wife to be extremely cautious and quiet but by this point, her nerves were jangled pretty hard. Her children sleeping in other parts of the cabin and an unknown quantity knocking at the parent's bedroom door to the outside? Hell no.

Mama bear armed herself, and heart in her throat, went to the bedroom window. She hoped that she could see around into the niche where the door resided by the hot tub – but alas, her view was obstructed by the general layout of things in the way the building was built – it was about that time that the knocking began again but this time, accompanying the knocking on the door, footfalls began – *on the roof.*

They never did hear footsteps on the deck, just that knocking at the door and those terrifying footfalls overhead from the cabin's roof. Something she figured was impossible considering any time she or one of her family members had set foot on that deck outside around the cabin, their footfalls had reverberated throughout the entire cabin.

So how could anyone be on the roof, and how could *anyone* have gotten to the door to knock without her hearing them on the deck first?

The woman plucked up enough courage that she went to the door and was about to unlock it when her husband stayed her hand and said that wasn't the best idea.

Her next step was to go out to the living room, and switch on every single outdoor light she had access to from switches on the inside. She peered out the windows, going around the entire cabin to look, but no one and nothing was there.

They never saw anything, and the sounds had stopped.

To this day, the woman is convinced that the two incidents are tied together. That whatever had been outside screaming bloody murder, and whatever had knocked on the door and walked across the cabin's roof, were one and the same creature.

With nothing out there, and no longer feeling as brave as she had when she'd gone to the bedroom's door to the outside, she and her husband switched off the lights and went back to bed – but still she lay awake in the dark, anxious for daylight to come.

It probably wasn't an hour more before her dog came and woke her out of the light sleep that she'd uneasily managed to fall into herself. She got up, dreading the fact that her dog needed to go out to pee.

She was absolutely terrified to take her dog out, but she didn't want it to use the bathroom in the beautiful cabin that they were just renting, so she again took up her firearm and in the other hand, took a knife from the kitchen – which girl, I know you was scared – but really?

She went out with the dog and let it do its business, but she says that the whole time they were out there, there was the heaviest, creepiest, most intense foreboding feeling that she has ever felt in her life, and the dog was absolutely fixated and staring off into the woods where the screaming had come from, just growling, hackles raised, the entire time it was out there with her.

They made it back inside safely, and locked the doors, checking that everything was secure and managed to go back to bed… but sleep was elusive even though the remainder of the night was quiet and uneventful.

The next morning, bags packed and loaded, the family made one last circuit of the cabin and its porch looking for any sign that anyone or anything had been there – but they found *nothing*.

Grateful to be going home, the woman swore that as much as she enjoyed the rest of their stay in that cabin, that after that last night of being there, she and her family would *never* return.

To that, I say, I'm with her – there are some experiences in Appalachia even I won't try to mess or play with and this is certainly one of those examples.

Pigeon Forge

SKY HARBOR CABIN

Sky Harbor lies a little bit between Pigeon Forge and Gatlinburg, but apparently more on the Pigeon Forge end of the spectrum or whatever – so we're going to put this here.

This happened to a woman and her family around 2017 when her husband, son, and in-laws rented this *gigantic* and beautiful cabin in the Sky Harbor area.

When they arrived, the place was *everything* they had hoped for in a family vacation destination, and they were excited. The place had more bedrooms than they could choose from, a giant recreational game room, a hot tub, and just about every amenity that you could want for your mountain getaway in the Smokies… and lucky for us, one of those amenities was *ghosts* – although I think this family might disagree with my assessment. According to them, that was one amenity they could do without!

To give you a clue on where this cabin might be, the woman who rented it said that from the porch of the thing, you could see the *entire* spread of Pigeon Forge down below – and from the description of it, I would hazard a guess that it was a fairly modern type cabin, meaning a relatively new build at the time. Not exactly someplace you roll up on and immediately think it's haunted. Far from it, in fact.

Now, the in-laws took the main floor bedroom downstairs while she, her husband, and son took a couple of the bedrooms up in the loft area.

First night, everyone goes to bed, and she said they'd been laying there for a little while when she begins to hear sounds coming from downstairs. Almost like someone is knocking at the front cabin door.

She wakes her husband up, who had fallen asleep before her, (typical – I envy the shit out of men for that particular talent. Seriously. 7,000 position changes and a sacrifice to the old gods, not the new, and I *might* fall asleep inside an hour – but more often than not, no.) and she asks him, "What are your parents *doing* down there?"

…

…

…

It's okay. I write romance novels for a living as my day job. My mind went there, too.

Her husband just mumbles something about her just hearing or imagining things and tells her to go back to sleep.

(Dude, you're lucky she loves you and that you're still married. I'm just saying.)

A short time later, her son comes into their room and tells them both "You guys need to quit shushing me!"

Mom and Dad were understandably both confused and demanded to know what the ever-loving fark he was talking about – neither one of them were shushing him.

He told them that he could hear someone softly going '*shhh!*' at him.

This wasn't her or her husband, but she just kind of shrugged it off. She fully admits this freaks her out – but she just tried to wave it off for herself as much as her kid and just told her kid that neither of them was doing it, and to go back to bed, which he did.

Over the next couple of nights, both she *and* her husband heard the noises from downstairs. Sounds like knocking, banging, and chairs being dragged across the floor. One night, they even heard the hot tub come on all by itself on the patio out back.

Both just kind of assumed it was her husband's parents but they both thought to themselves it was awfully late for them to be up, but hey – they were on vacation, so she and her hubby agreed just not to say anything.

On their last day at the cabin, they're all packing up and getting ready to leave and her son went out on the porch to play. With her son outside, her father-in-law approached her and said, "We need to talk."

I legit hate it when people do that, don't you? I'd rather face a full-on demonic entity rather than the drop my heart does into my damn toes at those four little words.

This is when her father-in-law spills the beans that he and *his* wife had *also* been hearing the strange noises within the cabin at night and throughout their stay. The knocking, the banging, and the hot tub coming on all by itself.

Now the husband chalked that up to it just being a mechanical failure of some sort, or a short in the system or something – and while that's a *possibility*... in conjunction with the other activity in the cabin, I'm voting ghosties.

The father-in-law really buried the lead on this one, though, because he then told her and his son that one of those nights he was lying in bed listening to the goings-on outside the bedroom, he started to hear scratching sounds *inside* the bedroom with he and his wife.

...and they sounded like they were coming from under their bed.

[Insert surprised Pikachu face.]

What surprised me even more than this tidbit of information was that dude was actually brave enough that he *rolled over* in the direction of the sounds to look; and when he looked, he said that he saw a little girl, standing or sitting *in the floor*. Not *on* it, but *in* it. She was also pretty much nightmare fuel with long dark hair really dark eyes, with her hands and arms outstretched to him like she wanted him to pick her up.

Nope. I don't like that.

Neither did he, apparently, because he said upon seeing this, he turned right back over because he followed the rules – he saw that thing and *no he didn't!*

Of course, it wasn't long before the urge to double check came over him, and when he looked back over his shoulder – just as quickly as the little ghost girl had appeared, she was gone.

He did what any intelligent adult of his age would do in this situation, and quickly had himself convinced that he hadn't seen anything and that it was just a dream – a really realistic dream, but just a dream.

Mother-in-law kind of blew his theory out of the self-starting hot tub's water, however, when she said no, that she had heard the scratching noises, too. Just as he had described, but that they had to be batshit crazy if they thought she was going to open her eyes and look for what was making the sound with all the other weird shit that was going on night after night leading up to that one.

The family said they'd never been believers in ghosts in the paranormal, but here it is seven years on and they *still* talk about that haunted cabin, and with no earthly explanation as to all of the goings-on and what her father-in-law clearly said that he saw that night; they're certainly reluctant believers now.

High five, little ghost girl. High five.

AN ALARMING STAY

This one is from a man, age unknown, who said this happened to him when he was twelve or thirteen. He said that his parents had rented a cabin in Pigeon Forge for a family vacation one year, something they had done many times before, but this particular cabin wasn't one that they had ever stayed in before.

He said it wasn't super fancy or anything, but that it had all of the amenities his family had been looking for, for their trip, and that it was nice enough.

The cabin had an alarm system on the doors to it, and the father set it before the little family of three settled in on their first night of what was to be a five-day vacation to watch a movie together.

It wasn't long into the movie before the alarm for one of the doors began to go off, as though someone was trying to enter the cabin. This was obviously alarming to the family, and the dad got up to check things out – of course, no one was out there, but they couldn't get the system to turn off.

So, they of course, called the cabin's management company and the management company sent a maintenance guy out their way right away.

He got there, checked things out, and said he didn't know what was up because there was nothing wrong with the system buuuut, this was probably the fourth or fifth time he had been out this way for the same complaint in a month or less, thus assuring the little family it was definitely *not* them.

Now the fam thought that was a little odd, but they didn't think anything of it, but by the time all was said and done, they were tired and the hour was growing late, and so they just decided to go to bed.

Different strokes for different folks here, my little strangelings; the man telling this story looped us in the know that the family sleeping arrangements were a little less than conventional but for a very good reason. You see, his dad snored a lot, and *loud*. Loud to the point that no one could stand to be around him if they wanted any sleep of their own, and so to that end, Dad took himself down to the basement level bedroom, while the son stayed on the main floor and mom went up to a bedroom on the second floor.

Now the man telling the story said that he went to sleep, but that at about two in the morning he was woken up by a noise outside his bedroom's door which was where the kitchen was here on the main level.

His door stood open, and he could see the light from the refrigerator door and watched as the fridge door opened and closed, and opened, and closed, and opened and closed, doing this pretty much non-stop as though someone stood there bored and just opened and closed it. He wasn't at the greatest angle to see *who* was opening and closing the fridge door, but he said he could see shadows moving in the light from it and he said that he just sort of assumed it was his mom or dad out there doing it.

He said that he eventually heard footsteps retreating across the kitchen floor and away from the fridge and make their way up the staircase where his mom was, so he brushed it off in his own mind as being her.

…until the next morning when he asked her, what had she gotten for her snack last night?

Mom looked at her son and told him, "It wasn't me!"

He told her that he thought sure that it was, and that he'd seen her go up the stairs.

The family promptly checked out, he said – never to return again.

Smart family.

If my twelve- or thirteen-year-old told me something like that, and

I know I hadn't been anywhere near the kitchen the night before, I would have noped on out of there with the quickness, too!

I Don't Quit, But I Won't Clean That One!

A young lady would sometimes help her mother, who was employed by a rental company to clean the cabins they owned after the guests had vacated them. She went with her mother on one particular day to this cabin in Pigeon Forge, and had the following to say about her time there:

She said that this particular cabin is similarly laid out to many of the others mentioned in this portion of the book. You enter a living space, with a kitchen and dining area beyond on the main floor. Standard stuff, she said, and on this particular day pretty normal – as in nothing felt different or weird on her arrival.

It wasn't until she started to head upstairs that she reported things feeling... *off*. In fact, she described it as being a whole different feeling upstairs than down on the main level.

Up there on the second floor felt heavy, and she reported that she near instantly fell prey to a *severe*, skull-crushing headache and the feeling as though her chest was tightening up. She said she heard a door close, all on its own. Not like it slammed, but it definitely drifted shut, and rather than just resting on the strike plate like most doors do when they happen to drift shut on their own, this door *shut*, as in closed completely, the mechanism giving an audible *snick* as the latch clicked home.

She starts cleaning the bedroom on the second level, despite the uncomfortableness and eventually, not long into it, she hears her mom call out to her.

She hollers back, but her mom doesn't respond. Shrugging this off, she just went ahead and finished up cleaning the bedroom, figuring she would just find out what her mom wanted later.

Once she was through, she promptly went back downstairs to find out from her mom what her mother had needed.

Her mom was confused and said she didn't know what she was talking about, she hadn't yelled for her.

Obviously, she thought this was weird, but she ultimately shook it off and started up cleaning again. She was into things for a fair bit when suddenly, she could swear *something was breathing on her*. She could feel it, on the back of her neck. She whirled, fully expecting to find someone looming behind her, but of course, there was no one there.

This frightened her badly enough that she noped on out of there and decided she would just head right on back downstairs to her mom and help her out the rest of the time they were there. You know, with her mamma in the room – where she wasn't alone, because *hell no*.

She was downstairs helping her mother, telling her what she'd experienced upstairs and letting her mom know she would please like to hurry it up so they could get out of there, when *SLAM!* It came from overhead; a door upstairs had slammed shut.

Her mother and her stared at each other wide eyed and without any preamble, called one of their male coworkers to get him to come over and check things out and to make sure there wasn't someone else in the cabin with them.

No sooner did he come through the cabin's front door when all three of them heard sounds emanating from overhead, as though someone was moving around, and even perhaps *furniture* around the bedroom upstairs.

Their male coworker went up to check things out, and when he returned, he said nothing was out of place, but that the closet door in that bedroom, the door handle was jiggling on it a bit. Of course, there was no one in the closet.

He helped them to finish the cabin forthwith and the trio got out of there as soon as possible.

When they got outside, or sometime after they had left the cabin, the woman who had experienced the most activity found scratches on her legs and her back that had no earthly explanation. It was at the appearance of these scratches that she and her mother both decided, *nope!* They didn't *quit*, but they were *never* going back into that particular cabin again – someone else could clean it.

Sounds to me like someone needs to cleanse it, not just clean it.

There's Something in That Cabin

In 1991, a family took a vacation in the Smokies with their brood of children. There was a father, a mother, three boys who were, at the time, 8, 10, and 13, their 16-year-old sister and one of her friends, another girl in the same age range, and her parents.

It was to be a five-day vacation, and this story comes from the then-10-year-old-boy; we'll call him Brian.

Brian said that their first night in the cabin was uneventful, that it was a little eerie, but that was easily chalked up to being in a strange place far from home.

On their first official day of vacation, they headed down into Gatlinburg to do some sightseeing and shopping. It was there that Brian was totally stoked, as his dad bought him an archery set. He couldn't *wait* to get back to the cabin and set up some targets among the trees out back.

As soon as they got back, that's *exactly* what he did. Pinning targets to trees and setting them up in various places before commencing shooting and getting acquainted with his new bow.

Now where he was shooting at was next to the cabin and its basement, where there was a window that he could see from the spot he was standing in.

Everything was going just fine, when out of the corner of his eye, he saw something in the window of the basement – a flicker of movement, or something he realized hadn't been there before.

He turned to look more fully and saw something that absolutely sent chills throughout his whole body.

There, in the window, was a pure white figure of a man standing inside the cabin's basement, eyeing him from the basement window.

He said this absolutely terrified him, and he ran immediately to find an adult.

The first one he found was his dad, and he told his father exactly what he had just seen and begged him to come quickly.

His dad immediately went with Brian to check things out, and once in the cabin's backyard, discovered the only door leading into the basement was locked, with a padlock on the *outside* of the basement door. There was actually no way to get into this basement door from the outside.

Brian's father dismissed him, but Brian insisted that he knew what he saw: The white figure of a man, standing in that window watching him!

Unfortunately, his dad didn't really think anything of it, his dad being a jokester type just thought Brian was trying to get one over on him and prank him or some such and left his ten-year-old son to play, disappointed and creeped out in the back yard – going inside to rejoin the other adults.

The sighting was put aside and all but forgotten about until the next day.

Brian's older, 13-year-old brother was in the kitchen the next day, making himself something to eat. He uses a can opener in the process, and lays it down on the counter, and went about preparing his food when all of a sudden this can opener *flew* off the kitchen counter by itself.

Unfortunately, he didn't tell anyone that this had happened, he just kept it to himself for the time being, but after more time went on, and more activity surfaced, it became a much relevant piece to the puzzle in understanding *this cabin be haunted, yo.*

He would eventually come clean about this incident, by the end of the vacation, after a slew of other paranormal events took place.

For the next day or two, things were quiet – not much else happened, or if it did, it was so low-key the family either didn't notice it at all or dismissed it as some other naturally occurring phenomenon with a perfectly sound and worldly explanation.

It was their last night in the cabin when they were all lying down and getting ready for bed.

Brian said that he and his brother were on the second floor in the loft area, on the pull-out bed that he was sharing with one of his brothers. Next to this room was his sister's room which she was sharing with her friend that was along for the trip.

Now Brian had a light on in the loft area and his room, while his sister's room was dark – which he could tell, because her doorway wasn't but six feet away from where he occupied.

He then said that out of nowhere, his sister and her friend both just start *screaming*. That they jump up, running out of their room, straight past Brian and their brother, and bolt downstairs to their parents.

To this day, Brian says that he hasn't seen *anyone* more terrified than his sister and her friend were in the moment that they fled that room.

It took the parents a while to get the girls to calm down enough to tell them what had happened, and this is what they said when they did:

Brian's sister was lying in bed on her back, her friend laying on her stomach next to her.

At some point, his sister had opened her eyes to see a full-bodied apparition of a woman just hovering above her and the bed, staring her in the face.

His sister nudged her friend, and told her to turn over and to look, asking her friend after she complied, "Are you seeing what I'm seeing?"

Her friend confirmed it, but also pointed out that there was a second apparition in the room – that of a man, standing at the foot of the bed.

That's when they both bolted up out of bed and ran for it.

Their dad, being the kind of joker that he was, didn't buy it – still convinced his kids were trying to pull a fast one on him. Still, despite that, the kids were all scared enough that they refused to go back upstairs, and all opted to huddle in one of the downstairs rooms together.

Brian's dad, being the practical joker that he was, snuck back up to the second level to make creepy noises and to throw some pillows around, trying to get a laugh out of his kids – which Brian said he was grateful to his dad for trying to bring levity to the situation and now as a grown man, he misses his dad for his laughter and joking ways, but that it didn't do much to make the kids feel better.

The next morning, as everyone was packing up their stuff, they run into the guy who was the caretaker of the cabin, coming in to start the process of flipping it after the family's stay for the next guests that were coming that night.

Brian brought up the things they had experienced the night before and throughout their stay, and the caretaker looked at Brian's dad and said, "Aw, yeah – the reason the basement door is padlocked is because years ago, a newlywed couple was here staying for their honeymoon. For whatever reason, the guy thought it would be a good idea to pick up his new bride and carry her down the basement steps. He lost his footing, both of them fell down the steps, and both of them ended up dying from their injuries."

He then went on to say that you could still see bloodstains from the incident on those same basement steps and in the basement area.

Brian said he was absolutely floored by what the caretaker had to say and that more than anything else that had happened during their vacation had convinced him that he had indeed seen a ghost.

CHOCOLATE BEAR LODGE

A pair of young newlyweds around the ages of eighteen and nineteen were looking to take the honeymoon of their dreams out in the Pigeon Forge and Gatlinburg area after coming into a little bit of money to pay for the trip together.

They found an affordable cabin off King Branch Road on the Pigeon Forge side of things called Chocolate Bear Cabin and decided that this would be just perfect. Nice and cozy, a romantic getaway for just the two of them.

Upon their arrival, the first thing the couple noticed about the place was that the driveway was exceedingly steep. One would even say precarious to traverse. A nightmare in and of itself, really; leaving them to set their parking brake just to feel some small measure of security in leaving their vehicle parked out front.

It was so bad that just to be on the safe side, the gentleman half of the couple found some stones to chock the tires with to ensure that even if the parking brake failed it wouldn't roll back and off the side of things.

The second thing they noticed was that the basement portion of the cabin was boarded completely up with signage declaring things like 'do not enter' and 'employees only beyond this point' the doors padlocked with sturdy locks and hasps.

They thought that to be odd, that every window and door was boarded, covered, and locked up tight and that the rental company or whoever had gone a bit overboard with the signage stating that no one was allowed entry or beyond that point. However, they dismissed it in order to go up and have a look at the cabin's living space where they would be staying.

The cabin's interior living space was cozy and quaint; the perfect little place for them for a romantic little weekend getaway... but something felt... off about it.

The couple later described their feeling upon entry, like that of entering an old western saloon – the music stops, all eyes turned on them and the tension in the room so thick you could cut it with a knife – which was just silly honestly. Obviously, they were alone, just the two of them, and there was no one there to stare at them or whatever. Still, the feeling was a palpable one and not one that they could easily shake.

In addition to feeling as though several pairs of invisible eyes sized them up, the two also felt quite the icy chill come over them upon stepping over the threshold. A chill they had no earthly explanation for.

Between the steep pitch of the driveway, the cabin's isolated feel, the creepy cordoned off basement, the feeling of being watched like they were, and that cold chill – to say this young couple was nervous was quite the understatement, but both just sort of went with it and decided they'd paid for it, and the payment was non-refundable at this point, so they might as well make the best of things.

Besides, it probably was nothing more than the both of them having first time being away from home together jitters.

Yeah.

That was it.

(I'm rolling my eyes; in case you couldn't tell.)

They unpacked their belongings and put them away, deciding it was still early enough in the day that they could go down into Pigeon Forge to enjoy the evening there, and so they left again, and when they started back down that steep driveway, the further they got from the cabin, the better they felt, all those feelings of heavy dread of just moments before melting into the ether.

Of course, the minute they returned from Pigeon Forge and climbed that steep hill, parking outside the cabin once more, those rough feelings of dread and foreboding returned.

Still, the couple pushed those misgivings aside, again chalking it up to both of them being only around eighteen and this being their first time truly alone together and away from home.

They went inside, and the girl professing that she was tired, went in to go lay down while he opted to spend just a little bit exploring the rest of the cabin.

He checked the rest of the place out, minus the basement which he said they had locked up like Fort Knox from the inside, too; until the last place left to look at was the upstairs loft area.

He wandered over to the bottom of the steps, but that was as far as he got. He later went on to say that no matter how hard he thought about it, and tried to get his body to move, he just couldn't bring himself to take that first step up onto the bottom stair riser – let alone any other steps after that first one that might be required to climb the staircase.

He said the feeling of just straight fear and dread kept him stationary and he just could not do it.

As he looked up the stairs, he noted a small triangular window up in the loft area, and for whatever reason, that window instilled in him such a creeping dread. As though the longer he stared at it, the more he expected eyes from the window to be looking back at him.

The whole thing gave him the heebs something fierce, and rather than press it or force himself to do what the silent alarm bells in his head were warning him against, he decided that he might as well go to bed, too.

He laid down beside his young bride, and rather than make a big deal about it, just made a low-key and passing comment about the cabin being a little on the creepy side.

To his surprise, she agreed with him, almost a little too vehemently. She agreed that yes, the cabin was *very* creepy, and that she didn't know the why behind it, but that *something* sure wasn't right about it.

They decided it wasn't worth talking about beyond that – after all, they still had to sleep here, and it was right before bed.

They decided to just go to sleep and forget about the pervasive feelings of wrongness permeating the Chocolate Bear Lodge for now.

Surely tomorrow would be better.

They lay close together, cuddling in the dark, and both were just on the edge of sleep when they heard it.

Whispers. Like two or more people having a full-on conversation, but quiet enough so as to be indistinct.

They didn't want to believe the sounds emanated from inside the house, and thus, they convinced themselves it was people at the mini-golf course up the road. That they were just being loud and it was a trick of the acoustics both in here and outside where the sound could drift through the trees and bounce off the rock faces.

They were both just trying to rationalize everything at this point. Just hoping that somehow, some way, this cabin would get better when it came to the ambience.

No sooner had they gotten close to sleep a second time, than the bedroom they were in suddenly became overwhelmingly and swelteringly hot. The kind of hot where the air felt thickened and it was almost hard to breathe. So hot, that neither one of them could stand to lay a minute longer.

Both of them opting to get up and walk into the kitchen to check the thermostat, although nothing about it was out of sorts, and the rest of the cabin felt just fine.

They both resorted to leaving the bedroom door open and to taking cold showers to alleviate their overheated feeling. Both were hoping that the next morning, things would be better. That it wouldn't feel as oppressive in here, and that the strong feelings of dread and discomfort would be gone.

Alas, it was not to be. The young man saying that when they woke up the next morning, his young bride looked *ill*. So pale and distressed that he thought honestly, she should be taken to a doctor.

She insisted that she was fine and was determined not to ruin their day's plans. They rose, dressed, and she powered through and they left the cabin. No sooner had they left the property, than she began to perk up, and both look and feel much better.

By the time they got out into the Smoky Mountains, she was right as rain and they spent a wonderful day together enjoying the Smokies and the park.

But no sooner had they returned to the cabin, and she mysteriously fell ill again.

She said not to worry and asked her new husband to run into town and get her some medicine from a pharmacy while she tried to just lay down and to rest for a bit, to see if that would help. She was sure some aspirin or Tylenol would help. He agreed, kissed her goodbye, and ran down into town.

When he returned, however, he found her sitting outside the cabin at the little picnic table. Something that he thought was odd, but that she refused to talk about. He pressed, she evaded the subject, and said she just wanted to take some medicine and could they please just go to bed?

He relented, and they did, but like the night before, the whispers and the talking started, and once again the room became unbearably hot and this time? They could see shadows passing in front of the dim lights from outside, coming through the blinds. Like someone was walking around the place.

Just as suddenly as the noises had begun, they ceased, and there was a knocking at the cabin's front door.

They were both terrified, but his wife said, "You have to check that out."

So, he got up, and made his way to the front door, and he said as he approached it, he could see a shadowy figure on the other side of the frosted glass, indistinct and about the size of a finger, wavering closer and further away, as though rocking forward and back.

He didn't open the door, but rather went to the kitchen window and peeked out – and of course, saw no one outside on the front step. Saw nothing at all.

He decided not to tell his girlfriend. He went back to bed and the next morning; they packed up and headed out. It was as they were descending the steep driveway in their car that she came clean about what she had experienced the day before that had made her wait outside at the picnic table for his return.

She said that as she was lying in bed, trying to rest, the room had become unbearably hot once again. So, she had taken herself outside to sit at the picnic table, and as she'd sat there, an old man in a pickup truck had come up the driveway. He'd stayed in the truck, but had rolled down the window, and had started to talk with her. She said he was a nice enough old man, and that she hadn't felt threatened at all. That he'd asked all of the usual pleasant small-talk questions, like, "Where are you from?" and "How's it going?" just making general nice conversation.

At some point during their small talk, he stopped and asked, "What's your boyfriend doing up there?" and she told the truth like a dumb teenager and said, "He's actually at the store grabbing me some medicine."

She said that the old guy had looked at her perplexed and asked her, "Then who is that up there in the window?"

When she followed his gaze, she too saw a dark silhouette of a person in one of the windows, and that when she turned back, the older man had looked unnerved, and just suddenly drove off.

She said she had been too scared to say anything about it when he'd returned, and that's why she'd been so quiet.

The man that told this story said that the Chocolate Bear Lodge has changed names several times since he and his bonny bride had stayed there, and that he wasn't even sure if the same management company owned it or whatever – but from time to time, he would look up reviews for the place to see if anyone else had experienced anything paranormal or inexplicable. He found it interesting to note, several of the lower star reviews mentioned that the cabin was cold when it shouldn't be, which he found curious, as that was the exact opposite problem he and his girl had.

As far as I know, the Chocolate Bear Lodge is still available to vacation goers – just under a new and unknown name.

It's also just the first of several haunted cabins mentioned on King's Branch Road – so read on my little strangelings. The paranormal party is just getting started.

GATLINBURG

The Cabin at the Top of King Branch Rd.

Same street, different cabin at this point. This time, like our first story, the cabin was occupied by a couple out of Nashville, just looking for a romantic getaway… unfortunately, their experience left them *wanting to get away!*

They couldn't even spend a whole night in the place.

While I'm not sure if this was the same cabin as the cabin in our very first account on King Branch Rd, I *do* have an approximate date, this incident taking place sometime in 2013.

Story goes that the woman in question and her husband were just looking for some alone time with one another for a weekend. They were frequent visitors to the area having vacationed here off and on for over thirty-five years – so this wasn't some city slicker newlywed young couple unfamiliar with the sounds etc. of the Appalachians. No, these were all but locals – heralding from just the next time zone away.

Now, they fully admit, when they tended to stay around the Smokies, they generally chose cabins or locations a bit closer to town that this – but again, they were looking to get away and connect and leave the outside world and any distractions from one another behind… so they picked a more isolated cabin this time around.

The trip was already off to a rough start for the lady of half of this cis het couple, the drive up to this particular cabin being steep and full of sheer drop offs and switch back curves. Her nerves were already a bit jangled – but adding to that, they didn't manage to arrive until *late*. It was 9 p.m. or so, and already after dark by the time they pulled up in front of the place – and it was as they had wanted: isolated.

They got out of the car, went up to the door, put in the code – and it doesn't work. Annoyed but undaunted, they tried a few more times and as luck would have it, whatever glitch in the system that was going on, worked itself out and they gained access to their cabin.

Relieved, they went inside.

It was a spacious, three level building. On the main floor, the kitchen and living room areas, the master bedroom, and master bath.

On the top level was a loft area with a pool table, and a pull-out couch that could be made into a bed if they had more guests or a family wanted to stay – and on the bottom level were two bedrooms with a shared bathroom.

So not the same cabin as 5150 or the aforementioned cabin on the same road – just to reiterate and make that clear.

Now, even though it was late – this couple decided *fuck it* and opened a bottle of wine. They were officially on vacation, after all, and they wanted to waste no more time in getting to relaxing than they already had. To that end, wine glasses and bottle in tow, they went out onto the deck for a nighttime dip in the hot tub before bed. (I like this idea.)

The husband changed into his trunks and opened up the wine, while his wife took her time getting ready. Taking the opportunity, while she changed into her swimsuit, to open up the hot tub, stage their wine, and take a walk around the perimeter of the deck that wrapped around the cabin, just to check things out and explore a little.

Now the wife, she was in the master bathroom changing, and rather than starting to unwind from the long trip in, she had a rather uneasy feeling come over her – to the point that she felt like she was getting wound tighter, rather than unwinding as she had intended. She had no explanation for this, other than a distinct feeling that she was being watched. The feeling was unnerving, and only grew in intensity to the point she was distinctly uncomfortable – the weight of some unseen gaze almost a palpable thing, an almost physical weight against her skin.

She did her best to brush this off, telling herself that it was just a new environment, a new-to-her and strange place and further out into the boonies than she was usually comfortable with.

No big deal, it would pass.

She made her way out into the living area where her husband was waiting on her.

In order to get to the hot tub on the lower outdoor deck of this cabin, they had to traverse the indoor set of stairs to the bottom level and go out through the doors to the outside onto the deck. However, as they headed down the stairs, she said that the lights in the cabin began to flicker.

The couple laughed it off, saying to each other something to the effect of it being spooky or creepy, but didn't think much of it at the time.

They got out onto the deck and switched on the porch or deck lights and nothing happened. The lights didn't work.

No lights. It's completely dark, and if you've never been to the Appalachians that far up or out at night, it gets *dark*, my little strangelings.

Now she was pretty creeped out by this, to the point she didn't even really want to get into the hot tub anymore, but her husband blew it off completely and said they didn't really need any lights and that it might actually be nice to cozy up in the hot tub with their wine in the dark.

After all, it would be fine. There wasn't anyone out there but them. Besides, they didn't have to stay too terribly long. Just a few minutes to relax stiff muscles from the drive and to drink a glass of wine each before going to bed.

After only about three minutes in the hot tub wifey was ready to tap out. She couldn't explain it, but she had just this *overwhelming* sense of dread. Fear wrapping its hand over her nose and mouth until she felt as though she were suffocating with the emotion. She just felt *anxious*, and she just couldn't stand to be in the water any longer.

She began to argue with her husband about how much she just wanted to nope right the fuck out of there, but again he was like, *babe, chill*, it's all good. Everything is *fine*. Just relax!

They stayed a few minutes longer, but with every second that ticked by, she just felt more anxious. When her husband finally had enough of the hot tub, they both got out and dried off. They went back to the door that they'd come out onto the deck through – and it wouldn't open.

They wiggled the doorknob, they pushed, they pulled, but it wouldn't budge.

Panic mode engaged.

This went on for several minutes, their anxiety rising – there was no other door, or even a window that would open for them to get back inside, and it wasn't like they had brought their phones out here near the *hot tub*.

They were trapped out on this deck in this cabin, out in the fucking boonies and *oh, shit*!

It makes me anxious just thinking about it, what about you?

As if not being able to gain reentry into the cabin wasn't bad enough, the entire time they fought with the damn door, the lights on the inside began to flicker again.

They began to really panic, when one of them reached for the doorknob *one more time,* and lo-and-behold, it twisted and the door opened up like it hadn't been stuck fast just the moment and for several minutes before.

Wordlessly, the pair went back inside, returning upstairs to the master bedroom and bath. They took a shower together, as much to calm their nerves and to try and relax from what was supposed to be a relaxing time in the hot tub, before they retired to bed.

As they lay in the close dark with one another, just as they began to drift off into sleep, they both smelled the unmistakable odor of cigarette smoke.

Neither one of the two were smokers, nor anyone else was in the house – so what was this, now?

The odor was potent, the couple describing it as though someone were standing in the room with them with a lit cigarette, so strong that one could believe it was intentionally being blown in their direction.

Obviously, no one was in the room with them, and they reported there was no *visible* smoke anywhere, but the odor was there and was just that *strong*.

Just as soon as the odor had kicked up, so too did the *sounds* from the loft. The distinct sounds of billiard balls clacking together and off the sides of the table, accompanied by voices and conversation taking place – although the words were too indistinct to make out what was being said.

Cue the *actual panic*.

It was after midnight by this time, and even still the couple immediately got out of bed, packed their shit, and noped right the fuck out of there with all of the haste. They went back down into town and got a hotel room instead. One with steady lighting and no phantom sounds or smells.

The experience they had was intense, and they swore that they spent barely a handful of hours at the cabin and that they wouldn't go back to that place if you paid them.

Meanwhile, I'm over here trying to figure out which one it is and the nightly rate. I'm totally down to party with Caspar and his homies. Seriously, take my money. Take my money, now.

THE CABIN ON KING BRANCH RD.

In 2018, a man and his family rented a cabin on King Branch Road between Pigeon Forge and Gatlinburg. Typically, these cabins are meant to be a relaxing getaway from the hustle and bustle of city life, but this stay would prove to be anything but.

It started with a rapping, as if someone gently tapping, rapping *from the inside of the walls*. You know, just your general poltergeist activity. A rap rap, here. A tap tap, there. Here a knock, there a knock – but before long *everywhere* there was a knock, knock.

Annoying, but low-key, and easily dismissible by the foundation settling or even wondering if you were really hearing anything in the first place.

Things escalated, though, when the man was showering in the upstairs bathroom adjacent to the master bedroom of the cabin. It was as he was doing his thing – lather, rinse, repeat – he paused and listened. *Really* listened, and he could swear that he heard the distinct sound of footsteps moving around in the master bedroom. Still, he was able to shrug this off – thinking it was his wife, or one of his kids. Not thinking much of it beyond that, as he finished washing up and got out.

He got dressed and wandered on downstairs, and it occurred to him and he asked his wife and kids what their wandering about in the master bedroom had been about.

The wife and kids admitted their confusion, confessing that *none of them* had been upstairs in the last little while. That they'd all been right here.

In addition to this unexplained activity, the televisions in the cabin would come on in various rooms at random all hours of the day and night. So too, would Amazon's Alexa which was wired into the home – belting out gibberish or answering random questions that hadn't been asked by him or his family.

Most of this was fairly ignorable or explainable – the wiring maybe was off or done incorrectly. Alexa was on the fritz – none of it happening with any major frequency or audacity to make them want to flee in terror or anything.

It was on their last morning in the cabin that the strangest and most blatant phenomenon occurred.

This family was one that took their shoes off in the house, and out of habit, they took their shoes off and lined them up inside the door – but on their last morning within the residence, they woke to find their shoes deliberately moved out from the wall in a diagonal line out into the room.

CABIN 5150

This story comes from around 2005, from a family vacationing from parts unknown in one of the larger cabins up around Gatlinburg.

The cabin was described as being one of the larger ones, enough to have a grand staircase and a loft area with a game room in addition to several bedrooms, a full kitchen, and other amenities typical to this mountainous region's getaways...

The family was a bit on the larger side, the woman telling the tale there with her husband and children, the oldest of which was a little girl who was three at the time. The grandparents of this little girl were present, some adult siblings and their teenage children as well. Your typical extended family vacation or gathering.

It had been a long drive for the woman telling the story, with her husband and small children. Their first night in the cabin spent relaxing, their toddlers playing on the grand staircase, and in fact, quite enamored with it, when the woman's three-year-old little girl came up to her and asked her mama, who the *other* little girl was, pointing up the stairs and to the loft area.

She was *very* insistent that there was another little girl present, and her mother was just as adamant that there was no one there. Still, this didn't sound like just an imaginary friend type of a deal and so she asked a few probative questions of the toddler – questions like what did this little girl look like?

The toddler replied that she looked like her, except taller and wearing a white dress or nightgown.

Soon distracted by other things, the woman dismissed the incident as a fluke, and it wasn't long after that everyone retired to bed.

The next morning is when things got weird.

The woman was up and making breakfast when her teenaged younger sister slid up into one of the seats at the table or counter complaining about "Why did you let the kids into my room last night?"

The older sister, perplexed, asked what her younger sister was talking about. Saying that she hadn't let her kids do anything the night before. The *other* sister, who also had her kids with her on this vacation said something to the effect of "Don't look at me, I didn't let my kids into your room last night, either. What makes you think there were kids in your room?"

The younger sister said that she'd been lying in bed with her back to the door when she heard the bedroom door open. She said that as the door opened, she could hear children laughing – like little girls. She said she didn't bother to turn over, figuring it was her young nieces, and that she just told them they needed to get out of her room so she could sleep. She said she heard the door close and that the laughter and giggling stopped, and she just figured her nieces had listened to her – still, she was annoyed they'd been allowed to run rampant to wake her up at all.

The older sisters, annoyed with their younger sister accusing their children of misbehaving when they hadn't, were certainly offended, and all but accused their teenaged younger sister of making things up – but the narrator of this story admitted that she was certainly starting to feel uneasy, especially given what her daughter had said the night before, insisting there was another little girl in the house when there most definitely was not.

It was at this point, her parents entered the kitchen. They had stayed on the bottom level of the cabin, in a bedroom that'd been located off of the cabin's game room, where a full billiards table took up residence.

The women and girl's mother said by way of greeting something to the effect of: "Girls, y'all are going to have to stay upstairs tonight after your dad and I go to bed. I'm not about to have a repeat performance of last night. You all kept us up all night carrying on and playing pool. We couldn't sleep for those balls clacking together. I won't have it tonight."

The girls all exchanged confused looks with one another.

"Who was playing pool?" the teen asked, annoyed. "I'd have played if I'd been invited."

"We didn't play pool," her sisters said looking at one another, the confusion clear on their faces.

"I went to bed before you and Dad did," the teenaged one said. "So, it wasn't me."

"It wasn't us, either," the two eldest daughters declared.

"Somebody was," their mother insisted, saying that the billiard balls had pretty much been making consistent noise off and on all night.

"Mom, we never even came downstairs!" one of the daughters insisted.

Now at this point, the three daughters of age were shaken, and none of the three believed that their mom believed them, but they all certainly believed each other – because they knew for a fact that they hadn't gone downstairs or played pool the night before.

They all had undergone a long drive the day before and had intended to go to Dollywood today, so there was no way they were going to stay up so late the night before doing all of that walking.

The woman and her family finished breakfast, the topic of conversation moving on to other things before everyone moved off to shower or otherwise get ready for the day.

The woman opted for a shower, then went back to her room to get dressed for the day, rooting through her bags to find a tank top that she knew she had packed two days prior specifically because Dollywood was going to be *hot* at the time of year they were there.

She found the tank top, one with thin spaghetti straps, but when she unfurled it, it was to find the straps had either been torn, or cut –

much to her annoyance because she *knew* nothing had been wrong with the shirt when she'd packed it.

That was apparently enough for her. They went to Dollywood the next day, had their fun, and stayed one more night in the cabin – but the morning after that, they didn't even finish out their vacation. They packed their belongings and left.

It wasn't long after this woman returned home that her mother called hysterically crying. It was as her mother was unpacking her suitcase, that she too found some of her belongings cut to ribbons – two pairs of her undergarments.

Up until that point, her mother hadn't bought into the spooky bullshit – but that was something enough to convince her, because she *knew* those undergarments had been whole when she'd packed them only days before.

She was certainly afraid now, the 'what if's' running rampant through her head about *what if one of her grandchildren had been hurt*. Looking at the state of her clothing, she was thoroughly convinced that they'd done the right thing in leaving early and that something sinister had been in that cabin – perhaps not even child ghosts at all, but something *pretending* to be children.

Now the title of this story is the only detail about the cabin that the woman remembers. She said it was owned by a property company then, that no longer owns it today – but that something about the cabin was '5150' – either the address, or the cabin number itself through the property company; that part she couldn't recall but she did remember 5150 specifically because of some Van Halen album. (The reference is lost on me, I'm not a huge fan of the band even if I do like some of their songs.)

At any rate, the cabin is still out there somewhere – I'm pretty sure it survived the Gatlinburg fires... just couldn't tell you which one it is. If I knew, I would divulge that information. I don't like to gatekeep knowledge of spooky places. I *do*, however, staunchly advocate being respectful of haunted locations and the people who own them. Leaving places in precisely the same condition or better than you found it.

If you happen to vacation in a cabin in the Smokies around Gatlinburg with the same characteristics as this one, my little strangelings, keep your eyes and ears open. If you think you've stayed in cabin 5150, contact me with your stories please? Contact information will be at the back of this book.

HEAVEN'S EDGE CABIN

This is another romantic getaway turned nightmare story from February of 2021, my little strangelings. In this story, a woman and her boyfriend were driving in for a romantic evening or weekend alone together – when – and this is fucked up – about thirty minutes from the cabin they had rented, they got a call from the rental company saying that the cabin they had initially booked was no longer available due to some kind of issue with plumbing or some such maintenance issue – but not to worry, they had them all booked in a different cabin for the same weekend…

Which, for me, as a paranormal investigator – RED FLAG!

It's February – so Valentines Day weekend, we have a couple, just like every other couple in the region, looking for that romantic cabin getaway and at the last minute *you have an empty cabin available?* Why? Why is that cabin available – seriously, my little strangelings! You have to ask yourself these questions because I'll bet you dollars to doughnuts the answer is, because the spare cabin is haunted as fuck, no one can make a night in it, and so they try not to book it unless a circumstance like this comes up because the company would rather roll the dice than refund any actual money.

How do I know? Because a haunted ass hotel straight up told me that's what they do with the haunted room – that they leave it to the very last unless it's requested rather than deal with all the problems guests will call down and complain about – but that's a story for another time and the hotel in question isn't even in East Tennessee.

You'll have to wait for another book for that or find it on my TikTok channel @soundparanormal (Shameless plug! Go watch everything if you didn't get here from there.)

Anyway, even though the trip wasn't a *complete* loss, being only thirty minutes away when they received this call, the couple was still, understandably, less than thrilled – especially considering they had no idea if this new cabin had any of the amenities that they'd booked their initial cabin for.

They arrived at the new cabin, and before the car was even in 'park' the woman reported feeling 'eerie' and that the atmosphere around the place was unreasonably heavy and creepy. Something just felt… *off* about the place according to her.

They went up to the door and tried the code that the rental company had given them and it didn't work… nor did the next one they received… nor the next – which was very strange according to the woman on the phone with the rental company. She ran them through several more codes and finally, access was seemingly granted and the couple was able to go in to check out their new weekend digs.

Remember, they hadn't so much as seen pictures of the place before their arrival.

Upon entering, they find the first bedroom just inside the main entryway, off to their right. They started there, checking things out, but didn't stay long in there – as the story goes, the atmosphere in that first room, despite being a somewhat decently sized room, felt *heavy*, almost claustrophobic and like the air was thick.

It wasn't just her, either – her boyfriend remarked on the feeling of the room and they were both in agreement – it was a whole lot of nope. They'd pick a different room, thank you very much.

The kitchen and living area was downstairs here as well, but they opted to go up to the second level to check things out up there.

Upstairs, they discovered a strange sitting area. Strange in that it was set up like a living room to watch a television but there was no television present.

They did find another bedroom up here, though, and they said it felt much better in there and decided that would be the one that they would use.

They spent some time getting unpacked and settled in – you know, everything just sort of going to plan. Nothing out of the ordinary.

They enjoyed the rest of their day, thus far satisfied with their accommodations, even if it wasn't precisely what they had booked, and eventually as the evening wore on, they took themselves upstairs to bed.

The first night in the books, they felt okay – their initial discomfort all but forgotten, but the *second* night – that was about to become a totally different story…

It was later on in the evening, and the woman had to do some training for work on her iPad, so she took herself downstairs while her boyfriend remained upstairs watching a football game, I assume, in the bedroom on the bedroom television.

She said that the entire time she was on her iPad for work, she could just *feel* eyes on her and like she was being watched. She also described the familiar sensation that we have all had at one time or another, where we are focused on something – in her case her iPad and whatever training videos or questionnaires she had going on it – and you're looking down and *feel* rather than see someone else enter the room. But of course, when she looked up – no one was there.

She said that she felt that same sensation over and over, that it was a pervasive and invasive feeling of constantly being under watch and like someone kept entering and exiting the room with her – even though no one was there.

Like so many before her, she ultimately dismissed these feelings as just ones that accompany being in a new and unfamiliar place – and shook it off as her mind playing tricks on her.

At some point, she decided to take a break from her work, and she found the cabin's guest book, and started flipping through it.

She immediately noticed, that weirdly, several pages of the book had just been unceremoniously ripped out and that they were missing – legit, this is my surprised Pikachu face over that one. I know it's easily mistaken as boredom, but again, what did I tell you, my little strangelings!? This cabin was backburnered by this rental company, they *know* it's haunted! They *have* to know – and this just clinches it for me… but I digress.

Nevertheless, she persisted, flipping through the guest book – and lo-and-behold, she found not one, not two, but *four separate reviews* in this book stating this place be haunted AF.

I told you so! I be vindicated on some level, even though we all know that none of us would be here without some spooky element to the story – but yeah, spoiler alert – haunted cabin is haunted.

Some of the things she read in the book described crazy and weird noises throughout the cabin at night and not just your typical house settling sounds, either, but things like what sounded like a kid rolling a ball down the staircase's steps. There were reports of the downstairs bedroom door, the creepy one they passed up immediately, the door opening and closing of its own accord.

While these things *did* freak her out to a degree, they also made her feel better! As in, it wasn't just her imagination – she *was* feeling the things she felt. There's nothing in the world like having your feelings validated when you all but half convinced yourself that you were just being a little bit nuts, am I right?

Of course, after reading all of this, she closed the book, set it aside, and decided, hell – she didn't really want to be downstairs alone anymore. She got up, taking her stuff with her, and made her way upstairs to her boyfriend and just hung out with him for the rest of the evening, still watching the football game – but she didn't say anything about what she had found in the book downstairs.

Truthfully, I probably wouldn't have either. I tend to keep stuff to myself like that to see how things play out for the people around me without biasing them to any of it – that probably makes me some kind of a bad friend or a bitch, but in the interest of the scientific method and avoiding confirmation bias I'm totally okay with that. I'll save some of y'all a seat on the bus to whatever Hell you believe in. I'm helpful like that.

The game ended, they enjoyed their evening and each other's company, and eventually it was lights out and they turned in for the rest of the night and went to sleep. They drifted off like normal, without any issues, that is, until sometime between midnight and the wee hours of the morning.

Bang!

She shot up in bed at the loud noise only to discover her boyfriend beside her fighting it out with *something* in his sleep. This obviously scared the bejesus out of her, because according to her he was straight *throwing hands* at some invisible force in his sleep. It was like he was in the throes of a fight to the death on his side of the bed.

It was during the course of this struggle that it happened again, he twisted, flinging his hand out and *bang!* His fist connected with the nightstand, making an identical noise to the one that'd shattered her sleep.

Only this time, it seemed to shatter *his* sleep, because he shot up in bed too – just in time for the power in the entire cabin to go down.

At this point, they're both just lying in bed, unsure what to do but damn sure *terrified*.

What was happening?

From downstairs in the kitchen area, the two of them could hear the sounds of *people* and things being moved around, even though they were sure that no one was physically in the cabin with them.

As if that wasn't bad enough, they could hear loud noises out on the balcony adjoining their room! Which was, as you recall, on the second floor and very high up off the ground with no outside means of access to the ground level.

Now keep in mind, her poor boyfriend still didn't know about what she'd read in the guest book downstairs, about the place being haunted... and she said that the pair of them were literally so scared by the goings-on around them, that they literally just laid in bed, side by side, frozen with fear to the point they couldn't even bring themselves to speak on the happenings around them.

They laid there, all night, until sunrise, the longest night of their lives, and as soon as the sun came up, they packed their bags and headed for the door – but not before she stopped and wrote their entire experience down in the guest book – you know, for management to tear those pages out, too so they could hide the fact the place was haunted AF because money.

It wasn't until they were off the mountain and headed for home that she spilled the beans to her boyfriend about the contents of the guest book – at which point, he confided in her, that while she had been downstairs in the living room and he had been upstairs watching football – he had felt the same thing she had. That eerie sensation of being perpetually watched, and how his attention had been drawn from the television to the door on more than one occasion, just certain someone had walked through it into the space – only with no one visibly there.

He then dropped the knowledge that the reason he had been fighting in his sleep, was that he didn't realize he was asleep at the time – he legit had thought he had woken up to a large man standing over them both in bed and that he had lunged and her boyfriend was locked in a battle with this large man before actually waking up – a nightmare within nightmare, which I find probably one of the more interesting parts of this story. Especially the part where he described the man, very specifically, as wearing a flannel shirt in overalls with both of his big hands wrapped around the boyfriend's neck choking off his air. The boyfriend had indeed, to his knowledge, been fighting for his actual life!

They both vowed together in that moment, that was enough for them and swore never to book another vacation in the mountains again – let alone to spend the night in the region.

So, there you have it, my little strangelings. If a rental company or hotel changes your booking last minute during a busy season or let slip that they are putting you in the last vacant space or room in a hotel or area, buckle up – you may very well be in the cabin or room that they consistently *can't* rent out due to the paranormal activity.

Or, you know, since you're here, you can do what I do and actually *request* the haunted space.

CADES COVE & WEARS VALLEY

The Cabin of Their Nightmares, Wears Valley

When this family found this cabin in Wears Valley, they thought they had found the cabin of their dreams for a dream vacation out in the Greater Smoky Mountains National Park.

Turned out, it would be both the cabin and the vacation of their nightmares.

Let's go back to 2016, when this family rented a cabin out in the Wears Valley community to enjoy the natural beauty of the Smoky Mountains that surrounded it.

The area, ironically enough, was called 'Tranquility' and it would prove to be anything but after the long, eight-hour-plus drive for this family from Maryland.

After arriving the did what one does after a long drive like that. They unpacked their car and went inside this picturesque cabin nestled in the Appalachian Mountains, and just sort of tried to unwind from the long drive before settling in for bed that night, but only after following the owner's *very explicit* instructions that the alarm need be set *every night* of their stay.

So, alarm set accordingly, the family went to bed, and all drifted off to dreamland.

At 2:30 a.m., the peace was shattered by the screeching alarm system.

The phone started ringing shortly after, the security company on the line asking if everyone was alright, that the alarm system had been tripped in the cabin's recreation room or area, and that they thought someone might be in the house.

Forthwith, the dad went down and checked everything out but found nary a soul nor anything out of place. The alarm company did note to whoever stayed on the line, that none of the window or door alarms recognized a breech, which was odd – very odd.

Eventually, the alarm company apologized politely for the disturbance, and chalked the alarm going off as some sort of malfunction in the system, wishing the family a good rest of their night.

The next morning, the family got up, got dressed, and went out for breakfast. The mother noting that when she left the master bedroom, she shut a pair of double doors related to it. But, of course, when they returned, it was to find both doors standing wide open – but she *just knew* she had shut them! So, what the heck?

She thought it was odd, but then convinced herself, *well, maybe I thought I closed them, but didn't.*

In hindsight, we know better, but in the moment, I can honestly admit I would do the same thing.

The family went about their day, and later that night, mom was just taking a long, hot, relaxing bath in the soaker tub she had access to here, which was in the master bedroom's bathroom, when all of a sudden, all of the lights winked out, plunging her into total darkness.

She yelled for her husband, who came running in, and confusedly, flipped the switches on the lights back to the 'on' position.

While she was alarmed by the lights turning off on their own, her husband waved it off saying that it was more than likely that the light switches in here were on a timer that they didn't know about to save the homeowner on electrical costs from guests forgetting to turn them out. That it was no big deal.

Later that night, the couple were woken by their three daughters arguing, the older two mad at the youngest for leaving the bathroom light on. The three of them sharing the other master bedroom in the big cabin. Except the youngest sibling was arguing back that she not once had gotten up to go to the bathroom, that her sisters were being assholes, because what she had been doing was getting up to turn the blazing bathroom light *off!*

So, later that night, or a subsequent night – that part wasn't made clear – the family is all gathered in the living room watching a movie, when suddenly, every light in the kitchen just suddenly went off at the same time.

The husband sighed and got off the couch and went to find the breaker box, as several lights controlled by different switches had turned off simultaneously, so logically speaking, it *had* to be a breaker or a blown fuse, right?

So, he's at the box flipping breakers – but nothing's happening. Mom follows the next logical step, and calls up the rental company to let them know, 'hey, the kitchen has lost all power what do you want to do?'

Rental company or owner says, 'so, sorry – we'll have maintenance out to you first thing in the morning' which is alright, given the hour. Family goes to bed, and lo-and-behold – as promised, maintenance is on their doorstep bright and early the next morning to deal with the electrical issue in their kitchen.

He goes straight for the breaker box, flips the breaker and all of the kitchen lights immediately come back on, no problem.

[Insert surprised Pikachu faces from the family.]

The husband insists that he tried that the night before to no avail, that he flipped the same breakers several times and the lights just wouldn't come back on – what the hell?

The maintenance man just chuckled and told the family that that was alright, that this sort of thing happened all the time, and not to worry about him coming all the way out there – that was, literally, his job.

He did add that not only did it happen all the time in this cabin, that they never could seem to track down the root cause of *why* – and so they just dealt with it as it came up.

Later on the *next* night, the family was all present within the cabin when the lighting and electrical in the home started acting up *again*.

This time throughout the entire cabin. The lights turning off and on in this room or that at random.

Mom was even standing in front of the mirror in the master suite, and both lights on the vanity to either side, just sort of winked out at the same time, as though someone had just pulled the plug on them. Of course, she yelled for her husband, and just as he entered the bathroom, the lights came on just as suddenly as they'd gone out.

Mom gave her husband a baleful look and said she felt decidedly uneasy, declaring that this house was either haunted or even scarier, had some *serious* electrical issues – and that neither one was a very appealing prospect to her.

They went to bed, but just before climbing into bed, mom went to her daughter's room and pulled the doors to it shut, firmly, to ensure they latched. She also closed the bedroom doors to her and her husband's room, again ensuring that they were firmly latched.

She went to sleep, however, when she woke for no apparent reason only a couple of hours later, it was to find both of the bedroom doors standing wide open as though she hadn't touched them at all.

She woke up her husband and pointed it out to him, and he affirmed, no; she wasn't crazy. He remembered her closing the bedroom doors too.

This set both of them even further on edge, but with nothing else to really do about any of it, they went back to bed.

The next day, before they went out sightseeing, the family closed every single interior door to the cabin and setting the alarm before leaving. Making a note to do so, to see if anything would be amiss when they returned.

They returned approximately five hours later, entering the cabin to find that every single door they had made a note of closing before leaving the premises was now standing wide open.

Still, they didn't go directly to the paranormal at the discovery. Instead, convincing themselves that someone was somehow *in the house* or had broken in while they were gone – despite nothing else having been touched. – and they searched that whole house from top to bottom. Every nook and every cranny – but to no avail. Finding no evidence at all of anyone having been physically present or in their space.

All except for one door within the basement, that remained securely locked.

Mom called the rental company again, and informed them of their situation, also telling them that they had dinner plans out of the cabin that evening and asking could they *please* send someone out while they were gone to check behind the lone locked basement door for any possible intruders.

They said they would send someone out, but that locked door was the owner's personal storage space or room, and that no one should have access or be in there. Still, if it would make them feel better – then, for sure, someone would be out and they would receive a call when the inspection was thorough.

Short time later, the family set the alarm and went out to dinner.

As promised, they received a call from the rental company while at dinner stating their man had gone out to take a look and that the locked room was totally empty – that no one was in there. She did offer, by way of explanation, that sometimes these old cabins were drafty, and pressure changes could sometimes dislodge certain doors and cause them to swing open.

Yeah, maybe one or two doors – but *all of them?* I don't buy that for a minute my little strangelings. The odds of that happening are astronomical.

Mom didn't buy that for a minute either but thanked the rental company for coming and having a look.

Late that night, after everyone had gone to bed, everyone was suddenly woken by a loud bang, emanating from somewhere within the cabin… but the security system remained silent.

They searched the place, but all they found is that when the bang had apparently occurred, it was accompanied by all of the kitchen lights coming on.

The next day, before they left on another one of their adventures in the park, they closed all of the interior doors to the cabin *again*. Making a note of it and discussing the odds on whether they would find them open again as they had the day before.

One of them had the idea to double down at this point, and even whipped out their cell phones to prove to themselves and each other that they weren't crazy. Snapping pictures as they closed each door and what doors they closed to what rooms.

Sure enough, when they returned hours later, the master bedroom door stood wide open.

At this point, no one so much as went to the bathroom alone. Especially mom, who had had the most experiences in the master bathroom.

Things escalated for the family that night, when mom and Dad's slumber was shattered by the sound of their three daughters *just screaming*.

They bolted up in bed and ran for the girls' room.

All three girls who were sharing the same bed looked utterly terrified as they explained that they had all felt a heaviness on their feet, just like someone had laid across the foot of the bed, over each and every last one of them, pressing them into the mattress below the covers.

Not only that, even though the bathroom door was shut in their room, they could see the light had come on inside it, the glow coming through the crack between the bottom of the door and the carpet.

Thankfully, this would be their last night in the cabin. Even so, the girls weren't having any of simply going back to bed. Terrified, they stripped the bed of its blankets and pillows, opting to make a palette on their parent's bedroom floor so that they could be near Mom and Dad.

The girls were so scared, in fact, they even wedged chairs underneath the door handles of their parent's bedroom doors to make sure they couldn't come open.

They got up the next morning relieved to be getting out of there. They had been looking forward to this trip so damn much, but with all of the creepy shit happening, they could all agree that it'd turned into some sort of a nightmare. One they had no reason or desire to ever come back and repeat.

Still, for some reason, as all five were loading into the car, the mom decided to snap a couple of pictures of the place as they left.

It wasn't until later that she realized that in one of the photos, standing in one of the tall, thin windows in the right of the frame, was the apparition of someone standing inside the cabin, looking out at them. Most who see the photo positing that it appears to be some sort of a little girl.

GREAT SMOKEY MOUNTAINS NATIONAL PARK

It's so big that it spans into Western North Carolina, but when it comes to this book, it almost *had* to be a sub-region within the region of East Tennessee. I know, maybe I'm being a little bit extra making this its own subsection, but you know what? That's right. It's my book, and I do what I want!

Seriously, though. I love this National treasure of a National Park, and I spend a lot of time driving through slowly to just sort of meditate and think when I'm otherwise feeling blue and have some extra time on my hands.

It's my second favorite spooky place to go behind Old Gray Cemetery… and I'd like to introduce you to some of its ghosts…

The Haunted Ghost Town of Elkmont

Elkmont was, once upon a time, a thriving town within what is now the Great Smoky Mountains National Park. When the government came through, buying up land to create the park, many of the people within Elkmont refused to leave. Eventually, the town was steam rolled under the juggernaut of forward progress, the government simply waiting for the rest of the families who remained within the town to die out. When that happened, their goal was achieved, and thus Elkmont officially became a ghost town; going from what was once considered a posh little resort town with its hunting lodges, to losing its title of crown jewel of the Smokies to Gatlinburg.

Today, Elkmont is silent and empty, the underbrush creeping in and taking over, Mother Nature reclaiming the cabins and lodges. It's also now a favored hiking destination within the park, but it seems that not all of the residents may have gone. Oh, sure, the living did, but some of Elkmont's dead may yet still remain.

There have been stories told by hikers and visitors to the town, of unrelenting cold spots that linger on the trail and within the town, no matter how high the summer temperatures may soar. Chanting can sometimes be heard, drifting through the trees along many of the hiking trails, no matter the time of day or night – often times attributed to the Indigenous peoples who wandered these lands long before Elkmont was even conceived.

Hikers sometimes report the sound of phantom footfalls behind them on the trail into Elkmont, as well as within the town itself; only when they stop and turn, no one is there. The woods surrounding the town growing eerily silent, and a pervasive feeling of being watched becomes overwhelming. When the hiker continues along the trail or moves throughout the town? Those phantom footfalls resume, right behind them.

In addition to these phantom footfalls, old-time music can be heard drifting from abandoned buildings and through shattered windows, floating on the light breeze accompanying the rustling of the tree leaves. Eerie, with no discernible direction or position to pinpoint it to.

Doors and windows swing open and slam shut of their own accord, and encounters with full-bodied apparitions dressed from the town's heyday have oftentimes been reported by visitors.

Sometimes, visitors to the abandoned town experience a phenomenon where they blink, and rather than the decrepit falling apart, quiet reclamation by nature that they should see upon opening their eyes, they're met with a town that's very different; full of life and thriving. They report the buildings are suddenly whole and intact, the streets and pathways maintained and clear of fallen leaves and creeping undergrowth. They say they see warm light glowing from windows that were cracked or broken only a moment before and the *people*. Hustling and bustling about just as though it was a normal Tuesday for them in their old-timey era appropriate clothing from the 1900s, to the 1930s.

Just as soon as the visitor blinks once more, the sounds of a thriving town stop, and it's back to being just as forlorn and abandoned as it was the moment before the strange vision.

While I've been to Elkmont's old cemetery, I haven't been to the town itself – but after discovering this information and these stories, I can't wait to get out there for myself.

The Roaring Fork Motor Trail, Gatlinburg

If you're reading this, I'm *sure* that you have heard the old legend of Resurrection Mary out of the Chicago area.

Just in case you haven't, here's a quicker 'n shit rundown of the story: Woman named Mary went to a dance sometime in the 1940s, but never made it home. Car accident, I think it was – but don't quote me on that. She was buried in Resurrection Cemetery outside of Chicago, and ever since, motorists passing by the cemetery at night, see a distressed girl in a dress as though having been out for a night of dancing wildly flagging them down. She asks for a ride home, gets into the back seat, and when they arrive, and the driver goes to drop her off, she's gone.

There are some iterations of the story where the driver, bothered so severely by the interaction, goes to the address she gave them to drop her off at, and knocks on the door to ask the occupants of the home about her.

It's her parents, and the mother has a wildly distraught reaction to the person at the door asking about her dead daughter. Sometimes, in the story, she just says that Mary is dead and not to bother her anymore, and the person that drove her glimpses a photo of the girl that had been in their car before the door is shut resolutely in their face.

It's one of the quintessentially American folklore tales and urban legends that has been making the rounds since the phenomenon started and has given rise to many more 'hitchhiking ghost' stories from all over the country… which brings me back to The Roaring Fork Motor Trail and it's very own 'Resurrection Mary' – except *this* hitch-hiking ghost predates Resurrection Mary by over *thirty years,* and so it should be a lot less Resurrection Mary and a whole lot more Roaring Forks Lucy.

That's the name of our hitchhiking ghost girl, by the way, and the story of her haunting starts sometime around 1910 with a young man riding through the area on his roan horse, looking to find himself a bride.

The legend begins with the young man riding down from his home up in the mountains to go to a church's 'protracted meeting' which was something like a revival, only lasting longer, I guess? I don't know – I was raised Catholic, but I'm not Christian anymore and the Bible-Belt Christians and their ways are pretty much a mystery to me – so be kind, my little strangelings. Not everyone was raised in the South or knows how these things work.

I digress, but it was important this time, so, yeah.

So this dude goes to this protracted meeting, or whatever the thing is, for this church that wasn't necessarily *his* church, but that was sort of how he was playing things. Going from church to church around the area and riding further and further out from home to pick up chicks – which I guess in 1910 was the Tinder or Bumble of its generation.

I mean, I can dig it.

Anyway, he goes, he gets shot down, or rather no chicks seem interested in his country bumpkin ass, and honestly – he seems like a nice guy and fuck them stuck up bitches, my dude! You can find better!

So, he fucks off back toward home, and man – it's cold, it's raining, it's dark, and it's going to make for a long fucking ride and a long fucking night to get back to where he's going.

He's plodding along atop his big-ass horse feeling sorta sorry for himself, when up ahead, he spots this girl on the side of the road.

It's raining, she's sorta not dressed for the weather, and he says she's carrying a sharp stick or something, likely to ward off a big (Wampus) cat, or a bear should she encounter one.

He draws up next to her and is like, "Yo, honey – what 'cha doing out here dressed like that? You're gonna catch a death of a cold!"

She was like, "Yeah, hi, homeboy – I'm fine, I think."

He's all, "Nah, you're not fine, can I at least give you a ride home?" and she's like, "Bet, that would be epic!"

(Yeah, okay, I'm pulling this dialogue outta my ass, but I don't know how they talked in 1910 – so just go with it.)

So, this guy helps this girl up in front of him on his horse and immediately notices a few things. She's pretty. She's warm – and I mean, like *really* warm, and did I mention she's pretty?

He nudges his horse back into action and makes small talk with her. Learns that her name is Lucy, and that she doesn't live *too* far up ahead.

He takes her home, and they even share a little kiss goodbye, the flirting getting a little hot and heavy between them. She dismounts and goes up to the house and he watches her go inside.

Cool.

He goes home, gets in in the wee hours, and crashes out hard. The next morning he's up and his mamma is making breakfast and he tells her excitedly all about Lucy.

She's like, "That's great, son! You talk to her parents?" and he was like, "Mom, it was the middle of the night – I wasn't waking those folks up."

His mamma was like, "Best get your ass back down there and talk to 'em, ask for permission to court their daughter before you get too far into her."

He agreed it was whatever in the 1910s of it all proper to do, and mounted up later that afternoon to head back down the mountain to the house he'd dropped Lucy off at the night before.

An older man and woman opened the door for him when he knocked, and you guessed it – yes, they knew a Lucy, she was their sixteen-year-old daughter who had *died in a house fire* up the road around about where he'd picked her up – sometime the year before.

Well shit.

If dude didn't have bad luck with the ladies, he wouldn't have any luck at all is what I say. I guess he *really* got ghosted before ghosting was even a thing. How's about that?

Our boy's story is only the *first* documented story of a living breathing human encountering the ghost of Lucy. A legend that endures today, thanks to The Roaring Fork Motor Trail having been erected along the same dirt tract that her home was once on; you know, *before* burning down with her in it.

Lucy is still being spotted along this stretch of road, even today, my little strangelings. Typically known in Paranormal circles as a 'Lady in White' she appears in a white dress or gown – my guess is an old-style nightgown as she *did* die in a house fire at night according to legend. She is also barefoot which also tracks for her mid-night immolation.

There's nothing really else about Lucy that stands out, other than the fact that she's a girl of about sixteen, ethereally beautiful, and walking barefoot alongside the motorway in her nightgown.

I mean, I guess that's pretty weird by today's standards.

If you've seen Lucy or know a story of someone who has, I'd love to hear about it. My inbox is open for all sorts of things.

LECONTE LODGE, LECONTE PEAK

The LeConte Mountain is the tallest peak in the Smoky Mountain range, and at its top, is a rather unconventional hotel – *ish*...

You see, you can't drive to the LaConte Lodge, there are no roads, what there are, are hiking trails a plenty, though.

An experienced hiker can make it from one of the several trailheads to the LaConte Lodge in around three and a half hours and they say, you can make it all the way back down, if you wanted to, in around two and a half hours if you pushed it – but if you're here, my little strangelings, I don't think you're the type to want to make the trek back down in the same day. You might miss out on all the paranormal fun.

Many guests of the lodge complain of feeling watched the entire time they are there. They report a heavy feeling, and a pervasive feeling of unease that just never seems to let up.

Part of that might be chalked up to the fact that you are thousands upon thousands of feet above what you would consider civilization. There's no signal up there, either – as there's little to no signal for anything but a satellite phone within the confines of the park. Again, there are no roads up here, and only a few trails, so it's about as isolated as you can get up there.

Many an intrepid guest who have made the trek and stayed the night here report that at 3:33 a.m. *exactly*, they have woken up to the utterly terrifying visage of a little girl sitting on the foot of their bed.

They only see her for a few moments, and then she completely disappears.

No one knows who she is, or how she got there, but she's always just sort have been a thing in this cabin at the top of the mountain, which isn't very hotellike.

If you're an experienced hiker and decide to make the trek up there, you should look things up online as I believe there is some kind of pre-booking process you have to follow. Additionally, this ain't no hotel. If you're going up there, you need to backpack all your supplies in and out with you.

Food, water, sleeping bag, etc. Yes, there's a shelter by way of cabin, so you don't need a tent – but there's no running water, or electricity, and so you're pretty much just glorified camping with a little ghost girl and whatever cryptid nightmare fuel Matt has in store for you later on in this book.

So, if you go, send me all your pictures, videos, and a rundown of any spooky shit you encounter while you're there to the contact information section at the end of this book. I'm afraid I have some permanent injuries that would make doing so for myself too excruciating to make it worth it to go personally.

I has a real big sad about that. Especially with how I've heard that no one has essentially gotten down from this place without a story of something creepy happening to tell.

Go, go, Appalachian Spooky Shit.

CADES COVE

The history of this place is fascinating, my little strangelings.

Established in the 1800s, Cades Cove was a small, but thriving, community right up on through the early twentieth century.

Today, only around eighty of its most historic buildings remain, from churches to cabins, and while there are fourteen documented cemeteries throughout Cades Cove, only eleven of them have documented locations, three remaining a mystery or lost to time. One thing that isn't lost to the annals of time are the ghosts of this place.

Cades Cove has quite a few ghost stories and paranormal happenings attributed to it, so it's getting its own wee little subsection to contend with at least its varying ghosties. It's also going to make several appearances flitting within and without the Critters & Cryptids section and may even have a brief cameo in the Folklore & Unexplained section.

Hell, it's already made an appearance up above with one of its stories.

Without too much more pomp and circumstance, turn the page to get into the ghost stories of this unique and picturesque location nestled within the Great Smoky Mountains National Park.

The White Lady & Other Hauntings of the Primitive Baptist Church

When you enter the Great Smoky Mountains National Park, don't forget to stop at the visitor's center and to grab a daily parking pass before embarking on your adventures. You're going to need one if you want to stop for any length of time to enjoy taking photos or to hike up one of the short trails to one of the waterfalls.

Likewise, if you're going through Cade's Cove, stop and get the Cade's Cove Tour booklet from the visitor's center, (10/10 highly recommend, as of writing this, it's only $1.25 for one and all proceeds benefit the upkeep of the park.) before you make your drive to the Cade's Cove portion of the park.

Stop 4 in the booklet will tell you all about the history behind the Primitive Baptist Church and its little graveyard set beside it.

I'm here to tell you about its ghosts.

This is one of the most prominent ghost stories of Cade's Cove, and it's shrouded in a mystery.

No one knows who the spirit of the woman that haunts the Primitive Baptist Church is, nor do they know why, of all things, she chooses to show herself by stepping and pulling herself out of the *wall* of the church.

Picture this:

It's a lovely fall evening, the sun is setting, the Cove is a riot of oranges and yellows, growing muted as the area is dipped in dusk.

You're walking along, the white building of the Primitive Baptist Church just up ahead, the deepening shadows as night begins to fall, drifting lazily from the sky like the falling leaves, casting the stately old, whitewashed building in hues of blue, the shadows deepening from gray to darker gray, and you decide: hey, let's go look inside!

You walk up to the front step, and you're touring the inside of the spartan interior of the old church, the browns of the bare wood turning muddy and dark with the dying light, when you circle the altar and freeze.

Your friend is standing there, looking at you like you've grown a second head – but you're not looking at them. You're looking *behind them*, at the woman in a white, old-timey dress, glowing with a faint and eerie light, as she pulls herself free from the wall to the outside of the church, and drifts on her ghostly walk through the little graveyard outside the windows.

You've met the lady of the church – and it has got to be one of the most profound and bizarre paranormal experiences of your life.

That's what people report here at the Primitive Baptist Church. The woman is a complete unknown as to who she is, why she is there, and more bizarrely, why she comes out of the church's old wall instead of a doorway.

Could it be she isn't coming out of the wall at all, but rather a doorway from the *original* log building structure that once stood where the Primitive Baptist Church stands today?

We'll never know. Nor will we ever know why she seems to be more active during the fall months, but when she isn't seen coming out of the church's wall, she's seen wandering the church's little graveyard set next to it, drifting between the stones. A melancholy figure whose name and story has been lost to time.

The White Lady of the Primitive Baptist Church isn't the only type of spirit to linger here. Ghostly laughter and the sounds of playing children have been heard, and people who have taken photos inside the church have come away with the blurred figures of children who weren't there at the time the photo was taken in some of their photographs.

Balls of light that are bluish-white in appearance have been seen in the little graveyard outside the church, following one another like children at play – too big and the wrong color to be fireflies.

Sometimes you can hear the faint echo of hymns being sung or the preachings of a most fervent pastor echoing on the breeze coming from the church. There's no speaker system playing these sounds, my little strangelings, which some have assumed – indeed, Cades Cove lacks both electricity and cellular signal for any recordings to be effectively played, plus the park service has no time for shenanigans like that with all of the visitors, campers, and wildlife to keep track of in the park.

While the Primitive Baptist Church appears to be the most haunted portion of the Cove, it isn't the *only* haunted location.

The Haunted Cave

Once upon a time, Cades Cove was a thriving community nestled in what is now the Great Smoky Mountains National Park. Like any thriving community, it held men, women, and children and, of course, this was in a time well before such entertainment as video games and cell phones – and kids, especially boys, will be kids and oftentimes sought out adventure.

Enter one of the naturally occurring phenomenon that East Tennessee and the Appalachian Mountains are famous for – caves, and particularly one cave known today as *Haunted Cave* in the Cades Cove area.

Now, since closed to the public, the Haunted Cave is actually like many of the caves in the Appalachian's – not just a single cave cutout into the rock, but an ever-deepening warren of an entire cave *system*.

You can imagine that parents from around Cade's Cove threatened to tan their children's hides should they be caught fooling around in there – but again, kids will be kids and tragedy did indeed strike when two boys disobeyed their mama's and their papa's and went in there anyway.

It was the early 1900s – what else was there to do?

The story goes that two boys, we'll be a little cheeky and call them Sam and Dean, went into the caves, and got themselves lost in the dark. While Sam somehow found his way out, Dean never did. These were young boys as the old story goes. No more than ten or eleven, and while Sam got to go home, Dean was never found at all.

Nowadays, when the modern lighting system in the cave is turned off, you can plaintively hear a child crying and screaming in the dark. Begging for help, and how he just wants to go home.

It's a harsh and heartbreaking tale, and though it's a cautionary one, I do believe it's rooted in fact over fiction.

If you somehow find yourself in the Cove after dark, and you happen to be in the area, you might just hear him faintly on the wind and if you follow that terrified little boy's voice, you might just find yourself outside the mouth of a cavern or cave. I caution you, my little strangelings – don't go in. Dean is long since passed, and you don't want to join him in his fate.

The Phantom Cabin

This ghost story isn't about a ghost in a cabin. In this final tale about haunted cabins, the cabin *is* the ghost!

There's tales told by many a park visitor, that as you drive the Cade's Cove loop, or ride it, or walk it, on the days that it's closed to motor vehicle traffic, that you can sometimes spot a creepy looking cabin off the road set back some into a field or into some trees.

Here's the thing about this cabin, my little strangelings – it isn't really there.

Anyone who has stepped off the motor trail on the south end of the loop to go check this one out, claims that as they approach it, they either look down to make sure of their footing and when they look up, it's gone as though it'd never been or it disappears in the blink of an eye. A few have even claimed that it's disappeared right before their very eyes!

If you find yourself in the Cove, driving, hiking, or biking the loop, pay attention toward the end of the loop on the south end. Look off into the woods, and if you spot the phantom cabin, try to snap some pictures of it before you go down to check things out.

It'd be something next level if you catch the thing disappearing on film.

PART 2:
HAUNTED CEMETERIES
&
GRAVEYARDS

There are a lot of dead people in the world, my little strangelings. Cemeteries, churchyards, and graveyards dot the south and can be found in some of the strangest of places, and who doesn't love a good ghost story about one of these little towns or cities of the dead?

Here's the thing, though. Not every cemetery is haunted. Just because the dead are, well, dead and gone and buried there doesn't mean the place is packed and rife with ghosts. Quite the opposite actually. Usually, it takes maximum effort to find enough haunted cemeteries in order to even make a section in a book like this out of them.

Indeed, it's going to be a pretty short section, but with how steeped in lore and bloodshed the south is thanks to the Civil War, and atrocities like the Trail of Tears, as well as all of the other fucked-up shit that people do to each other – we've got enough haunted cemeteries, graveyards, and mausoleums to make this section a good one.

I happen to like cemeteries, by like a lot, and spend quite a bit of time in them not just for the spooky factor, but for the fact that they're peaceful, no one tends to bother you in them, and the monuments are just plain gorgeous to look at.

Still, when the light of day is drawn out from between the graves like the tide getting low, and the shadows fill between tomb stones and monuments, that's just when things start to get good for us, and boy howdy do I have some good stories for you here in East Tennessee. So, turn the page and let's get to it. Hope you have a flashlight and your courage because things are about to get scary.

NORTHEAST TENNESSEE

EAST HILL CEMETERY, BRISTOL

So far north and east in East Tennessee, around a third of this particular cemetery is actually in Virginia – but hey, the other two-thirds is in Bristol, Tennessee and this is my book, and I do what I want. I say it counts, so it counts, and here we are!

A spirit that haunts this cemetery supposedly haunts the back of it, and that is the ghost of Evan Shelby, a Revolutionary War General. It's said that shortly after he was buried, that hunters in the area began to see his spirit. A vision of the old general standing in the tree line; there and then suddenly gone, faster than the blink of an eye – almost so fast that you could convince yourself that you hadn't seen anything at all, but for the fact that you know you just did.

One of the first burials that kicked off East Hill becoming a bonafide cemetery was that of little five-year-old Nellie Gains. She was interred here in February of 1857, and was soon joined by two other area children.

Not long after, a gentleman walking past the new cemetery, late one snowy evening, stated that he heard giggling and the sounds of children playing wafting out from the fence line surrounding the burial place. He stated that he peered into the dark into the burying ground where he saw balls of light flitting after one another, the sounds emanating from them – ghostly specter children at play.

The final story attributed to this cemetery concerns a lady from Morristown, TN.

Her great-grandmother was supposedly buried here in East Hill, and she reached out to some local volunteers to help find her grave. One of the volunteers found it, and sent her pictures, but that wasn't enough for her. She wanted to see for herself – which I can't blame her. I did the very same thing with my great-grandparent's grave on a visit to New Jersey a few years back.

She got in her car with a notebook and her camera and headed for East Hill and spent all day looking.

Hey, it's easy to do. Cemeteries this old and big tend to sprawl, and there are rarely ever maps with sections and plots on them to follow. Sometimes, it's just you and rows and rows of endless markers and you just have to take them one at a time.

On this visit, the woman had to admit defeat – the sun was getting low, and the cemetery was going to close soon – and she, like me, wasn't the sort to be a trespassing bag of dicks.

She was about to get into her car when she made one last wistful look up at the hillside and froze.

There, standing next to a low shrub, was a woman. Older, with iron gray hair, beckoning to the younger woman and insistently pointing down at something beneath the shrub.

The woman about to leave hesitated, and the older woman on the hillside gestured more insistently that the lady visiting and looking for her great-grandmother's grave come see.

The woman did what I would have done. She firmly shut her car door and struck out, marching resolutely up that hill in the other woman's direction.

She marched up the hill to the iron haired lady in the pale pink dress, but the footing in a cemetery can be challenging. Chuck holes, and burrowing critters, uneven footing and dangerous rocks and dips literally try to reach out and break your ankle.

The woman, as she neared the older lady, took her eyes off the older woman for just a second to watch her footing and when she looked up again? The older lady had disappeared.

Undaunted, and certainly unnerved, the younger woman made her way to the spot where the woman had stood and looked under the shrub, and that is where she found her great-grandmother's flat stone marker, partially obscured by the little plant's overgrowth.

It was as she laid eyes on the marker that it clicked.

Her great-grandmother's favorite color had been pale pink, and everyone in the family had said that she had been buried in her favorite pale pink dress.

I love this story. Even if there is likely no way to replicate the sighting and it was just a one-off thing specific to the woman seeking her ancestor's grave.

It's just another cool reminder that there is, indeed, magic in these hills.

At any rate, replicable or not, the story of the witches, Evan Shelby, and the ghost children of East Hill Cemetery still leave plenty to investigate should you have the fortitude to check things out.

Going back to what I said about this place earlier, though – don't be a trespassing bag of dicks, my little strangelings.

East Hill Cemetery *does* allow for after-hours shenanigans yearly by way of a Historical Ghost Walk Tour. Look into going on one of those, your money is well spent in the preservation of this historic cemetery that straddles the border between Tennessee and Virginia and the volunteers on the ghost walk work hard for your donation.

Let's keep things above board, okay?

JOBE CEMETERY, JOHNSON CITY

This quiet, unassuming, little cemetery was closed off when I tried to get to it. Nevertheless, it's one of the most interestingly haunted cemeteries in East Tennessee. Why? Because not only has it spent the entirety of its existence as a burying ground, for some portion of it, it's been considered a *murderin'* ground, curtesy of a murdering hobo – or so the old legend goes.

It it's early days, Jobe Cemetery was surrounded on three sides by woods. Set back from the cemetery in these woods, was a fallen tree that sort of served as a makeshift table with a bench for hobos that traveled through the area during the early 20th century, during the era known as the Great Depression.

From this Hobo royal court, these men and women would flow out into the county and surrounding towns and cities to beg for money, food, and sometimes even work. At night, these men would return to the fallen sycamore behind Jobe Cemetery to drink rotgut whiskey and to gamble, and as we all know, drunken idiots and gambling make for a volatile mix. One that tends to end in blood, the life lost more valuable than any coin being squabbled over.

It's said that the ghosts of far too many men, murdered in this way, over a dispute over cards or dice, walk the historic Jobe family cemetery as a result of the violent deaths that resulted from the alcohol fueled volatile exchanges.

The Unicoi County Sheriff would round up the hobos and flush them out of the known camp from time to time, but the jail was small and legally, a vagrant could only be held for a short amount of time. Generally, these homeless transients would be escorted to the edge of town or the county the next morning and would be turned loose under threat of stiff penalty should they deign to return.

They knew as much as law enforcement that the threats were empty ones; that the Sheriff didn't have the authority or manpower to do much more, and no one knew this better than one particular vagrant the townspeople nicknamed *Old Dog*, after his lined appearance and drooping face reminded anyone who looked at him of an old basset or bloodhound.

Unfortunately, Old Dog might as well have been a rabid dog from the violent streak he held. He didn't have a bone in his body that *wasn't* mean, so say the old stories. In fact, the legends say Old Dog was responsible for the murder of at *least* thirteen men in Erwin. Most of them dying when the man pulled out a knife in a fistfight to finish things once and for all.

Here's the thing, though – Old Dog? He still hangs around the cemetery.

The stories say that Old Dog himself was murdered near the old sycamore, and that his hulking apparition can be seen wandering through the gravestones of the old cemetery on moonlit nights. He wears a coat far too heavy for the season, and an old slouch hat; and it's said that if he catches you looking, he'll come up on you bringing with him a winter's chill, hissing about how he's going to kill you.

If you run, you turn back and he's simply gone – but no one has been brave enough to stick around to find out what happens if you stay rooted to the spot.

I don't, under any circumstances, advocate that any of you try to tough this one out, my little strangelings. We don't trespass, and those spirits laid to rest in Jobe Cemetery deserve the respect of a restful eternity, even if Old Dog doesn't.

He's allegedly a murderer, after all. If that's the case, may he continue to rest in distress.

BETHESDA CEMETERY, MORRISTOWN

It was an especially beautiful October day when I visited this cemetery, my little strangelings, and I couldn't have possibly picked a better time of year! It was absolutely *gorgeous* on my trip through. The sun shining, the air crisp, and the blue skies stretching as far as the eye could see. It was quite stunning in counterpoint to the trees which were a brilliant riot of fall foliage.

This land and its remaining buildings saw action during the Civil War. One of the buildings even holds scars and repairs still visible today from taking fire from canons during the fighting here.

Another building was a makeshift hospital for the Confederacy during the war, and to this day, it would seem some of those Confederate soldiers remain...

Rumor has it that spirits of restless Confederates can be seen inside and outside the church. They have reportedly been aggressive toward visitors. The apparition of a crying woman has been seen on the far side of the cemetery. You can often hear her crying late at night.

People have reported phantom lantern light bobbing through the bushes and trees, late at night – and some intrepid investigators who chose to ignore the no trespassing after dark signs, have reported equipment failure. (Which I cannot stress this enough, my little strangelings, you shouldn't be trespassing – under any circumstances!)

Nestled in a residential neighborhood and surrounded on at least two sides by houses facing the gates and low tombstones – one of the notable things about this cemetery is that it has no perimeter fence.

However, it is clearly posted just about *everywhere* you look, that Bethesda is closed after dark, and I have it on good authority that the area is extremely well patrolled by local police if the signage isn't deterrent enough.

More than one neighbor, caretaker, and errant trespassing ghost hunter have reported the sounds of cannon fire and screaming in the vicinity of this cemetery and church. A residual auditory haunting from the fighting that took place here, I'm certain.

If you ever find yourself in Morristown, Tennessee, no matter what the time of year, I recommend this little cemetery as a stop to make. It's beautiful... although I wasn't able to locate the supposed witches' grave. It would have been nice to pay my respects to a sister.

That's right, this cemetery supposedly harbors the grave of a woman who was a witch. All the haunted cemeteries do – too bad, I couldn't find any information on her or what her story was... I think it's just a case of it's haunted, so of course a witch is buried there! It's been quite the theme when it comes to haunted cemeteries in the south, to the point it gets a little ridiculous sometimes.

At any rate, this cemetery was a good one, has just about the most activity to it of all the cemeteries I've researched for hauntings in East Tennessee, and I'm hoping against hope, should I ever come back to this to add to it for a second edition, I'll have more to tell you about it.

Until if or when that day ever comes, happy hauntings – and again, *don't trespass,* it makes the paranormal investigative branch of society look like a pack of assholes and has given us all the reputation that makes us persona non grata and I'm tired of fighting it – so be good! Let's try to turn that reputation around.

Red Ash Cemetery, Caryville

Once a booming mining town, when the economy collapsed, so too did it, leaving for a time, just the relics of its bygone heyday. Relics like the Red Ash Cemetery.

Red Ash was the recipient of many a tortured soul, mostly miners that died in both accidents and from the black lung that was, and still is, such a hazard of their occupation.

My great-grandfather on my mother's side was a coal miner in Ohio, so even my family hasn't gone untouched by the companies of the 18 and early 1900s.

Indeed, if you ask about haunted cemeteries in Tennessee, Red Ash is at the very top of that list. Every year paranormal enthusiasts traipse into the woods, following winding roads deep back into the holler to find this place and test their mettle against the spirits that supposedly lurk here.

Red Ash not only has a reputation for being the most haunted cemetery in East Tennessee, but it also has the reputation for being one of the scariest.

I'm sure that part of that is the fact that it *is* set deep enough into the woods where there are no streetlights nor porch lights from nearby residences to reach it. While you *can* drive practically right up to it, I was warned by several locals that going up that way either during the day or at night isn't a very good idea, and that if I were to go, that I'd best do it strapped.

It seems the living in the area, like the ghosts of the old burying ground, are none too friendly to outsiders for a variety of reasons; some of which is that even though prohibition is over, moonshining is still alive and well in the hills of East Tennessee and this new generation of shiners, like the old, don't want people near their stills. Additionally, some other, more nefarious cooking goes on up that way and there are sometimes makeshift meth labs out there and that is something you *really* don't want to tangle with.

In any case, you've been blatantly warned that going up there alone is inadvisable and that even going up there with a group of people is *still* inadvisable, but I know you're apt not to listen to me and honestly, I've done my best here. I'm telling you, don't go – but of course that didn't stop me from going.

I went up there in the broad light of day, with a companion, and yes, with a firearm between us should we need it.

It was a hot, May day; the sun shining bright with fat fluffy white clouds drifting lazily within an azure sky above the tree cover we had going for us. The shade was a welcome respite from the heat, and even more welcome, was that even though there were some creepy motherfuckers chilling at the head of the trail leading up to Red Ash, when we got there, we found an affable older gentleman that hung out with us while we took pictures and video of the old cemetery and talked about its legends.

I'm here to tell you, that even in the broad light of day this place felt *heavy*, the atmosphere among the low stones, like you were walking through something thicker, denser than just air alone. It was an interesting cognitive dissonance, my little strangelings. The feeling there and extremely valid, but by all appearances the cemetery a sun dappled and idyllic spot to the naked eye.

This is the one location that I'll grudgingly admit, might have something dark and unnatural to it – Moreso than just an angry or malevolent ghost.

The reports at Red Ash vary on the type of activity experienced within it. From shadow figures seen darting between graves and behind trees at night, to disembodied voices, and a shit ton of malevolence to come through communication methods such as an Ovilus, which is a new-to-me piece of equipment but promising, nonetheless.

Its function is to read and interpret energy fields, allowing any nearby spirits to manipulate said fields into getting the piece of equipment to spit out words.

Not only does this piece of equipment facilitate communication, but some models will even detect fluctuations in ambient temperature and humidity – further and more concrete evidence that an incorporeal being might be around.

Why did I say it like that? Incorporeal being?

Well, that's because not only ghosts supposedly haunt Red Ash, but there's potentially a demonic presence, and a Goat Man.

You read that right. A Goat Man – which I will not be getting into here beyond just the mention of him, because Matt and I agreed that if it's a critter or cryptid, that's his territory and so the Red Ash Goat Man will be handled in the cryptid section further along by Matt.

I'm just here for the ghosts…

There's report of a weeping woman at this location, one who hovers over and weeps inconsolably over her own grave.

In addition to shadow figures here, ghost lights have been reported, as well as wildly fluctuating EMF readings, despite the fact there are no power lines etc. nearby. EVP's have been captured, as well as photographic evidence of shadows, ectoplasmic mists, and varying other artifacts such as orbs.

Now, I know, I know – I'm a tough sell on orbs. There's just so much that can replicate the phenomenon of orbs from water vapor and dust particulate to small insects hanging in the air – but every once in a while a photo will come across my feed that makes me perk up because that it *clearly* not a bug or any of the other aforementioned phenomena.

What I look for when it comes to orbs in a photo is that one, it must stand alone. If you have a row of them, especially during daylight hours, that's not an orb, sweetie – it's probably lens flare. If there are hundreds if not thousands of the little fuckers in the picture? Yeah, that's probably dust or water particulate. Misshapen and not perfectly spherical in shape? Too easily dismissible as a flying insect.

No, what I look for are solo orbs, usually in a still photo, varying in color from everything around it, bonus points if there is some tell that it's in motion.

Of all of the hundreds if not thousands of photos and hundreds of hours of video evidence I have taken ghost hunting, I myself have only captured what I would consider an authentic orb, just once.

Your opinion may differ from mine, and that's fine. Everyone's lived experience and mileage may vary.

That being said, I've seen some pretty convincing orb photos out of Red Ash. They're out there. Look for yourself and you be the judge.

The reason I went off on my diatribe about orbs on this one, is because Red Ash is home to ghost lights, specifically blue in hue and color, which appear bobbing among graves and flitting through trees, spherical in shape, that resemble, you guessed it – orbs.

There's also an apparition of a man that has been seen here, likely a coal miner by hazarding a guess at the way he's been described to be dressed.

Disembodied footsteps, rustling, and voices have also been heard here. And as I mentioned from my own lived experience – there is a heavy discordant energy that permeates the space, as though this hallowed ground has somehow found itself corrupted.

It's not a good vibe here, my little strangelings, and that's not something I say lightly. I don't believe in over-hyping or sensationalizing a site that is already sensational enough. This one deserves all the caution and the warning labels, though.

Feel free to jump on ahead to Matt's section for the Goat Man half of the stories of this place or get there when you get there in your own time. It's your book now, you bought it, and you can do what you want with it.

Likewise, it's a free country. You can go where you like when you like – but parents, I would consider excluding your kiddos from this particular location. There are so many more for them and I mean it. I hated it here. For sure, I'll go back, otherwise what kind of paranormal investigator and lore keeper would I be?

Still, investigate responsibly and stay safe, okay?

CENTRAL EAST TENNESSEE

First Presbyterian Churchyard, Knoxville

The oldest cemetery in Knoxville, the First Presbyterian Graveyard is closed to the public in order to protect the very old and fragile stones – but, due to its setup and location on State Street, you can still visit this historic site right up close on at least two sides from the public sidewalk as we did this fine, sunny, late March, day.

One of the most interesting rumors about the 1700s era graveyard, is that no one is actually buried in it! There is a widespread belief, that when the current First Presbyterian Church building's foundation was laid, it was over the original (or at least a good portion of it) graveyard and that only the most notable historical figures of Knoxville were actually moved – but to where, there is no speculation or knowledge. The rest of the bodies were just built upon and only the stones moved to the plot of graveyard we now see today.

Considering that the plot lines on documents dating all the way back to the 1790s haven't changed, I highly doubt that this is the case for First Presbyterian, but by the same token, stranger things have happened. (I'm looking at you, Lake Lanier, but that is totally another story for a different ghost bite, cemetery file, book, or day.)

Aside from the deep-rooted rumor that no one is buried at all here, there are also whispers and gossip abound about a black, hooded figure that presents itself on the deepest and darkest of moonless nights, sweeping between and through the graves dramatically, terrifying all that have seen it. It certainly isn't a living person, as this figure has been known to appear and disappear in a blink, as though magically apporting a la the wizarding world. At once, they're striding through the graveyard and then winking out of existence to reappear frighteningly closer, or further away.

There are a few theories attributed to this apparition. One, that it's a guardian, or death itself, sent to look after the standing stones. Another is that it's one of the denizens of the graveyard that was supposedly moved to parts unknown... and three, and my personal favorite harkens back to the Bakers-Peters House legend of good ol' Abner Baker.

What does he have to do with First Presbyterian, you might ask?

Well, he was the last man buried in it – according to historical records anyway, and long after the graveyard was closed to further burials at that.

The story goes, that after Abner Baker murdered William Hall, the former Union soldier who had either dimed his daddy out, or had been part of the posse that had been sent to apprehend his daddy but shot and killed him instead, ol' Abner was taken to the jail where a mob stormed the place and hung him from the tree outside the old courthouse.

(We'll get to that digression in a minute, I'm trying to stay focused here. Focus with me!)

Abner's uncle was, at the time of Abner's death, an elder or some kind of a man with sway within the First Presbyterian Church and as such, Uncle-What's-His-Face got special permission to have Abner interred in the First Presbyterian Church's graveyard. His gravestone is one of the tallest that is present among the old stones, a standing obelisk with the top busted off; but don't worry – it wasn't the work of vandals, the broken off top was an intentional design of the time back in the Victorian era – a symbol of a life cruelly cut short.

Anyway, it was while I was sifting through the ghost stories surrounding the churchyard that I found out that Abner may be the figure spotted within it, and that in addition to the haunting at Baker-Peters House and the graveyard we're talking about here, that he's also been spotted in the deep of night hanging from the tree outside the original courthouse.

(There. There's that digression I was getting to.)

So, we get three ghost stories at the expense of *one* dude here in Knoxville, how cool is that?

Well, okay, it's cool for us but clearly not so great for Abner Baker… but hey, them's the breaks in this field. Somebody has to die in order for us to get ghosts and the more traumatic the death usually gives us a guarantee of a haunting good time…

To be honest, I think it's prettiest to think so that Abner is back at his childhood home with his dad, who he clearly dearly loved. I don't know who the figure is in the First Presbyterian Graveyard, but I don't think it's him. As for the ghost seen hanging from the tree outside the original courthouse? Oh, I think that's Abner, too, alright. I just don't think it's *Abner*, if you catch my drift. Like, I don't think it's his consciousness or whatever – not like how he haunts the house. No, I think the ghost of the hanging man is just a residual haunt. A recording on time and space itself, if you will. You know, just to recap if you haven't found me on social media discussing such things in a Sound Paranormal Fledgling File. (Shameless plug, go find me!)

Anyway, that's what's up at the First Presbyterian Graveyard – a place where supposedly many gather and have seen the dark and ghastly figure wander through the stones on Halloween! Until Knoxville PD shoos them away for loitering, that is.

You can find this slice of Knoxville's haunted history just across the street from the State Street Garage downtown, which is usually free to park at on the weekends and is very reasonably priced during the week!

OLD GRAY CEMETERY, KNOXVILLE

Established in 1850 Gray Cemetery was named by Henrietta Reese, the wife of the first president of cemetery trustees for Knoxville. She suggested naming it after the English poet, Thomas Gray, whose poem *Elegy Written in a Country Churchyard* captured her imagination. The poem perfectly fit the vibe of the location of Old Gray at the time, and without further discussion, the name was adopted and stuck.

Gray Cemetery became *Old* Gray in 1892, after *New Gray* Cemetery was established in another part of town, but that's a topic for another day.

Located at 543 North Broadway in Old North Knoxville, Old Gray Cemetery is the final resting place of over 9,000 souls including 26 Knoxville mayors, 8 congressmen, and no less than 3 US senators. It's also the home to more than a few ghosts.

One of the stories more notably attributed to Old Gray as a haunted cemetery is the story of Virginia Coxe. She died at the tragically young age of 41 back in 1906. Virginia and I have a couple of things in common, one of which is we're both accomplished novelists. Indeed, Virginia finished her second novel, *The Embassy Ball*, while living here in Knoxville.

Her bereaved husband had this beautiful angel statue commissioned for Virginia after her passing and it stood, perfect and whole, until sometime in 2011; that's when vandals chose to desecrate the monument to Virginia's memory by burning candles on it, but more egregiously by breaking off the statue's right hand... the hand that, undoubtedly, Virginia wrote both of her novels with.

It is said that Virginia's restless spirit wanders the headstones and tombs of Old Gray at night, looking for the vandals who desecrated her grave and for her lost right hand so that she may continue her writing. I'm not sure that Virginia cares all that much after so long dead – but that's just my take on things. Aside from sharing a love of the written word, and my being the same age as when she passed, we have at least one other thing in common should the story be true... I spend a lot of time haunting Old Gray myself, as it's pretty close to home; however, you will never catch me there at night –

One, its gates close at the appointed hour whether you're inside or out, and two – there's rumor and whispers of a malevolent spirit locked within Old Gray's gates at night, one known as a *Black Aggie.*

I had never heard of such a thing before moving to Knoxville and encountering stories of Old Gray, so I took interest right away in what this thing could be. It led me down a rabbit hole, my little strangelings, as every web search I conducted traced back to the same thing: A legend about a grave marking statue in the Washington DC area by the same name. A topic for another time down the line if I can ever get to it to see it in person.

While the searches were dominated by the statue erected, originally in 1926 in the Baltimore, Maryland area, and the undying urban legend surrounding it – I finally found an explanation for the Black Aggie in the context of a spirit haunting a cemetery. Indeed, a relatively obscure thing in southern folklore that arrived by way of Scotch-Irish immigrants. A Black Aggie in *this* context is derived from the old stories of *Black Annis*, which is the terrible, blue-skinned ghost of a witch that haunts the Scottish Highlands.

The Black Aggie of Old Gray, however, is reputed to be the spirit of an unfortunate witch or woman doomed to haunt the cemetery she was buried in after being shunned in life by her neighbors, dying rejected and alone. Indeed, a terrible fate, and one that twisted her soul turning her into an evil bitter ghost with glowing red eyes set deep within the sockets of a skeletal face.

Oh yeah, and like the Black Annis legend before her; she eats people. People stupid enough to go into her cemetery at night. So, that's another reason you won't find me in Old Gray after dark. I don't identify as paranormal snack food – just your run-of-the-mill cis, het, white woman.

Boring, I know.

There is one story that was related by two boys sometime in the 1990s about Old Gray's Black Aggie – the boys were amateur ghost hunters, and that's me being really kind... what they really were, were a pair of idiots. One night – armed with a case of beer and a polaroid camera, they headed out to Old Gray Cemetery to see if the stories of the Black Aggie were true and to try and capture the entity on film. (See, they dumb.)

After a while of snapping photos and wandering among the graves, the boys grew bored and went back to their car (stares in 'don't you dare.') where they cracked into their case of beer and started drinking. Eventually, fueled by alcohol and their teenage stupidity – they started to make disparaging remarks about the ghost and cutting up, as teens are want to do.

(So effing dumb.)

Eventually, mother nature called to one of the boys who exited the vehicle and wandered back inside the cemetery to relieve himself. (I can't even.) It was as he was taking his leak against one of the gravestones, (the disrespectful little shit) he noticed a black, deeper than shadow, darker than night substance begin to ooze from the cracks around the stone and up from the earth.

He said the ooze collected and coalesced into a humanoid form, and terrified, he tucked and ran back to the car, leaping inside and screaming at his companion to get out of there.

It was as the boys backed out of the cemetery, one of them *supposedly* snapped a photo of the entity chasing them – but of course, these boys are the only ones to have ever seen the photo and we're just supposed to take their word for it. (Yes, this is me, rolling my eyes.)

Still, for years and years, both before and after this supposed incident in the 1990s, the Black Aggie has been the top told ghost story and legend of Old Gray Cemetery – teenagers willing and daring one another to camp outside the cemetery gates, or worse, trespass within them at night to antagonize and try to see her.

To that, I say: leave a bitch alone! – clearly, she's already had it rough and doesn't need any more douche-baggary in her un-life. Get off her lawn!

That, and if I've said it once, I've said it a thousand times, my little strangelings – although maybe not thus far in this book: *We. Don't. Trespass.* Period. End of. Trespassing is a dick move and what gets paranormal investigators shut out of locations and gives them a bad rep. We don't need any more of that. We like hunting ghosties, so it's much better to ask permission than to beg forgiveness and to leave any potential investigation sites either in the same condition or better than you found it. (You see some trash left by a trash human, pick it up!)

Anyway, there I go digressing again… hopefully by now you're used to it.

As for visiting Old Gray yourself, go during the day – if the gates are open off Broadway across from the church, then Old Gray is open. It's a beautiful cemetery, especially in spring, winter, and fall – you won't be disappointed no matter what time of year you go.

GREENWOOD CEMETERY, KNOXVILLE

This seemingly very modern and unassuming cemetery off Tazewell Pike in Knoxville, TN doesn't look like it would harbor much by way of ghosties or things that would go bump in the night. Strangely enough, I actually found it by accident from the comfort of my living room recliner while I was catching up on one of my guilty pleasure television shows, *Paranormal Caught on Camera*.

You best believe my head shot up and I paid attention when I heard the general announcer for the show say 'Knoxville, Tennessee!'

The video clip in question seen in season five, episode fifteen, shows a local man in a cemetery at night in what appears to be its unlocked receiving vault. Now for those of you not in the know, receiving vaults aren't generally utilized as much today as they were in the past. It was an above-ground vault that was often times set into a hillside of a cemetery that facilitated keeping bodies over winter and through the colder months when the ground was frozen and it was much too hard to dig.

They aren't as required anymore due to the advent of heavy machinery such as front loaders and back-hoes that make quick work of digging through even the toughest of frozen ground nowadays.

Anyway, back to the video clip...

So, this man is in the Cemetery at night and in what appears to be an unlocked and empty receiving vault. The walls are brick, the floors are tile with several tiles missing over the cement beneath, and there is only one way in, and one way out of the vault – and that is through twin rusty metal doors the like you would expect to see in a horror themed video game set in an abandoned asylum or something.

The vault is well lit by a light in the investigator's hand, likely emanating from his phone, or from a source that was with his phone as he was filming himself. In his other hand, he holds a K-2 Meter, utilized to measure electromagnetic fields, both their presence and their strength.

He's inspecting an 'L' shaped patch of missing floor tiles with his camera and you see his foot scrape some dried leaves out of the indentation left by their absence, when all of a sudden, a wild and horrid metal screech is heard behind him. He whirls! Facing the rusted metal doors of the vault and pauses, nervously, no doubt – I mean, I would be! Full confession, my little strangelings, I can be quite the pansy and you wouldn't catch me dead in that receiving vault alone at night!

He approaches the door, states for the camera and the benefit of all of us watching that someone or something has just scratched on the barely ajar door. He calls out, "Hello?" and pushes open the door revealing the deep dark of night beyond. We catch a glimpse of brick and ivy of the outside wall of the vault and he declares in a hushed tone… "There's nothing out here."

I, like you, breathed a bit of a sigh of relief, he turns to the open vault door and then shines his light and turns the camera the opposite way of when he first came out, showing the other direction of the outside of the vault… and there's nothing out there, just like he said.

Still, he goes up to the outside of the open door and points out a deep scratch in the metal. You can see it, but barely as he says, "Looks like something was drug right down the door," as the insects softly sing in the background. He pans up the outside of the doorframe toward the top and exclaims, "Oh, look! That's claw marks!"

Three distinct claw marks reside on the outside of the door, starting at the top down to about the door handle.

The man goes back into the vault and continues trying to communicate with whatever is in the cemetery. He has an app open on his phone, which has been blurred by the show, and a female voice emanates from it in a mechanical voice saying 'push' and you hear

Josh say, "Push? Push what?" when all of a sudden, the vault door that he'd left open in front of him is pushed shut, the door slamming, with Josh still inside the vault.

Yeah. That would have been a whole lot of NOPE from me, too. I feel you, there. I mean, I'm made of some tough stuff, have been in quite the interesting situations personally when it comes to the paranormal, but that? I don't know about all that!

Now, as to just why the man was there in the first place...

Earlier on in the segment, he introduced himself as Josh, and that he was on-site due to hearing from some of the nearby locals to the cemetery that there was a large black shadowy mass that had been spotted inside the cemetery's low walls and gates. A huge, hulking combination between a shadow figure and what had been described as a black cloud. Onlookers had told him that it had the distinct form of an entity or person, but that it was absolutely *gigantic* in stature and with enough substance to it that it could and did block out streetlights as it passed in front of them at night.

Having an interest in the paranormal and being a paranormal investigator, Josh decided to, well, go investigate – and have a look for himself.

Here is where I'm going to stop and be your paranormal investigative den mother, my little strangelings. Please, don't do what Josh did in this case – no, not go into a cemetery at night, that's perfectly fine as long as it is one of those cemeteries that's open twenty-four hours, which they *are* out there, and this case, Greenwood in Knoxville was one of them at the time that Josh was there in September of 2021. (You should definitely check to make certain that still is the case before you go anywhere at night – we don't trespass, no, no, no!) I'm not sure if that is still the case as of the publication of this book, so I would double check that – but no, the point I am actually trying to harp on here is that you should never, ever, go anywhere be it cemetery, building, or property at night *alone* – and I promise you, I am not just saying that because I am a big ol' chicken, either.

There is always safety in numbers, my little strangelings. Be it from the living or the dead; and let's face it, the living are and always likely will be a much bigger problem for you than the dead ever will.

I digress... I do that a lot... by now you should really be used to it...

Cut to Josh back outside the vault, a braver man than I, as he swings the door that just slammed shut back and forth on its hinges and says, "This door has to weigh at least two-hundred pounds and it just *flew* shut..." and he's right, it did – we all just got to witness it with our own eyes merely moments before.

He says he felt like something was watching him and he states that he doesn't know if whatever it was was trying to keep him in or was trying to scare him out, or whatever, but that "whatever it was, it was up to no good."

The talking heads have their heyday talking about it after that, and their viewpoints were fascinating, as they always were – the clip was replayed half a dozen times before, and the theories were abound – but my mind was already made up.

I wasn't going to be satisfied until I went and checked this place out myself.

It wasn't long after I saw the clip that I went to Greenwood Cemetery – during the day, and with two friends, to drive around and see if we could find this vault. Which we did, but it wasn't entirely in a place where it was quote "the first thing you see" according to the show.

No, it was tucked in the back of the cemetery, and up on an elevated tract, set back in a hillside as most receiving vaults I've seen are. My friends and I did see and identify the scratches in the rusty metal – they're still there – but here is the part that genuinely surprised me.

I had expected that the door wouldn't be that heavy, or that it would swing fairly easily and I was wrong. I was wrong on both counts.

Josh wasn't lying in his footage – that door was *heavy*, and what's more, no matter how hard any of the three of us tried to slam that door the way it had been slammed in Josh's footage, we couldn't replicate the speed or the strength required to get it to do it.

I tend to approach most things I see on television with a heaping level of skepticism – but on this, I was pleasantly surprised. Josh was telling the truth. There wasn't anything short of a *very* strong man, or a supernatural entity that could make that door do what it did that night in September of 2021.

(…and Josh, if you're reading this, I would like to buy you a drink and listen. I want to know all about what you felt and even more about what you heard about that place to lure you there at night all by yourself! Contact information will definitely be in the back of this book!)

SOUTHEAST TENNESSEE

ST. LUKE'S EPISCOPALIAN CHURCHYARD, CLEVELAND

Technically, this one is just north of Chattanooga in Cleveland, Tennessee, but this is my book, and close enough for my tastes to lump them together a bit. I just didn't feel like calling this one an 'outlying area' as it is right next to Chatt and right along the I-75 corridor.

Anyway, the spooky, I'm getting to that...

The churchyard at St. Luke's Episcopal Church in Cleveland, TN, has a remarkable mausoleum at its back. There is also just one person interred here – a little girl by the name of Nina Craigmiles.

I'm getting a bit ahead of myself here, let me go back – all the way back to Nina's very short-lived life.

She was born to sea captain John Craigmiles and his wife, Adelia Craigmiles on August 5th, 1864, in what was then, the small town of Cleveland, Tennessee.

She was the apple of her daddy's eye, and likewise, the apple of her maternal grandfather's eye – who spent a good deal of time with Nina while her father was away.

It was a common sight to see – little Nina with her papa as he made his rounds in his horse drawn buggy to see his patients and make his house calls. Often times, little Nina would urge her papa Gideon to make the horses go faster between houses and calls. Something her grandfather often indulged her in, even allowing the young girl to take the reins every now and again.

Today, you would never see a grandparent turn over the steering wheel to their seven-year-old, but this was the 1800s of it all, and I remember a time, not so long ago, when grandparents would set their grandchildren in their lap and let them steer the car – so this doesn't seem too far out of pocket to me...

It was a fall afternoon, and little Nina Craigmiles was with her papa, or maternal grandfather, Doctor Gideon Thompson. St. Luke's Day, to be exact – which apparently is on a day in October.

This day was set apart from most of their jaunts, in that the weather was quite tempestuous and Dr. Thompson thought better of taking his, then seven-year-old, granddaughter out into the storm.

He must go, there were patients to be seen to, but he did try to leave Nina behind... at first.

Little Nina begged and pleaded with her papa to please, please, pleeeeease, let her go with him – and against his better judgment, Dr. Thompson relented.

It would be the worst mistake of his life.

No one knows what spooked the horses. An errant clap of thunder? The train's horn in the driving rain? That part is unclear – what *is* clear is that Dr. Gideon's team of horses affixed to his buggy *did* spook and lunged at the most inopportune time – directly into the path of an oncoming train at one of the town's railroad crossings.

Gideon Thompson was toppled from the buggy and thrown clear – but both horses and little Nina didn't fare half so well. They were struck by the train, killed brutally and instantly; and Dr. Thompson, though he survived, was badly injured.

Nina's parents were inconsolable – neither one more than her father, who immediately commissioned a church to be built within town – not her grave, but the *whole-ass church*, my little strangelings!

Thus, St. Luke's Episcopal church was built in memory of little Nina Craigmiles, named for the saint whose day it was when she died, and behind that church, an elaborate mausoleum of Carrera Italian Marble was constructed; specifically, to house little Nina's broken body and to house little Nina alone.

Some important dates to set the timeline for you:

- August 5th, 1864, Nina Craigmiles was born.

- October 18th, 1871, on St. Luke's Day, Nina Craigmiles was killed.
- One year later, on St. Luke's Day 1872, St. Luke's Church was consecrated in her memory after having been built by her father.

As soon as the church was completed, John Craigmiles did a few interesting things. First, he unlocked the church's front doors and destroyed the only key to ensure that anyone at any time would be welcome to enter. He also had a special niche created within the church that he called Nina's Niche, and he directed that fresh flowers be placed within that alcove for his daughter daily.

Finally, he planned and began to execute a mausoleum be constructed on the church grounds for Nina and the rest of the Craigmiles family upon their death.

It was three years later that the lavish memorial to his only daughter was completed at a cost that would be equivalent to 1.1 million dollars today.

The mausoleum was stunningly constructed of the finest Carrera Italian marble that John Craigmiles money could buy. Famously, this marble type is known for being purest white, with faint bluish and grayish veining that shadows beneath the smooth white stone beautifully.

However, it wasn't long after the completion of the mausoleum and Nina's interment within it, that something very strange took place...

On the mausoleum, in the archway above the door on the right-hand side, appeared to start *bleeding*.

A red stain appeared on the stone, one that couldn't be explained. At first, it was supposed that there must be some kind of mistake, that something had gotten onto the marble. Of course, Nina's father was incensed by the red stains, and ordered the marble thoroughly cleaned. However, when nothing at all could be done to scrub it off, he had that section of the mausoleum completely *rebuilt*...

...and yet, the red stains returned.

And they didn't return just once, my little strangelings; nor was it just twice, but after *three* separate attempts at rebuilding, Craigmiles had to admit defeat.

It was assumed, logically, that the red staining had come from iron deposits within the marble, and at one point – that theory was put to science; a bit of the marble carefully chipped and scraped from the spot and sent to a laboratory as a sample for testing.

There were no traces of iron found within the samples taken.

There were no traces of iron found within the samples taken.

There were no traces of *anything* to explain the red staining of the vault, in fact; and to this day, the bloody red staining on little Nina Craigmiles' mausoleum, remains a mystery, completely inexplicable... but for *one* explanation... one of *paranormal* origin.

Could this be a haunting? A physical manifestation of poor little Nina's horribly violent, bloody, and tragic death?

Or... could this be a powerful subconscious manifestation of a father's grief? A grandfather's guilt?

Whatever the case, the red staining above the door remains visible to this day, and it *does* indeed look like blood, my little strangelings. I've seen it myself on a sunny June afternoon just before I sat down to write this.

I took several photos and videos of the spot, and indeed, a quick Google search will yield a multitude of photos of the strange phenomenon.

The Craigmiles' vault is located directly behind St. Luke's and is the only interment here at the little churchyard. Once a year, they open the doors to the mausoleum around easter Sunday for some such religious reason surrounding the resurrection of Christ. It is the only time of year that you may see inside, and I do believe that next year I shall make the trip, because the sarcophagus that holds little Nina's broken body is a sight to behold. A beautiful work of art in remembrance of a vibrant and beautiful little girl the whole town used to call 'Princess Nina.'

GREENWOOD CEMETERY, CHATTANOOGA

You're not seeing double, my little strangelings. This is a separate yet coincidentally similarly named cemetery from Knoxville's Greenwood Cemetery. A lot of cemeteries are named like this. I can't tell you how many 'Greenwoods', 'Bethesdas', 'Mt. Olivet's' and other names that have been used and reused between cities and states. Some of them it's because they are run by the same memorial service and funeral home chains... but that is neither here nor there.

This particular Greenwood Cemetery is still an active cemetery that first opened in 1891, with its first interment occurring in 1892. I was first drawn to visit it when I found it third down on the list of 'Eleven Most Haunted Cemeteries in Tennessee.'

I was enamored by the short paragraph of information contained in the online article which basically told of the old legend that a wealthy family lived across from the cemetery on a lake. The wife became infirm and eventually wound up wheelchair bound. Her husband, having fallen in love with another woman, wheeled her into the lake to drown so that he could be rid of her.

While not a haunting specific to the cemetery itself, legend has it that on certain nights, twin grooves resembling the tracks from the woman's wheelchair can be seen leading into the lake. The markings inexplicably coming and going as she haunts the edge of the water leaving the tracks in her wake.

A slight variation of this account calls this woman the 'green lady' and it is said that she doesn't haunt the lake, but rather the cemetery. Appearing as a green mist and leaving her wheelchair tracks in her wake across these hallowed grounds.

In either case, it has my attention as a fantastic take of selfishness, tragedy, greed, and is rather hopelessly romanticized – so you know that I'm there!

I made the side quest into Greenwood one afternoon on a return trip from Atlanta to my home in Knoxville, and while I didn't see any wheelchair tracks, I certainly did experience a fright! Though it had nothing to do at all with the paranormal, but rather turning down a track or road within the cemetery that turned out not to be one at all.

There wasn't enough space to turn around and go nose down the steep bit of track, and so I put it in reverse but the angle was too steep to see. My rear tire of my trusty Jeep found itself over nothing next to a retaining wall with a deep rut before it and it took putting her into 4WD and some rather fancy wheel work on my part to get her off her semi-high centeredness.

We made it, though, and thus a lesson was learned. Be very careful when driving through some of these old cemeteries – especially if you aren't in a vehicle equipped with four-wheel drive. Make certain that the road is actually a road before you turn down it, and always watch for hazards that aren't paranormal in nature, too.

Life is but a series of lessons my little strangelings, and I would rather embarrass myself with an admission like this a little in hopes that one of you learn from my mild stupidity so that you don't make the same mistakes.

Stay safe out there and turn the page for the next haunted East Tennessee cemetery on our list.

MEMORIAL CEMETERY, CHATTANOOGA

The stories surrounding Memorial Cemetery in Chattanooga, Tennessee straddle the line between ghosts and hauntings and cryptid territory, which I guess it's fitting that it's our last stop before we head into Matt's section of the book and Cryptid Country.

I'll start with the ghosts and end with the cryptid sightings and see if I can't get Matt to weigh in on that part before wrapping it up and heading into his sections of the book.

The most prominent paranormal activity associated with this cemetery surrounds a free-standing arch located within it.

The story behind this arch goes that a man wanted his grave marker to stand out above all others within the cemetery – to that end, he had the arch designed and placed where he would be buried. Of course, when the man passed, and the time came to be interred, his family had other ideas. Rather than follow the man's wishes in having the stone arch itself be his headstone, they had it moved, and placed it at the entry way to the family plot, giving him a modest headstone in line with the rest of the family's.

It is said that a shadowy figure is seen loitering around the arch at night – the spirit of the disgruntled man, making his displeasure known at the backstabbing and selfish ways of his family.

The spirit is described as a Black Aggie, but the back story doesn't fit the specifications for one. As you'll recall from previous cemetery entries, a Black Aggie is derived from that of the folkloric Black Annis of Scottish highland lore. While Black Annis was depicted as a blue faced hag with iron claws and a taste for human flesh – particularly the tender flesh of children; a Black Aggie is a dark, shadow figure type ghost that haunts a graveyard or cemetery and is believed to be the earthbound vengeful or spiteful ghost of a witch or ostracized person, particularly a woman, who was outcast and died bitter and alone.

So, while there is a shadow figure that haunts this archway in the middle of Memorial Cemetery, I don't believe it to be a Black Aggie in the traditional sense of the word – which is a very bitter, very angry, and very vengeful spirit – which sure, the dude that had his family back bite him has definitely every reason to check those boxes. Instead, I believe the spirit that loiters around the arch, repeating the same movements and just sort of chilling could very well be the dude from the local folkloric story surrounding the arch.

Indeed, a Black Annis seems to interact with the living, actively horrifying and going after them; terrorizing them, but the spirit of Memorial Cemetery has been described as either one, doing its own thing – ignoring or simply not recognizing the living as being there, or two, if it *does* interact with the living, it behaves less vengefully or terrorizing as it follows the person at a considerable distance, acting shyer and more curious than anything.

To that end, I'm somewhere in the middle on this one, if it be a residual or intelligent haunting. I would need more information to feel comfortable more firmly categorizing it as either or… but one of the accounts I've read certainly leads me to error on the side of intelligence.

I think it interacts with the living enough to qualify it as such, but again, it lacks the anger and vitriol to classify it as a Black Aggie.

The shadow figure haunting this particular arch isn't the only ghostly figure in Memorial Cemetery.

Full-bodied apparitions of an American Civil War soldier have been seen. Generally, he's thought to be the same soldier, and not different ones. It's thought that he may or may not be as high ranking as a general – but other than that, no one knows who he possibly is.

Finally, there's another shadow figure that lurks here, and it's definitely not malevolent, but rather curious. Nighttime security and some nighttime trespassers to the cemetery noting that this shadow figure follows at the perimeter of the cemetery grounds, keeping its distance, but also keeping the living within sight as it flits along gravestones, and between trees, along the perimeter fence line. Anyone who has encountered this particular shadow figure has said that it gives the very distinctive vibe of "What 'cha doing over there?" as it follows you.

Memorial isn't home to *just* ghosts, however. One security guard reported hearing sounds outside the main building one night and leaving out the front to investigate – as was his job, he shined his flashlight all around, and didn't see anything at first.

The rustling in the tree branches in the big tree across from the front entrance of the main building had him training his light with the quickness, where he said there, in the branches of the tree, he spotted a gray creature; gargoyle-like in appearance, the thing couldn't be more than two feet tall – and even though we aren't there yet, this thing sounds suspiciously to me like the Wears Valley WTF we encountered on our search for Appalachia cryptids for this book.

We wrote about the Wears Valley WTF long before I got to writing about the Memorial Cemetery – and to that end things are a bit out of order, but that's okay.

These two creatures sound suspiciously alike, but they're sure a distance away from each other – this one being sighted in Chattanooga and the other in Wears Valley.

Another thing these tiny terrors have in common, is they nasty. The guard said had gone running back into the information building after spotting this thing, locking the door and panting like hell, his heartbeat so loud in his ears it drowned out every other sound, and he could feel the organ battering the insides of his ribs. He got himself calmed down, convinced himself that he was crazy, that he hadn't just seen what he thought he'd seen – that it had to be a raccoon or something – not this grayish two to three foot tall, humanoid but not creature.

Yeah, it was just an Opossum or a Trash Panda – he'd only got a quick look after all, and his imagination had just taken off without him. Besides, now that his heart had stopped its pounding and the blood had stopped rushing in his ears, he couldn't hear anything out there.

Plucking up his courage, the guard ventured back outside, shining his light into the tree where the creature had been, and with a sigh of relief, found nothing there.

That relief was short-lived, however, when he heard a noise at ground level, and training his light in the direction it'd come from found this nasty little shit not but two feet from him – snarling and lunging at him and that was no raccoon!

The guard ran – and this thing chased him, all the way through the cemetery making rabid noises and looking like something straight out of hell, stopping at the cemetery gates as the guard ran through and out into the night well away from Memorial Cemetery.

He returned with the light of day, turned in his uniform, and quit. Vowing never to set foot in or near the cemetery ever again.

There's no more information about this little fuck other than the one story, and we honestly have no idea what it is or could be, although we explore some theories in the Wears Valley WTF section – but for us, it's aptly named by us because seriously... what the fuck is it?

With little shit gargoyle/goblin like creatures with big attitudes wandering around at night, best keep your visit to Memorial Cemetery to the daytime and it's posted hours, my little strangelings. Who knows what that thing is, and honestly, with it choosing violence, I don't think any one of us really wants to find out.

GATEWAY TO THE SMOKIES
&
GREATER APPALACHIA

WHITE OAK FLATS CEMETERY, GATLINBURG

Established in 1830, White Oak Flats bears the name originally given to the settlement that would later become Gatlinburg. It has some interesting ghostly tales revolving around its crude headstones with etchings that have barely survived and are mostly illegible today.

One of the prevailing theories is that the reason Lydia is seen in the Park Vista is that she is buried here, halfway between the Park Vista and the Greenbrier. It may be why she is seen not only in both, but on some lonely nights when the tourists are all abed and the strip is all but shut down except maybe a bar or two, that it's said that you can see her walking along, all alone along the sidewalks, sometimes pausing to look into the Little Pigeon River.

One of the other ghostly tales revolves around a woman named Mary, who died sometime well after the cemetery's establishment.

Mary was completely and unreasonably terrified of the dark all of her life. We're talking true phobic levels here – which are *ugly* and can take a *huge* toll on one's mental health. She was reportedly obsessive about not being left alone, or in the dark without some kind of a light. It is said, that after she died and was interred here at White Oak Flats, that on particularly dark nights, if you sit still and watch, you will easily be able to pick out Mary's headstone from the rest of the markers that still remain within the cemetery as it will begin to glow, with a soft, unearthly light.

I can only hope that the fact Gatlinburg has grown up so much like it has, and the advent of electricity and the fact that the town is quite regularly lit up after dark, has brought some measure of comfort to Mary in her afterlife. Enough so, that perhaps her headstone doesn't need to glow quite as much or often – although I would really love to see it.

Another story concerns a young, Confederate Soldier, who was struck down in his prime of life during fighting in the American Civil War. Shortly before leaving to fight for his cause, he married his young sweetheart with promises that just as soon as he returned, they would begin a beautiful life together.

He returned, alright – but in a casket, making it hard to make good on his promise. Still, despite that fact, to this day, mysterious bundles of flowers appear atop the soldier's grave; though no one has ever seen anyone there to leave them.

It is believed that the restless spirit of his grieving widow is the one to leave them. Even though she has long since passed herself.

Another little girl ghost is seen within the cemetery. Local legend says that she is seen wearing a blue 1800s style dress with a white pinafore, and that she can sometimes be seen at night running and playing through the tombstones at one edge of the cemetery. It's where her family is buried. Mother, father, and all three children including herself, who all tragically died within weeks of each other. Likely from one of the mosquitos borne illnesses that ran rampant throughout the South in the 1800s.

There are reports that she has run up to cemetery visitors in the broad light of day and asked them if they're visiting someone special before disappearing in front of their very eyes.

Then there's the story of one couple who decided one night to use White Oak Flats as a lover's lane.

It seems the spirits who reside there didn't take too kindly to the disrespect that the couple put on their final resting place.

The couple were in their car, getting hot and heavy, when they began to hear strange noises out in the dark.

At first, they chalked it up to just hearing things. You know, the whole paranoid about getting caught thing – especially being in a cemetery after dark like you're usually not supposed to… but the noises got louder, and louder, and suddenly, both halve of the couple, freaked out about what they were clearly actually hearing and what *wasn't* their imagination, were squinting and peering into the dark.

That's when they began to pick out shadowy figures darting through the graves and moving from tree to tree. The sounds resolving into drumbeats and growing in intensity. Speaking of intensity, an intense wind kicked up out of nowhere, plant matter picked up and battering their vehicle; grass and tree branches whipping out in the dark.

Then, it was as though the figures they thought they had seen had become some kind of corporeal but remained invisible and had taken up post to either side of the car. Pushing and ricking it back and forth on its tires. The couple screaming in terror as the driver tried desperately to get the car to turn over. They cranked the ignition, but nothing happened. The vehicles lights even refusing to turn on.

Then, as quickly as the maelstrom of paranormal activity had begun, it just... stopped.

The driver turned the key in the ignition again, and the vehicle cranked without one iota of trouble. Chests heaving with fright, the driver put it in gear and got them the fuck out of there.

To the spirits I say, 10/10 trolling and standing your ground. Bravo!

There is a multitude of paranormal activity attributed to White Oak Flats Cemetery by paranormal investigators. From shadow figures to full-bodied apparitions, to disembodies voices and EVPs captured. Ghost lights, and not just the glow emanating from Mary's tombstone, either – but honest to goodness ghost lights and floating glowing orbs not just captured on camera, but visible to the naked eye.

Spikes in EMF activity, and a whole host of other things are mentioned here too.

Pretty cool, I say.

OLD ELKMONT CEMETERY, GREAT SMOKY MOUNTAINS NATIONAL PARK

Once upon a time, Elkmont was the premier resort town of the Smokies, *not* Gatlinburg. Now, it's just another ghost town within the Smoky Mountains, and one of the National Park's favored campgrounds for the ability to camp and explore among the old ghost town's ruins.

I t took me a while to find any real stories about the ruins of Elkmont being haunted, but I *did* find at least one video talking about how the Old Elkmont Cemetery was supposedly *the* most haunted cemetery in the Smokies – kind of tough to beat out White Oak Flats for that title, but I thought I would see if the guy that posted it could wow me with some fresh ghost lore out of this old little cemetery that was shockingly filled with children more than adults.

The reason was readily apparent on the stone markers that had dates on them as to why the mass of child graves. Most of the end dates on the headstones between 1917 and 1918 – or when the Spanish Flu swept the globe in an epidemic that wiped out a good chunk of the population for the time.

Still, a pandemic wasn't enough to say why this was supposedly the most haunted cemetery in the Smokies, nor what type of activity supposedly takes place here; just that people experience things.

Really, the only information I found about *what kinds of things*, was a footnote not about the cemetery, but about the abandoned stone buildings and cabins of the original resort town, and the only thing I found about *that* was a pervasive feeling of being watched.

Annoying, right?

Enter *The Paranormal Sleuth* on TikTok, to save the day!

He had a short video talking about the activity in Old Elkmont Cemetery. Activity like disembodied voices, and full-bodied apparitions that supposedly haunt this old historic town's even older and more historic burial ground.

There wasn't much more detail than that, but it was enough to convince me – but that brings me to a point, my little strangelings:

Cemetery hauntings, for the most part, are few and far between.

I am going to do some digging into more of Elkmont, though. Apparently, it was a logging town before it was a ghost town, and between logging accidents, and some train accidents on record – it was a place rife with men dying in horrible and traumatizing enough ways that it *should* be haunted – but researching ghost towns can be a pain in the ass, my little strangelings. Mostly because 'ghost' is in the name but just because it's a 'ghost town' too, doesn't mean it is haunted but trying to look up any specific hauntings in one of them just leads you in circles to – you guessed it, 'yup, it's a ghost town' nothing about ghosts in it, just 'yeah, this is a ghost town' – while the internet is a great tool, it can be dumb and sometimes is only as smart as it's operator.

I guess I just haven't used the right string of search words to find what I'm looking for, but I'm going to keep trying. For now, this will be here waiting for a second edition should I ever get around to it and come up with enough requisite information to shove here.

For now, this is just your solid reminder that just because 'ghost' is in the name, and it's a cemetery – there's no guarantee there's anything spooky to it.

You know, except for the fact it's where dead people are buried, or just the reminder that nature is just outside the walls and doors waiting to reclaim the buildings built from its harvested flesh and bones, rocks, and trees.

I guess the existential dread those thoughts conjure up is at least worth a 3/10 on the spooky scale.

PART 3: CRITTERS & CRYPTIDS

Northeast Tennessee

RED ASH CEMETERY GOAT MAN

You find yourself in a cemetery late at night. The trees surrounding the small patch of tombstones cast strange shadows in the moonlight. There is a rustling in the tree line and you see a humanoid figure step out into the clearing. It stands at the size of a man or perhaps a little larger. This is no person; however, this thing walks on crooked legs with cloven hooves for feet. The creature has the head of a goat with curled intimidating horns. The very sight of this monster chills you to the bone. You have met a Goatman. I say "*a*" Goatman because these guys are everywhere. Especially in the Bible-Belt region of the American South.

There may not be a single abandoned bridge, railway crossing, access road, ranger station, or cemetery anywhere in the south that has not seen its fair share of rumors of satanic rituals and sacrifice. Them damn devil worshipping teenagers am I right? Show me rural graffiti in an abandoned space and I will find you at least one instance of a badly drawn inverted pentacle (if it is even inverted) and many generic "666" tags.

I mention all Satan stuff because I believe that's where the imagery comes from. There have been many horned figures in mythology but Christianity has a habit of adopting iconography and lore so we end up with demons and the devil himself with horns and goat-like features. The Greek god Pan is described as having the legs and feet of a goat while sporting horns. Pan was the god of a few things but one being shepherds and flocks. I include this little piece of information here because one of the origin stories for a Goatman legend is that a shepherd went insane and vowed eternal vengeance against teenagers because some of his flock got killed by a group of kids.

Goatmen across the country usually have some element of tragedy attached to their origin stories. A murdered slave, or a farmer that met an untimely end. Maybe someone who died because of unsafe conditions comes back to haunt the location of their demise.

These things more often than not come with a curse attached as well. Witnessing a Goatman in whatever location he is haunting or protecting may mean an ill fortune has been doled out to you. Hell, there are even tales of the creature just straight up pushing people off of bridges or frightening them so badly they accidentally injured themselves.

I ran across instances of mangled animal bodies being found near a Goatman area but these correlated with active train tracks. It is a fair assumption that trains have a higher kill count than a two-legged demon humanoid goat from hell.

We have established that East Tennessee has a wide range of creepy critters. Is there a Goatman hoofing around these parts? Well, you are damn right there is! I guess it's obvious since we put a chapter about him in the book.

Our Goatman calls Red Ash Cemetery home.

Red Ash Cemetery lies about thirty minutes northwest of the city of Knoxville. Caryville Tennessee was once a bustling coal mining town. It is now home to what some say is one of the most haunted locations in all of the state.

The surrounding area, including the graves, coal stacks, and railroad, are home to terrifying apparitions. Railroads seem to be a common factor in these legends and it is something I will definitely be looking more into.

Reports of floating orbs, ghosts abound, as A.J. described in her chapter about Red Ash, what she glossed over is that it is said to be guarded by demons. One of those is our friend The Goatman.

The Red Ash Goatman perfectly aligns with the descriptions of the others across the country. A bipedal humanoid creature that seems to be a hybrid of a goat and a human. It is said to stand over six feet tall (some reports have it closer to nine feet in other regions) on fur covered haunches. The torso of a human man and the head of a demonic goat with large, curled horns.

One eyewitness statement claimed that after exploring the area with their family they were leaving and their two kids suddenly ran to them scared out of their minds claiming to have witnessed The Goatman in the flesh... or fur rather. The kids reportedly described the creature exactly as other witnesses had before. Is this a case of children freaking themselves out in a spooky location? Did they really see the demon that guards the cemetery? There is no real way of knowing. I do know that something is definitely not normal about Red Ash Cemetery and the area surrounding it.

There are some who claim that, as paranormal investigations become more popular, it leads to an equal rise in sightings and the creation of new lore. This may very well be true but a counterpoint to that is perhaps the rise in stories is from simply having more witnesses and an easy way to spread information. You can't find something if you don't look for it, after all.

If you find yourself out looking for our Goaty friend I ask that you be respectful of your surroundings, the environment, and your fellow humans. If you choose not to, you may very well end up part of the legend itself.

Be safe out there, and happy hunting, y'all.

VAMPIRES IN OLD BUTLER

That's right we're covering vampires. Buckle up buttercups because things are about to suck.

The legend of undead blood fiends spans the entire globe. Almost every civilization has a story that fits the vampiric lore. This shit actually goes back well into antiquity but we are going to focus on more modern tales. The vampire story may span the globe but there's a small portion of it that hits home right here in East Tennessee.

I think we are all familiar with the dapper and suave image of the sanguine socialite. Typically, a man or woman who exudes charisma and seductive prowess. The creature being painted in a sophisticated light as opposed to being a feral demon pretty much started with "The Vampyre" written in 1819 by John Polidori. You've heard of that guy, right? Yeah, didn't think so, but I bet you have heard of Bram Stoker, whose novel Dracula in 1897 transformed the vampire legend forever.

Dracula has influenced countless pieces of media and is a great example of the evolution of mythology as vampires today are still held to some of the superstitions laid out in the book.

The descriptions of the creatures in most cultures are very similar. I think ultimately comes down to poor understanding of death processes and germ theory. The vampire's hair and nails are said to keep growing after death. The appearance of growth of course being from the skin retracting and shrinking and not some evil undead curse. A group of brave vampire hunters may find the corpse they have unearthed be bloody around the mouth. This is evidence of a recent meal by the demon! Not, yah know, the fact is that dead bodies, for lack of a better word, ooze fluids.

A common element has members of the locality become ill shortly after the death of our suspected vampire. Even with some claiming to have been visited by the dead in the middle of the night. Stoker plays into this well in Dracula giving him command of dreams and mesmerism. In my opinion, this is explained by two things. If I ever write a history book it'll be named after those two things. Disease and Mass Hysteria. It's got a ring to it, doesn't it?

We obviously don't want these neck biting assholes around so what are our options? Well, history gives us quite a bit to work with. There are numerous purported ways to prevent, deter, and ultimately dispatch those creatures of the night.

Vampires are said to be warded off by garlic and certain herbs. How bad would it be if you enjoy good flavorful food in life and end up a vampire afraid of garlic? Silver is another thing. It actually comes up quite a bit in folklore about many monsters. Silver was thought to be a "pure" metal and thus corrupted souls could not interact with it. A silver bullet is a pretty good remedy for a werewolf for the same reason. Mirrors ages ago were made with genuine silver backing, thus the whole no reflection thing. Likewise, it was silver that made up some of the original chemical composition of old-timey camera film, which is where we got the no appearing in photographs. Modern vamps keeping with this tradition would probably be able to see their reflection and take selfies with cameras since little no silver is used in either process now.

Christian religious items like holy water and crucifixes seem to have widespread use as well. I always thought it was a funny mental image of someone being attacked by a vampire older than Christ. You hold up your cross and throw your holy water and it's just confused about why it's damp and you have a model of a Roman execution method before it eats you.

You have distraction techniques like leaving knotted lengths of rope, or spilling seeds around for the monster to find. Apparently, they have a compulsion to count such spills (I mean the Count on Sesame Street shows us that!) They will also obsessively count and untie knots that they come across. So, while they are busy you can get the hell out of dodge.

There are prevention methods that were practiced. A person who passed away and is suspected of returning to the land of the living to wreak havoc on his neighbor might find the mouth of their corpse filled with stone to prevent biting. Maybe a blade across the neck so if you rise it's instantly back to forever sleep. I have to say these preventive measures were damn successful because none of those folks ever came back. That's a good success rate if you ask me!

Then, of course, we have Old Reliable. A wooden stake through the heart. Usually, it's not specified length or type. Just wood into the heart. You know what else that kills? Every fucking thing! I don't care if you are a vampire or just some normal person. Getting a table leg shoved into your heart is going to ruin your evening for sure. There's also the classic decapitation and heart removal. This will also be highly effective against any foe I would think.

There's one thing I forgot to mention on how to drive away and kill these suckers. How about flooding an entire damn town?

You read that right.

The Tennessee Valley authority back in the mid-1940s were conducting flooding in support of the Watauga Dam. The town of Old Butler put up a fight to stay dry but eventually in the latter part of 1948 the residents were relocated to where Butler sits today and the area was flooded. There's some lore out there that there was more to it than just normal infrastructure expansion. No, the town some said, had a problem with vampires. The area became so infested that all efforts failed and they took drastic measures. The TVA basically said, "well hell, let's drown two birds with one dam," flooded the area, and took care of vampire menace. I guess they were going with the old throwback legend that vampires couldn't cross running water, or that the water from the flooding would somehow keep them contained in their coffins or graves or whatever.

Old Butler surroundings have been relatively dry a few times due to drainage and drought, but the legend says if it remains so for too long the bastards will come back. (Vampires not the TVA, although they suck too with their rate hikes, am I right?)

It's a common practice to have entire towns flooded in this manner to build or maintain hydroelectric facilities, reservoirs or to prevent disasters. This almost always leads to decades of spooky shit and ghost stories because of the large number of lives uprooted and the flooding of cemeteries and graveyards. A lot of energy remains in those waters. This may be the only story of spooky happenings causing the flood and not the other way around. This is obviously unsubstantiated and based on rumors. It is hard to find anything about it but we included it because it's an interesting tale. I mean vampires are a fun thing to write about.

I normally close with wishing y'all happy hunting.

If you decide to hunt this type of vampire, bring a snorkel. I jest, please don't go looking for any iteration of these things. Still, if you find yourself on the shores of Old Butler, walk softly and carry a big stake.

Be safe!

THE SQUEEZER

Ok folks here's a fun one that hit me out of left field when A.J. told me about it. A pint-sized little mischief maker that I've never heard of.

There's not a whole lot to this little bastard but one story to share and I think the whole thing is hilarious so it's getting a small mention in this book.

The Squeezer is a small creature about the size of a soda can with huge spindly arms and fingers. The arms extend unnaturally as its primary motive is to get a hug while also scaring the hell out of you. I can relate to the little guy. I guess the hugs can maybe be fatal like a southern grandma who hasn't seen you in a long time. This creature also has a mouth on him and apparently some insecurities wish we will get into.

The story I was told is amazing. Two young girls are having a sleepover. All of a sudden, on the edge of the bed, there appears long skinny fingers gripping at the covers. Straight-up nightmare fuel, right? So, the girls scream their heads off and run to the adults…wait no, no, that's not what happened at all.

One of our duos of friends reaches to the other side of the bed for a baseball bat. She then proceeds to bash the ever-loving hell out of the creepy digits invading her slumber party. I love it!

It's not every day you hear about a little girl going full 1980s mobster movie on a scary creature. This girl is going places, not sure where, but don't stand in her way.

After the thrashing the fingers quickly retreat.

The thing that caused them a fright and got his knuckles fractured by baby Babe Ruth came out from under the bed and lo-and-behold spoke English.

It cried out for the beating to stop and when it did it presented its little cryptid self to the girls.

A tiny thing stood before them on the floor. It explained to them it was called the Squeezer. The girls laughed their ass off. That's an understandable reaction. I mean come on, some little freak tries to ruin your night and then tell you it goes by the Squeezer? I'd laugh at it too!

Well, the laughing just pisses off the mini monster even more and it starts yelling about how it needs to be feared, and it's nothing to laugh at. Typical tantrum from a tiny tyrant. I'm sure you've experienced something similar.

Dad barges into the room after hearing the late-night ruckus and tells the girls that play time is over. Cut out the rough housing and get to bed.

So, they do. Dad's appearance I guess caused our little monster to hide and the girls settled down. Not long after they got comfy cozy to go to sleep, a pair of fingers broached the side of the bed. It was back for more, eh? The girl reached for the bat but paused in terror as another set of fingers appeared, then another and another.

This thing brought friends. *That's terrifying.*

My opinion on this is if it is true, I would love to meet the thing. Of course, I would treat it as a Fae and not trust it as far as I could throw it – wait no that doesn't work here, because I could probably yeet this thing into the neighbor's fence. Point is, I wouldn't trust it but I *would* like to talk to it.

I'd ask so many questions, and to be honest, it would probably just get tired of me and fuck off back to whatever dimension it lives in. My face would be on posters on every Fae bar "Do not talk to this person!"

It would be great. I'd never have to worry about every Starbucks barista being one of the Fae ever again.

So, have you seen the Squeezer? Let me know through the contact section at the end of this book… and as always? Happy Trails.

SKINWALKERS IN EAST TENNESSEE

W*hat's in a name?* William Shakespeare wrote that. Well, for this creature we are about to discuss, there is a whole hell of a lot in a name. The people who believe strongly that this thing exists believe that even uttering its name will somehow summon it. Now we don't want that, but I think everyone will be safe reading this entry. I like to call it a Flesh Pedestrian, myself. If you build an altar and invite the thing over for a couple of beers then that's on you. A.J. and I hold no responsibility for anyone that gets eaten after reading this book. (I asked my lawyer friend about this and his reply was, "Are you drunk?" then he hung up on me, but I'm saying it anyway.)

Anyway, the common theme, it seems, in all of the legends that involve this terrifying cryptid is that it's shape-shifting. A good bit of lore states that a magic practitioner that is up to evil gains the ability to transform through gruesome unnatural acts. This rings a bell with the witch hunts and legends of witches kidnapping babies to use their fat for flying potions and other supernatural abilities. There're even stories of people who had to commit cannibalism being cursed to transform into this monstrous creature as punishment, but again, that's more Wendigo territory than Flash-Pedestrian – and believe it or not, a Wendigo didn't make it on to our Cryptid BINGO card for East Tennessee.

When it comes to Flesh Pedestrians, which are more Navajo legend and hale all the way from the Southwest, I gotta say, if you think you are far enough removed from this bad boy that you don't have to worry about bumping into him around here. Think again my friend.

This account comes from an anonymous source. That happens a lot in this field of investigation and I have nothing against it. I encourage anyone and everyone to tell their story. You don't have to name yourself at all. The important thing is the story is told.

Our reporter tells us that she and her wife were on a drive in the White Pines region of East Tennessee and our couple of heroines decided to take a little trip down to Douglas Lake. Our main protagonist had spent many an hour there watching the lake and found it a beautiful spot to relax and unwind and wanted to share it with her spouse.

They arrived at the lake right before dusk. The sun was beginning to set and they began to enjoy a quiet evening watching the small fish on the banks of the lake swim. All seemed to be well... at first. Suddenly, the environment around them seemed to shift. It wasn't going to be an easy-going evening after all, as a strange feeling hung in the air; something was very wrong.

The critters they had been happily watching in the shallows next to the bank of the lake suddenly fled for deeper water. When the wildlife around you decides to book it, you bet your ass you should do the same rather quickly. Being normal rational humans and not in a horror movie, the couple decide to take the hint from their surroundings and get the fuck out of dodge. It is probably a very good thing that they did.

They retreated to their vehicle. She states when she begins to turn over the ignition to start their car and make their escape, they see something that will change their lives forever.

Not ten yards away an animal is standing there. It appears to be a deer but not quite. The creature had pale skin and was abnormally large. So just a huge ass deer, right? Or maybe a Not Deer... we'll get to those on down the line.

What set this apart from a Not Deer is when our storyteller's wife yelled, asking if that was a wolf standing there before them. It was no wolf, nor a deer. The monster, according to our eyewitness, began to shift and morph into a human-like figure standing around six feet tall.

This is very similar to my own personal experience with a Flesh Pedestrian in the Black Hills of South Dakota. I will tell y'all about this story in a future book, I promise. The animal to human form is spot on of what I personally dealt with, which is why, even though an anonymous account, I wholeheartedly believe these women when they say what happened, happened to them.

The monster, according to them, after it transformed, had abnormally long fingers with nails or claws black as night. That is fucking scary. I don't care who you are.

So, she does what any afraid and rightfully upset person does, she gets the hell out of there.

Later on, she goes to her dad. Dad hears the story and goes silent. He tells her to not mention anything and just drop the whole thing. Dad relays a story from his youth that he heard of an elderly gentleman running a ferry to a nearby island that once encountered something that made him stop everything. Was this a run-in with a Flesh Pedestrian?

You be the judge.

To wrap this particular tale up, our anonymous source says that in her youth, they frequently went fishing around this lake. She remembers one time that they had only just got to the lake and had maybe been fishing for less than a half an hour. Her and her sister found some deep claw marks up on a tree. Now, she admits it could have been a bear that made the marks. The parents saw the claw damage on the tree high up beyond where it was logically possible for anything to mark and just booked it. She stated that they usually stay for a while but seeing that they left.

We have another story about this ambulatory epidermis. To be honest I had initially refused to include this story for several reasons. The reasons are all on me. A.J. presented me with the bones of the account, then I looked into it and well dismissed it because I didn't see how it added anything to the narrative. I was dead wrong after new witness accounts came up suddenly. So here follows the tale and witness testimony that made me eat crow.

Our brave reporter received a call from a friend in Petros Tennessee. That is pronounced Pea-tross for anyone inclined to choose the Spanish or common pronunciation. That happens a lot really, in my home state we have a town called Omega that's pronounced Oh-Meegah and of course Cairo Georgia is Kay-roh. That's neither here nor there, back to spooky.

The heroine of our tale begins to make her way to rescue her friend that needs to get away from his current family situation. It is always good to have someone that will bail you out. I like her already. She didn't have a way to go herself so she enlisted a buddy and said buddy's vehicle on this mission. They picked up their friend who needed bailing out, and the worst thing that could happen in unfamiliar territory does, the phone they were relying on for GPS dies. They soldiered on though using the memory of the area to kind of push their way to their objective. Unfortunately, the surroundings became strange and confusing. They may just be lost. The best bet was to find a place to turn around and that they did.

A junkyard provided the perfect place to reorient themselves. The vehicle began to turn back onto the road leaving the yard and an animal or something crossed in front of it. Now an animal darting across your way is not anything new in these parts. Hell, the driver was very familiar with the local wildlife and their tendency to throw themselves in front of moving vehicles. This thing though. This thing was different. It wasn't like any animal witnessed in these parts.

The creature was described as initially being on all fours but was a pale gray thing with spotty patches of fur. My mind goes to a mangy dog when picturing this monster. Headlights illuminated the terrifying thing as it does what you never want to see an animal do. It stands up on two legs. The standing up thing is what reminds me of my own experience with a similar creature. It stands up on two legs a bit taller than a normal human man. Here's the thing that puts a bow on this story for A.J. and me, the thing had no face.

Now before I knew about statements I'll share in a sec from another eyewitness, I dismissed this as light washing out the face of whatever this was. I no longer believe that is the case. I think this thing *had no face*. You'll find out why soon.

PARANORMAL BY REGION: EAST TENNESSEE EDITION

Our trio of intrepid friends obviously hauled ass out of there. Three people in that car. Three people reported the same damn thing. Something on all fours with patchy hair and pale gray skin stood up. Three people claimed it had no face. She was hesitant to come forward because folks would call her crazy. I get that, but I'm glad she did. I don't think she's crazy. I believe her one hundred percent. Her mind went to Skinwalker when questioning what this was and I'll tell y'all I'm right there with her.

Now, Petros is home to Brushy Mountain State Penitentiary. A huge, haunted as hell prison complex that since 1896 provided Morgan County with all its carceral and ghost needs. It is in this prison we find a story that sealed the deal for me on the Flesh Pedestrian tale we just told.

A.J. had a chance to chat with the lead paranormal tour guide there whom I'll refer to as Ms. Jamie. She told A.J. about a sighting that clicked so many puzzle pieces that A.J. had to call me in the middle of her meeting with Ms. Jaime about the ghost show up there at Brushy.

One night, on the third floor of the prison, she witnessed something terrifying. She stood on one end of the cell block staring down the gangway. She states at the opposite end, a creature was there on all fours. Well, she described it as hunched over but it could very well have been completely down. This monstrous thing was pale gray and blotchy looking from the distance she was from it. Every Flesh Pedestrian story including my own has the following element: the thing stood up. It rose up on two legs and as it did so, it dragged its long arms across the floor. Want to know the best part? It had no face. *It had no fucking face!* All of this lines up completely with the other story! It was like some perfect cosmic alignment that my co-writer researching her own story gets the holy grail of a confirmation.

Whatever spooky spirits are guiding us on this literary journey are amazing. So yeah, Petros Tennessee has something lurking in the shadows for sure. Ms. Jamie didn't end there with her information. She provided amazing first and secondhand accounts in other parts of this book. She's officially my adopted aunt now, she doesn't know it unless she reads this book but it's true. Thank you, ma'am!

Believe these stories or not. The hills of Eastern Tennessee hold some very dark things. Now, while I'm sure there are some of you out there, rolling your eyes and sayin' "A Skinwalker? Really?" I do just have to point out, according to old Navajo and Diné Indigenous people – one of these things is human, or much like a Wendi-boi, they started out that way.

The Flesh Pedestrian is, at its base, a shape-shifting witch with evil purpose and intent, using the foulest and darkest magic there is to achieve this. They aren't good people, but they *are* people – and gone are the days where you walked and went on horseback to get from here to there.

So, why not Flesh Pedestrians in South Dakota, or as far reaching as East Tennessee? People are people, and a Flesh Pedestrian in human form is just as capable of buying a bus, plane, or train ticket as you or I.

Shit, serial killers get around – why not these happy bastards? Travel is easier than ever.

So, the next time you see an abandoned-looking Volvo sitting off to the side of the road on your way to the great outdoors, I bet you'll wonder: is it abandoned, or is there a Flesh Pedestrian out there?

I'm just fucking with you, family. It's probably just a Volvo... not a mystical evil being's delivery system from its point of origin to the great outdoors of another part of the country.

Or is it?

At any rate, my friends... be safe, and happy trails. Especially if you find yourself in Petros, Tennessee.

CENTRAL EAST TENNESSEE

THE KNOXVILLE GREEN WORM

This is one cryptid that has given me some trouble to be absolutely honest. The eyewitness accounts are very few and far between. The list of hidden and horrifying things that lurk in the darkness that I've got are numerous and could easily fill a whole book on their own, but very little information is available floating around out there about this specific, strange, and wriggly weirdo.

There's a certain human instinct to avoid serpents and worms. I mean there's a whole religion about some asshole snake and an apple. The thing that's more based in reality, however, is that usually legless slithering things probably have a bite that'll kill you, and that's just straight facts. I figure that's more than enough reason to avoid things like snakes and serpents.

I reckon worms are included in the whole fear of raw, wriggling, critters because we automatically associate them with dead things. The scientific term for fear of worms is Scoleciphobia and I think that's valid as hell.

Take the Mongolian Death Worm for instance; but no, I mean seriously take this fucking thing because it's horrifying. Giant worms lurking beneath the Gobi Desert that terrified and allegedly killed whole grown ass men.

The prime minister of Mongolia in 1922 described the thing as, "… shaped like a sausage about two feet long, has no head nor leg and it is so poisonous that merely to touch it means instant death. It lives in the most desolate parts of the Gobi Desert."

PARANORMAL BY REGION: EAST TENNESSEE EDITION

That's according to Roy Chapman Andrews' 1926 book: *On the Trail of Ancient Man.*

The Mongolian desert ain't the only place with tall tales of these slithering horror shows.

Antarctica also has tales of giant worms oozing under the ice. I mean, where's Kevin Bacon when you need him? The film Tremors had to have been influenced by some of this right?

It's over 6900 miles (nice) from the Gobi Desert to Eastern Tennessee. It's 9,081 miles to the Antarctic as the crow flies... and yet, Eastern Tennessee has some weird worm worries of its own it seems.

Eyewitness accounts describe a glowing green segmented worm like creature burrowing into soft undergrowth around these parts. The monster wasn't a huge intimidating ordeal but rather something a bit smaller. Less than a foot across and bright green squirming its way into the earth.

However not-scary that may sound, it certainly spooked those that saw it. I can't blame them at all. If I were in the woods in East Tennessee and saw some glowing green worm making its way through the soft wet mud, I would most likely not tell anyone for fear of being mistaken for crazier than I already am. All I've got to say is *Bravo*! to those who share their experiences by the way, if for no other reason than I got to spend an afternoon learning about these creepy crawlies for this entry into this book. Not going to lie, if it were me, I would probably leave very quickly and question whether or not my coffee that morning was just coffee after seeing something like that.

Growing up in the flatlands and swamps of the coastal plains' region of the United States, we did a lot of fishing. Part of that was catching our own bait. The best bait for some of the fish were earthworms.

Grandpa taught me how to catch worms for fishing. He called it "Gruntin" for worms. Find some soft soil. Shove a small stick in the ground and take a rock and scrape it across the top of the stick. This sends vibrations into the dirt. The worms think it's raining and come up to be caught for fish bait. That's how grandpa explained it anyhow. The best place to get bait growing up was the graveyard. Probably because it was close to a creek but looking back, I'm pretty sure this whole exercise has something to do with why I'm so damn weird.

Anyway, I'm glad we never bothered anything like the Knoxville green worm; but I do reckon it'd catch a hell of a catfish at the size of that sucker the way it's described.

What d'you reckon?

WAMPUS CAT

There are many things that can either kill you or make you have a very bad time in the hills of Eastern Tennessee. Supernatural and Natural there are just creatures that want to end you. That's just kind of how it goes up in the mountains. That's how it goes in a lot of places where the natural world meets human expansion.

Nature is beautiful and majestic, right? You see a sunset or a nice tree and you just kind of smile. You succumb to the beautiful scene in front of you. Except everything wants to kill you in nature. There is a dangerous edge to everything you see. There is no forgiveness in the natural world. Tread lightly for you are most definitely on the menu.

The Wampus Cat has so many origin stories and iterations it's easy to get lost in the fact that it's just another big scary animal legend. I say to you, dear reader, it is so much more than that. This thing is a very scary, and I believe, a very real concern.

Imagine this you are having a great time camping and hear something stirring outside your tent. The fire is dying and embers dance around in the darkness. Blazing eyes brighter than any fire meet your gaze in the deepest part of night, underneath the trees. The Cat Distribution System has fucked you royally.

What you see step from the shadows is a giant, six-legged panther-like creature. It hisses with its gaping maw of razor-sharp teeth and you breathe your last breath that isn't a scream before it pounces on you.

The Cherokee name for the creature is Ewah. There are many variations of the origin of this terrifying feline.

One of the legends surrounding the Wampus is that long ago, an Indigenous woman witnessed a secret ritual that she shouldn't have seen. The punishment for her was that she was cursed to stalk the earth as a monstrous cat forever.

There are other tales that the cat is a witch that is trapped in a beast form and hunts the woods in a bloodlust.

Here's a great example of the Wampus Cat in East Tennessee.

On the then western edge of the city of Knoxville sat the Middlebrook house built in 1795. The area around it known as Middlebrook Pike would in 1894 be the scene of a great Wampus Cat tale.

In the summer of 1894, the heads of cattle that were recently slaughtered began to mysteriously disappear. These things are not exactly what you would call a valuable item but nevertheless someone or something was stealing away with them. The general consensus was that it was probably not a weirdo with an affinity for livestock heads but an animal. I guess a weirdo animal is exactly what they got.

Hunters sat out to kill the head stealing menace. They were not prepared for what they ran into in the dark forest surrounding Knoxville. Reports came back of a massive white feline-like creature that moved like a serpent. It struck terror into the hearts of the seasoned outdoorsmen. They claimed that it shook off any bullet that was fired at it. (Because I swear guys, I totally hit the thing you saw!) The conclusion was made that this thing was so fast, weird, and immune to the crack shots of our hunters that it must be a ghost.

Rumors spread like wildfire around the town and soon people were up in arms to take down this spectral monstrosity.

Two teenagers decided that they would have a go at the mystery and made their way into the woods. They sat quietly and waited. The idea was to basically use themselves as bait for the creature and see what turned up. Something did turn up and when they produced some light to see the monster it quickly ran away. The teens went back to town to tell everyone that yes there was something in them woods but it was only a bear. It was a white bear but just a bear.

Here comes the fun part of the story. Treasure! Hearing the teens' account of the monster being a normal, if not some mutation of normal, animal, a lot of folks accepted it and were like ok then we got us a freak bear to kill. Enter the cartoon legend portion of our story. An old timer hears this and absolutely refutes it. He claims that he has seen the creature since the Civil War and it was guarding the fortune of a wealthy traveler that was killed by the Cherokee years and years ago.

Well, all you gotta say is treasure to have everyone and their uncle to take up arms and head out into the wilderness. Hell, even Knoxville's own mayor Melvin Thompson headed out into the woods with basically an arsenal to get this thing. Thompson, however, was sadly disappointed when he did not get to shoot or even witness the thing. Roving bands of armed money hungry hunters were unleashed on the woods. This led to pretty much what you would think it would lead to. Chaos and property damage.

The surrounding woods of Middlebrook Pike were a cacophony of gunfire and trampling as the halfwit heroes searched for their target. Crops were destroyed by the people haphazardly traipsing through fields and unfortunately two cows were accidentally shot during the massive monster hunt and subsequently had to be butchered. Eventually the people had damn well enough and called for the whole thing to be shut down and all visitors to the area be banned if they came looking for treasure or a ghost cat.

Later years and up to the modern era there still are reports of howls or strange creatures moving cat like through the trees. Tales of the Wampus Cat living in caves along the river watching folks as they go about their leisure. There are even some stories of it living beneath the city itself giving credence to a name I ran across for it: The Underground Panther. Watch out sewer alligators.

The fact is, this isn't the only big cat cryptid creeping around the dark corners of the earth. Humans have reported all kinds of large felines throughout history and continue to do so today.

Whatever is out in the woods of Appalachia probably won't be won over with a bag of kitty treats or some tuna.

Never hurts to keep a little catnip on you, nonetheless. I have said it before, and I will say it again, if I am ever found mauled and ravaged in the forest rest assured my last words probably involved "psp, psp" or "who's a good boy?"

Keep an eye out for kitties and be safe on the trails my friends.

BEARDEN ELEMENTARY SYP

Normally a creature sighting that doesn't have multiple sources or cannot be verified in some way just kind of gets thrown into what I like to call File 13. (File 13 is the trash by the way.)

These following accounts had enough of an impact on both of us that we felt that it should absolutely be mentioned, however briefly, here in this book. The title of this entry Bearden Elementary SYP comes directly from an annotation by A.J. while researching. SYP stands for Shit. Your. Pants.

I believe that it is very well titled because that is exactly what I would do if I came across this thing. So, let's get into the sighting and we will discuss what I think it may have been.

On a dark and spooky night (Sorry, I've always wanted to write that,) A couple of friends decided to do what young folks tend to do when boredom is high and the sun is low. Hang out in a park.

Making their way and not really having any plan in mind, they walked and shot the shit in the darkness. That's when they saw it; a few yards away, standing taller than an average person, was a white almost skeletal figure. Its head and hands were disproportionately large to its frame and its eyes a menacing "black-red." The two friends fled in terror back to their vehicle as it felt like the creature was in hot pursuit. They reached their car and managed to escape.

The next day, one of the individuals reported in the daylight there was nothing amiss and it was an open field. No structures or signposts that could have played tricks with their eyes. Both witnesses independently described the monster and both were remarkably similar.

The same area and roughly the same time frame gives us another eerie encounter of what can only be described as the same creature. A couple of friends exploring an abandoned building in a small field are met with a putrid rotting smell. (There's that smell again. I'm telling y'all; *pay attention*. The nose knows.) The smell was followed by the appearance of a creature that matches the description of the above encounter. This pair of friends, of course, likewise fled. The witness claims to have not told anyone out of fear of being ridiculed. He was happy though to share this account anonymously online. I believe them. I believe all of these folks saw something terrifying in that neighborhood. Specifically, in the park right next to Bearden Elementary in Knoxville, TN.

In my youth, I spent many a night in random parks, playgrounds, and cemeteries doing what I assure you was totally legal and wholesome activities. I have never experienced anything as scary as these witnesses. What exactly did they witness though?

The Rake is a cryptid that is said to have pale or gray skin. A large head and long arms and legs. This thing is typically described as crawling or crouching when observed. Perhaps our unfortunate friends above caught one while it was standing and stretching. The creature, if it was a rake or not, may have been employing a tactic used by everything from bears, to raccoons, to house cats; standing up to make itself more intimidating. I'd say it worked like a charm in these cases.

This is all to say: be safe out there on your next adventure. You don't have to be in the deep wood for the horrors to find you. Stay safe and let us know if you have ever seen anything similar, not that I'm going to go personally looking for it.

RACCOON VALLEY PTERODACTYL

There are a few things in nature that a modern human will recognize on an instinctual level as a threat. Those of us that are the outdoorsy type will recognize a sudden silence for example. If the woods get quiet then shit's probably about to get real.

I hunt and used to spend quite a bit of time out in the woods. Silence is one of those signs for sure, but also never underestimate your sense of smell. You can literally smell certain predators. Some smell like decay and rot, others with an overpowering musk, and then there's the old sign you're near a copperhead - the smell of cucumbers. Not sure why those slithery little bastards decided to shop in the '90s Bath & Bodyworks, but I think it's kind of cool that girls inadvertently chose to smell like a venomous snake there for a while.

As A.J. likes to say, *I digress...*

There are quite a few signs when you're all alone out there in the woods that'll let you know when an apex predator is around, but what about the things that don't care about the human position on the food chain? What about the deep fear drilled into our brains to fear death not from what's lurking in the black muddy waters or the thick brambles just outside our camps?

What about death from *above*?

There are countless legends of "monsters" hunting humans that swoop down and carry off children and the grown alike.

The Thunderbird for one. That's the cryptid that covers the Southwest up to the Pacific Northwest territories of Indigenous legend. I've heard told, that folks will absolutely cower if they see that shit!

But we aren't talking about the western half of the United States, we're talking about East Tennessee, and to that end the question is, what's going on around Raccoon Mountain?

Y'all see a dinosaur flying around? Don't lie, because there's been more than a few reports of just that. A pterodactyl to be exact. Or maybe a few of 'em, centered over and around Raccoon Valley, just outside Knoxville.

A large prehistoric winged creature. The wingspan of the monster is said to be as large as 3 to 11 meters! Oh, oh wait, I need to get that into freedom units. That'd be 7 to 35 feet.

Now, that's a big bitch; and I know if you saw it, you'd report it. Well, maybe not. We don't tend to talk to the government 'round these parts. But I'm asking now. Y'all please report what ya see... especially to me. I ain't no government lackey, just another feller like you, born right on down in the swamps of South Georgia – a country boy through and through.

There's something out there I know there is. There's a cave or holler around Raccoon Mountain that holds a winged creature we ain't seen since the dawn of time itself. Now, how it came to be here, or how it survives is anyone's guess. Still, it's been spoken of and stories handed down for generations and mark my words, with as many cameras as is in everyone's pockets these days, it's only a matter of time a'fore we see it.

Wings so wide they blot out the sun, leathery and brown, and big enough to give that yellow bastard on Sesame Street a run for his money.

I ain't got much more to say other than if you're around Raccoon Valley, to keep your eye on the skies. A pterodactyl. Ain't that somethin'? I'd sure like to see that.

Cryptid Guy here packing up his binoculars and walking away. Y'all know how to contact me. Show me them dinosaurs!

SOUTHEAST TENNESSEE

THE SUGAR FLATS MONSTER

This one I'm a little skeptical on, but It's also one of my favorites because of actual tangible physical evidence. I don't want to get ahead of myself though, so let's run down this noggin scratcher of a cryptid.

January 5, 1989, on a chilly night a pickup truck on Sugar Flat Road will go down in crypto zoological history. A creature with what was described as blueish hair and ape-like appearance was in the wrong place at the wrong time and ended up losing a fight with a truck.

Sugar Flat Road had what could be called a "lovers' lane" a place to get away from it all and get into your partner so to speak. Well, our story involves two lovers, one married, but not to whom they were on this little carnal adventure with.

The hour grew late and it was time to return home so as to not arouse suspicion.

Our secret lovers began their journey down the winding roads to their respective homes. They were met by something more terrifying than any jilted lover. In the road before them stood two figures. The truck screeched its brakes and ran headlong into …something? Was it a deer in the lonely back roads? What the hell had they just witnessed and subsequently run into?

The driver exited the vehicle with a flashlight. Between the moonlight and the glaring red of the taillights of the truck that cast a ghastly shadow onto the road it was hard for him to see behind his vehicle.

But there was something lying in the road. Something that was definitely not a deer.

There was a thing almost humanoid covered in fur. He approaches the body and from the woods he hears a terrifying animal-like cry, a cry the likes of which he had never heard before.

Ignoring the cries either from fear or adrenaline he grabs the dead thing and drags the fallen creature to the side of the road.

The driver wanting to cover his affair and his own ass more than reporting killing some weird animal decides to take his liver home and go home himself. At home he can't shake what he saw. He proceeded to do exactly what I would do and look and see if the bottom of a bottle of whiskey held any answers for him. Also like me he didn't find much there. He tried to sleep but kept being drawn back to the scene of the cryptid hit and run.

In the early morning hours of the next day, he sat out to the scene where he unceremoniously dumped ol' monster in the woods. He found the body and started digging a grave. Because that's what you do right? Bury your problems. This thing he thought wasn't a person it was an animal so it should be treated as such. That's when he got the bright idea that, well if it's an animal, I should have a trophy.

He looped the things head off with a shovel and kicked the body into the shallow grave he had dug. Class act here folks. He then took the head to a local taxidermist. The taxidermist being a fine upstanding citizen basically said "I don't know that the hell this is but I'll preserve it for you". Money is the universal language after all.

The head has its own crazy history of being displayed and lost throughout the decades from its original severance. It was displayed finally in 2021 and thought to be safe and sound until it disappeared again in 2023. The head displayed now in {(note to editor need to get location when I have internet)} is a holographic imagine of the supposed head.

So, do those puns I made at the beginning of this chapter make sense now?

Whatever this thing is it is said that its partner still roams the roads resulting in sightings to this very day.

Take care in the area and keep your head about you!

A.J. MASON & & MATT GEIST

Happy Hunting

The Tennessee Serpent

I love a good sea monster, don't you? I say sea monster, but any aquatic cryptid will do really.

Enthusiasts of such swimming monstrosities are in luck because there is an abundance around the world. The most famous of them all being of course Nessie over in Scotland. We have them here on our side of the pond as well. New England has Champ who haunts Lake Champlain. There is Lake Tahoe's Tessie, and Georgia has a coastal one called Altamaha-ha whose name is a play on the Altamaha River where it is said to reside. That's just a few! I have no doubt we will hit up these and more in the future but let's talk about the Tennessee Serpent.

This thing is unique to me because in all my research as an investigator of things that go bump, or rather, *splash* in the night, I haven't really come across one that was said to curse the folks who have a run-in with it. Death omens are not uncommon at all in folklore and legends but the stories about this thing seem to suggest that it's not necessarily a messenger of death but the actual dealer of it somehow.

The first encounter I could come across happened in 1822. A fella named Buck Sutton was out fishing on the Tennessee River for the last time in his life, he just didn't know it yet. I'd like to take a quick moment here to say that I admire his name. Buck Sutton is just a solid country name, and I'm inclined to believe his encounter. Buck was standing on the shore when something huge about thirty feet away made one hell of a commotion in the water.

He knew instantly that this was not a fish that he would be tangling with and there was no way his meager pole would be able to catch something like that even if he wanted to. Buck fled to tell his friends about the encounter with his heart full of emotions. A normal angler after seeing something like this would be filled with excitement or anticipation of a future haul, but not this one. Buck Sutton was filled with dread and sadness. When telling his friends his story he relayed that he was certain he was cursed because he witnessed the creature. He felt he was not long for this world and it turns out the feeling was dead on.

Buck passed away a few days later but no cause of death was recorded. It was rural Tennessee in the 1800s and you can't exactly expect every death to be thoroughly documented but come on! The guy predicted his demise after seeing a river monster. That's not nothing! Sutton may have been the first to fall victim to the Tennessee River Serpent but he certainly wasn't the last.

The accounts of a serpent in the river that once gazed upon, leading to death continued for several years after Sutton's untimely(?) passing. In 1827 a man described a serpent-like creature stalking his boat. A bluish yellow thing that nearly capsized him. He too felt cursed and apparently died a year later under mysterious circumstances.

I'm sensing a pattern here and I will get into my theory of all the death dealing at the end of this chapter.

How about another boat incident a couple of years after when one Jim Windom saw a large black fin emerge from the water and a creature swimming and turning the water around his vessel. He panicked and pushed fervently to the nearest shore. He knew that even though he made it to dry land that he was cursed as well, He did what any good Christian man that also believed in curses would do and spent the rest of his life dutifully attending church and praying every day. The rest of his life was about a couple of months. He died of complications from a fever.

These stories and more come from a historian E. Randall Floyd. Now he said that the reports of the monster fell off because of the prevalence of steamships in the Tennessee River. That makes sense from a wildlife perspective. The introduction of mass transit has absolutely disrupted many natural ecosystems all over the world. Why would this be any different?

Let's go back and talk about the curse a bit more. Was it the monster fish-serpent? Did these poor gents get so unlucky to cast their eyes unto some demon spawned hell creature that put some magic on them that they were destined to die in some undetermined amount of time? This may be a case of the confusion between causation and correlation. Just because something happens after something else does not mean it's related.

This reminds me of the whole ordeal of the Mummy's Curse. All those grave robbers, um I mean explorers, that perished after looting tombs. Did they die from some vengeful spirit? While as much as I like to think that some afterlife vengeance is the cause I have to think maybe it wasn't. Maybe it was the fact that they were in a foreign land with exotic diseases going into enclosed spaces surrounded by centuries old mold and poisons.

There is a very real possibility that a crazy cursed serpent stalks the river. There are indeed other river monsters out there for real. The rivers in the United States are slam full of giant catfish. Hell, the Tennessee River has one named Catzilla. I myself even have a big fish story. I dragged a giant catfish up onto the muddy banks of the Belle Fourche River in South Dakota who had a head the size of a basketball. The only thing that makes my story believable is I had a witness. My buddy was having a beer and watching me as it snapped my thirty-pound line and dropped me on my ass in the mud as it wiggled from the banks and into the rushing water.

Unlike me, with the mud soaking into the back of my pants, y'all keep vigilant and be safe on the waters my friends and as always…

Happy Hunting.

GATEWAY TO THE SMOKIES
&
GREATER APPALACHIA

NIGHT CREATURE OF SEVIER COUNTY

Having friends is important to me. A group of people who can all count on each other is a great thing. Everyone needs a pal but not everyone can seem to make friends. It's not always easy. Perhaps you have social anxiety and can't bring yourself to talk to anyone. Maybe you're plain awkward. Maybe your mother was a witch and cursed you at birth and gave your soul to the devil. Doomed and lonely you stalk the land seeking companionship but the very act of looking at your grotesque form causes any potential buddies to die of fright. Yeah, it's tough out there.

Legend has it there was a witch living in the forest. Now this is pretty standard mountain witch lore, a lady who basically knew how to fix anything with the right combination of herbs and other natural ingredients. Stomachache? She's got you. Chicken won't lay? Feed it this and call me in the morning or don't because phones weren't a thing back then. The point is she was a fixer. She did have a problem apparently though, she hated kids. She hated them so much so, that when she was about to have her thirteenth, yes you read that right, *thirteenth* youngin', someone suggested she should just give it to the devil.

So, she did.

On the day that cursed child was born it was said it landed on the floor and crawled itself out of the house and into the woods.

Holy hell y'all.

PARANORMAL BY REGION: EAST TENNESSEE EDITION

The lore around this thing rings a familiar bell and I'll get into that at the end, but let's keep going. Our monstrous abomination is actually a sweet guy it seems. Stories say in his youth he rescued a little squirrel. Now by the time of this supposed act of fondness of fauna the creature understood that its visage would cause everything up to and including death. Ain't that a bitch? Even animals can't look at you? The tiny pea brain of a tree rat (squirrel) can't fathom your image? Boy howdy.

There was, according to the stories, an interaction with a farmer. The tale says that a farmer working late in his fields felt a tap on his shoulder. He turned around. But he knew what was up so he did not look directly at his assailant. He focused his gaze downward. Looking down he saw scaly green feet! That caused him to flee. I don't blame him at all.

Here's the rub. This is an absolute retelling of the Jersey Devil. Right down to the thirteenth kid reference. That is a big part of the Devil's lore. I'm sure we'll cover it in coming books or presentations. I honest to goodness think this whole story smells of bull-shittery.

That's okay! Stories get retold and the only reason we have legends is oral history, right? The stories get passed along and this one just happens to be one that matches up to a well-known cryptid.

The Jersey Devil is a retelling of the Leeds Devil and the Leeds Devil is just basically "stay out of the Jersey Pine barrens" and yah know that in turn is the Boogeyman tale. A lot of cryptids can travel their origin in those stay-out-of-the-woods tales.

When I told A.J. that I was going to write this basically refuting it, her response was golden. She told me "Not everything is a thing, in this case we're just here to tell the story," and I love that. You should too!

So, wherever you are and whatever you're doing, I'll ask this of you: Please keep an open mind, *but question everything*!

Happy Hunting!

MR. FOOT

The most well-known cryptid that stalks the forests and mountains all over the world is Bigfoot. He goes by many names. Sasquatch, Yeti, Skunk Ape, and I, personally, refer to him as 'Mr. Foot' but that's just my thing. The fact is, it answers to a lot of names but also answers to no one. There is a storied history of this creature. Most commonly associated in the United States within the Pacific Northwest region, particularly Washington and Oregon.

The southeast shoulder of Mt. Saint Helens up in Washington State holds the beginnings of the legacy. In a 1924 encounter with so-called ape-men, prospectors in the canyon at the time said huge ape-like creatures attacked the camp they were staying in. Large boulders were supposedly thrown at the cabin and it was a terrifying encounter. Ape Valley, as it was later dubbed, was permanently altered by mother nature on May 18th, 1980, when the sleeping volcano in Mt. St. Helens decided to not be so sleepy anymore, blowing over 12 percent of her top into dust and ash that drifted over the states of Washington and Oregon, darkening the skies and coating everything with ash.

While Mt. St. Helens was the first recorded sighting of Mr. Foot, the most famous footage of all when it comes to this creature was captured much later than the 1924 encounter, but well before the eruption of St. Helens wiped 'ape valley' off the topographical map of Washington.

In 1967, the most well-known and recognizable footage of a sasquatch was captured. Now widely known as the Patterson-Gimlin film, A.J. happens to have met relatives of the Gimlin half of the dynamic duo that shot it. I'm sure you know the film I'm talking about. The upright ape creature walking through a riverbed with swinging arms and looks back at the camera? Yeah, that one. This film will be discussed in later books and outlets by me and A.J. but I will just say this; it is this investigator's opinion after research on the topic that the film was a hoax. This opinion is mine and mine alone is not in any way meant to represent anyone else affiliated with this publication.

(A.J. here, I call bullshit on this one, too! Solidarity, homie.)

Not only does it annoy me that the film that started the whole Bigfoot craze is, again, in my opinion, a hoax - it also irks me that Washington somehow got all the credit when the film was shot in Northern California - which I know, is still the Pacific Northwest, as A.J. likes to remind me, but still - how did Washington get all the credit?

I digress...

Now that we got a bit of Mr. Foot's history out of the way, let's look at Bigfoot over in these parts.

That's right, Mr. Foot's sightings may have originated in the Pacific Northwest, but he's just about everywhere when it comes to the continental United States, as well as Canada, Russia, and some iteration in the Himalayas.

Mr. Foot gets around, and he certainly is around in the hills and hollers of East Tennessee. Let's get familiar with our tall hairy friend that lurks in the Smoky Mountains, shall we?

The first tidbit I want to share is very vague and gives very little information but I thought it was humorous and as such, a good place to start:

A fella said he was camping somewhere near a body of water in the Appalachians in Tennessee and claimed to have the following encounter. (I know that really narrows it down.) He's out there enjoying his evening, cooking up the day's catch when he claims to have received an uninvited dinner guest. The darkness was falling as rapidly as it was rising through the trees, when a figure approached the campsite. The man's first thought was that it had to be someone primitive living or rough camping for an extended period of time because the approaching individual looked unkempt and shaggy in the low light.

Bringing that southern hospitality out to the middle of nowhere, the camper offered up this feller a plate full of fish, assuming his newfound friend was hungry and that's why he'd approached. The stranger took the dish of fish and walked away into the woods without saying a word. I mean, a 'thank you' would have been nice!

Something didn't sit right with our anonymous storyteller after this interaction, and so he decided to strike out in the direction the shaggy interloper had headed. He probably should have just stayed put and called it a night.

He claims he eventually came to a clearing where he witnessed several very tall fur-covered creatures standing in a circle in the darkness. Terrified and panicked he retreated. I'm assuming that he never got his plate back. Bigfoot does seem like the kind to have a stack of his neighbors' Tupperware containers stashed somewhere that he never intends to return but I don't know exactly how much stock I can put into this tale. Still, for some reason, I really enjoyed it. Maybe he witnessed a family of sasquatch doing their nightly routine and one was just feeling some fish and stepped out for some takeout from the local camper. Perhaps not, but it makes for a good story.

That had a lighthearted spin on it. It's very easy for your average person whether they believe in the existence of such creatures or not to see Bigfoot as kind of a character. The likeness of our crypto pal has been used in advertising to sell everything from snacks to soap. He's on stickers, patches, postcards, anything you can imagine. For a creature that is so elusive the entertainment industry seems to love him. Tons of movies both good, bad, and so bad that they're good have been published. He's even in some video games. There's always a new documentary series trying to find the guy in any given year, and while I do think this is wonderful and brings interest to the field of cryptozoology; if you ask me, it may be setting a bad precedent.

Whole the above story is kind of cute and full of feel-good vibes, the reality is much more terrifying. You'll recall our camper friend running for the hills at the sight of these creatures, and with good reason: these cryptids are among the most violent and territorial I've ever researched, and I believe would just as soon smack you against a tree than sell you dried meat products.

On the subject of violence, that 1924 prospector incident set the bar for close interactions. Multiple accounts of sightings in the Chattanooga region have an element of intimidation and terror tactics. Rocks and boulders being thrown at campsites are common. Trees being slammed with limbs to make loud knocking as a warning to hikers. The tree knocking is also theorized as a form of communication between individuals to warn others of humans in the area kind of like an alarm sounding. Then you have the vocalizations and screaming.

Animals tend to vocalize when they want to let you know to back off or they perceive danger. Crows will give away your position when hunting as a warning to turkeys. Bears will growl into your soul to tell you to back the fuck off. Even our domestic animals do it; ever get hissed at while trying to get Mr. Mittens into a pet carrier? Sasquatch, it seems, are no different. The most bone chilling and disturbing noises I have ever heard from nature are supposed recordings of Bigfoot calls and screams. That shit will rock you in the part of the brain that reminds you that you are a very small thing in a very big nasty world.

The Cumberland Plateau area of Tennessee has seen incidents of strange growls and screams waking campers in the middle of the night dating back to the 1970s. One minute you're enjoying a nice relaxing evening in the great outdoors while getting ready to turn in for the night, and the next you are greeted with an otherworldly scream coming from the forest. That would ruin both my night and my sleeping bag.

This part of Tennessee has its share of physical evidence as well. Structures and shelters consisting of foliage covered branches and small trees arranged in a teepee like configuration are found built from materials that are much too massive for an average human to do it by hand. The classic footprints are included here. The topic arises frequently that the lack of evidence such as bones or bodies means that the creature does not exist. I am strongly of the opinion that we know nothing of the societal aspects of Bigfoot. They may bury their dead, or eat them, they may migrate to one of the deep caves and die inside like an elephant's graveyard, who knows? For me, the absence of evidence is not the evidence of absence.

Speaking of physical evidence, let's get on to our next up close and personal encounter...

Deep in the Great Smoky Mountains a Park Ranger is having one hell of a week. I always respected Rangers and for a brief amount of time seriously considered it as an option after college. Spending my workday outdoors and upholding conservation and preservation of the natural world around us is a noble and very appealing pursuit. Finding lost hikers and dealing with idiot tourists who ask how the deer know to cross the road at the yellow deer signs just had some kind of romantic appeal to me. There's nothing romantic about this coming story.

The park ranger was on his routine patrol when he received a call from a family he had met a few days prior as they were entering the park. The family was concerned about a horrible smell at the campsite. The father assumed some animal had died near the camp and felt that the rangers should be alerted. Our Ranger friend here goes to check out the situation and one can assume he probably wasn't too concerned about what he would find. Perhaps some small animal had bit the dust and unfortunately happened to be next to a nice family's vacation spot. Upon arrival and talking to the family he definitely notes a horrible smell hanging in the air and begins to investigate.

Fifty yards into trees away from the camp is where he made his gruesome discovery.

The body of a deer lay torn and shredded. Now a dead deer isn't exactly a surprising thing in the Smoky Mountains. They live there, they die there, they get eaten, get sick, make poor life choices. That's nature baby. This dead deer was different. It showed no signs of predation and its legs appeared to have been intentionally broken. Something absolutely wrecked this thing and just left it there like a discarded toy.

That's not the only strange thing the Ranger noted. The smell, the whole reason he was out here to begin with didn't seem to be coming from the deer at all. It was there alright, but he couldn't pinpoint exactly the source where it was coming from.

PARANORMAL BY REGION: EAST TENNESSEE EDITION

He did what he felt was the most logical thing and dragged the sloppy mess of a deer carcass farther away from the campsite. He tells the family that everything was fine and the problem was taken care of and to enjoy their stay. No mutilated bodies round here folks! Enjoy your s'mores little Timmy!

The Ranger was clearing the scene and heading back on patrol when he received a call for service from the other side of the Park. A solo camper reported a foul rotten smell around his camp site and wanted someone to come check it out. Round two begins. He arrives and talks to the guy and it's the same exact deal. A putrid rotting smell filled the air as our ranger began his investigation. Just like the previous call he set out into the forest surrounding the campsite.

This time, however, his investigation came up empty. Nothing was there except the lingering stench.

A few days after these events on a gloomy, rainy day a third call comes in. This call will be the one that changes the Rangers' outlook on his choice of careers. The call comes from an elderly couple requesting assistance. The reason? You guessed it, a foul odor around the camp. If were the ranger in this situation I have to say that my experience the past few days would lead me to believe that something was afoot. (See what I did there?) He arrives on scene and begins his investigation. This time he pushes even further into the surrounding trees looking for the source of the terrible smell and I would imagine trying to keep calm and vigilant.

Deep into the woods he sees it. A deer standing in the rain. Behind the deer standing at around nine feet tall is a humanoid figure with black fur or hair. The ranger is trying to process all this when the creature grabs the deer by its throat and proceeds to rip the deer apart, spilling blood and viscera onto the wet forest floor. Mr. Ranger did what anyone would do, He noped the fuck right out of there leaving the old folks to whatever fate the deer hating monster may have in store for them.

I mentioned these things are violent right? This perfectly shows how these creatures are nothing to play around with. This thing ripped apart a full-grown deer like I would a mozzarella stick at happy hour. It was not hunting to feed itself. It was straight-up killing for fun. That is terrifying. Imagine what it could do to a person, you would be human soup before you could even react. They would find you in a puddle in the middle of the forest and probably rule it an "accidental" death.

I know what you're probably thinking. Matt they can't all be bad right?

I mean, do you really want to find out? - A.J.

One unfortunate hiker almost did find out. This story also comes to us from our national parks' finest.

A park ranger going about his normal day is dispatched to a woman with unknown injuries on a trail close to the road. The ranger responds and finds the woman lying on the ground. The injured hiker states that she thinks her leg may be broken but that is not the reason she is absolutely losing her shit right then. She tells the ranger that she was making her way back to her car when suddenly she felt something was off. The woman could sense something watching her, stalking her on the trail. This feeling of dread and caution is common from reports of humans being hunted by predators. Large cats produce infrasound which has been proven to give people a fear response. Hell, even some hauntings were debunked because of infrasound being produced by some malfunctioning equipment. We talked about Bigfoot vocalizations and this makes me wonder if there is some element of that in their calls.

She starts to panic and she turns around to what, if anything, may be sneaking up on her. What she saw on the trail shook her to her core. Standing there staring at her was a huge bipedal ape-like creature covered in reddish-brown fur. The hiker did what one does and turned and ran for her life. The creature began to pursue her, chasing her along the trail up until the cliché horror movie moment happens and she trips and falls. Laying in pain with a probably broken leg she looks up to see the ape-man approaching. If it were me laying there, I would surely think I was about to leave the mortal word at the furry hands of Mr. Foot.

Something surprising happens. Instead of tearing her limb from limb or stomping her into the dirt, the creature leans down and extends a hairy arm as if to offer her help standing up. This must have been confusing as all hell. Unfortunately, before the gentlemanly gesture can be appreciated, nature decided to make things complicated again. When the woman fell she had the luck of falling right next to a yellow jacket's nest. Yellow jackets being the bastards they are and never wanting to let a good opportunity to be an asshole with wings pass them by, proceeded to sting our injured heroine causing her to yell in pain. Her sudden yell startled the creature who in turn let out his own and ran away down the trail in the direction he came from.

Thus, ruining the meet-cute for the latest and greatest monster lover romance novel of A.J.'s dreams... damnit.

Eventually, medics arrive and transport the woman to the hospital where she was treated and expected to make a full recovery. The ranger and the medics noted that the woman did not appear to be under the influence of any mind-altering substances nor did she have any signs of mental illness or head trauma. The question here as in all encounters and sightings is, did this really happen? What would lead someone to fabricate such a weird story? I write science fiction and horror on the side so I guess that last question is kind of out there because people will make up shit for any reason.

Let's talk about the helping nature of the interaction. There are countless videos floating around of chimps "helping" handlers up onto obstacles and being good little furry companions. Chimpanzees are also brutal and go for the genitals and will eat your face. Experts that interact with greater ape species in wild or semi-wild environments have observed such helpful gestures. One that comes to my mind is a person working in chest deep water. An adult orangutan is above the man on the ground watching closely. The orangutan reaches his arm down to the man as if to say, "Hey let me get you out of the toilet ya big weirdo" The man sees this and ignores the helping hand. Folks will be quick to say aww and wonder why he did not let the big, sweet fella help him or even acknowledge him. Thats because like all things everywhere there's a zero percent chance that that shit wasn't a trap. The moment he reaches out to the helpful ape will be the last thing he ever regrets as his arm is broken and he is most likely drowned in the water simply because the orangutan was a little bored that afternoon.

Point is, be careful interacting with any living creature. Humans included.

I would definitely be remiss if I didn't include something about the local nomenclature for Mr. Foot. As we all know, Bigfoot is the common name for this cryptid, but he is known by many other names regionally. In the Pacific Northwest, he is Bigfoot or Sasquatch. In South Georgia and Florida, in the swampland habitats, he is known as the Skunk Ape, and in East Tennessee, up through parts of Kentucky, and down through parts of Alabama, he is also known as the Wooly Booger.

When it comes to our damsel in distress hiker out there in the Great Smoky Mountains National Park, however, there is one other possible explanation for this Beauty & the Beast like encounter on the hiking trail - and that's that our hiker didn't actually meet a Bigfoot, but rather a creature known in the Tennessee wilds as The Tennessee Wildman.

I feel that I would be doubly remiss if I did not include The Tennessee Wildman in this section of the book.

The Tennessee Wildman is supposedly a humanoid bipedal creature commonly described as having orange or dark red hair. Though standing much taller and more massive than the average man, it is said to be much more human-like in its appearance than Mr. Foot only with several differences in its behavior and morphology.

The similarities being what they are led me to mention the Wildman here, and both A.J. and I think it deserves its own little section with more detail. So, I'll see you there on the next page.

The Tennessee Wild Man

It's a good thing it's legal to marry your first cousin in Tennessee because I'm pretty sure that's what Bigfoot and The Tennessee Wildman are to each other; kissing cousins.

While there are a lot of similarities between the two creatures, there's just enough difference to convince me they're related, without necessarily being the same species. I view The Tennessee Wildman as a sort of 'missing link' if you will; a creature that by all accounts and descriptions is Bigfoot-like, but closer to the human end of whatever its genome is than Mr. Foot.

The sightings of The Tennessee Wildman date all the way back to the 1800s. Newspapers as far away as Maryland told accounts of an abnormally tall human-like creature terrorizing the good people of East Tennessee. The stories back then had a general theme of women being the target and that the Wildman would run away if confronted by a man. It is even said that in the late 1800s, a circus operator had captured a feral human as a sideshow act. The Wildman, some theorized, was an escapee of the big top. The sightings and encounters persisted for decades so either this thing is very old or perhaps there's a family out there.

The Tennessee Wildman apparently has a habit of not only going after women but also dogs throughout the years. One eyewitness in McNairy County in 2012 stated that an eight-foot-tall creature resembling a man with long reddish-brown hair with red eyes chased his dog. The creature then retreated into the woods with unusual speed and agility.

That's another common description in sightings. The Wildman possesses superhuman strength, agility, and speed. He is said to be able to bound from tree to tree with ease like what was reported by Robb Phillips in a 2015 interview regarding his encounter that happened two decades before. Robb and a friend came across a tall, hairy, and terrifying creature that was accompanied by a horrible putrid stench. (Sounds familiar, doesn't it?) The Wildman let out a terrible scream and leaped from one treetop to another. Phillips and his friend retreated in fear.

None of these exactly match up with Bigfoot sightings, though they may share some common elements. I believe that The Tennessee Wildman is a whole different animal.

I think that it may be some missing link in our evolutionary history. Either some isolated remnant of a species that developed independently outside of normal humans or a mutation that took a crooked branch off the ol' family tree. Hell, it's not so outrageous to look for so-called missing links. In 1935 anthropologist Ralph Von Koenigswald discovered some peculiar teeth in a drugstore of all places, and that led to the classification of a new animal. That animal is now known as the Gigantopithecus, a 600 lb. giant ape that resembles an orangutan whose bones have been found all over Asia.

It depends on your geographic location, but you could very well have Neanderthal DNA, up to 4 percent actually. Neanderthals died out around 40,000 years ago. All I'm saying is that there is a chance that the Wildman is distinctly separate from both humans and sasquatch. It could very well be its own unique thing.

What I believe wholeheartedly is that The Tennessee Wildman is out there. Keep your eyes and noses open my friends and happy trails.

FERAL PEOPLE OF APPALACHIA

I think it is safe to say that most of us, at some point, have thought about slipping the bonds of regulated society and running naked into the woods to live a free primitive life. I also think the majority of us wouldn't last too long without the creature comforts we have grown accustomed to. I know I wouldn't. I enjoy my air conditioning too much. You have to catch your own food, too; and I have no idea where nachos live or how to hunt them. I joke, of course. I grew up learning self-sufficiency and outdoor skills like I'm sure most of you have. I could make it, but it wouldn't be pretty and God damn, do I love a flushing toilet and my internet.

It's one thing to spend a week on a fishing trip, but an entirely different one to spend your whole life in the woods and never know anything else. I'm talking full-on feral existence.

There are some pretty frightening accounts from the hills of Tennessee about run-ins with just such feral folks.

In the early 2000s, a couple from Ohio were making their way down to South Carolina. They were both avid outdoor enthusiasts who enjoyed camping and hiking and taking in the sights. Driving through the Great Smoky Mountains and enjoying the majesty of their surroundings, it started to get dark. They, being familiar with roughing it, decided that the best course of action was to find a place to park and just sleep in the truck for the night and continue on in the morning instead of trying to find a motel or rest area along the way.

After a bit of searching, they find a logging road that appears to be somewhat overgrown and not frequently traveled. The couple decides this is the perfect place for their resting spot and they traveled up the road a bit and parked. Kicking the seat back and relaxing getting some shut eye was the plan, but sometimes the best laid plans... Well, you know where this is going. The wife falls asleep rather quickly but the husband is having a bit of a rough time and stays up a while. I don't know if you have ever tried to sleep in the driver seat of a full-size truck but it's not the most comfortable place, even with the seats back.

He contemplates grabbing the tent out of the back of the truck and sleeping out in the fresh air but something about that idea seems oddly dangerous for some reason. (Listen to your intuition folks! It more than likely will save your life.) He ultimately decides against the tent idea and eventually manages to fall asleep in the vehicle. It's a good thing he did, too.

Around two that morning, the wife wakes up to what she thinks is the noise of an animal walking around the truck. This isn't exactly the strangest thing given that they are parked in the middle of nowhere so she eventually falls back asleep after the noises begin to subside.

Not long after she jolts awake again at what sounds like several something or someone walking around near the truck. At this point she wakes up her husband to let him know that there is some potentially scary shit going on and he should probably be awake for it.

Hubby, startled awake by his wife, immediately turns the headlights on to see what the hell is out there. Illuminated by the light, four mud covered, ragged looking people stand in the middle of the road staring at them. The "get the hell out of here" factor kicks in big-time and the couple goes into retreat mode and begin to try and navigate turning a full-size truck around on a narrow mountain road. Every time the headlights move off of the four strangers in the road, they begin moving closer to the truck. They only stop their advance when the light catches them like the worse game of "red light-green light" you have ever played.

At one point, the figures are left in darkness for a good bit of time and when the lights swing back to the road ahead, what was once four becomes around a dozen dirty terrifying people advancing toward the truck. Hubby finally says fuck it and just throws it in reverse and begins to slowly make his way back down the road as best he could, using his mirrors in the middle of the night, while being pursued by insane looking feral mountain people. They don't teach that shit in drivers education classes y'all.

They are making their retreat when the truck hits something solid and runs it over. They stop wondering what the hell just happened. He puts it in drive and pulls forward hitting this thing again. The wild folks are still on the move and begin to try and surround the truck. The fleeing couple just gun it backward, whatever is behind them be damned. It was a log. A cut log that had not been there hours before when they had driven up the road. A log that had to be placed there intentionally. They were being trapped. Holy shit y'all. What would have happened if that log had jammed up, high centering and stopping the truck?

Eventually they make their way back close to the main highway where the lights and sounds of other vehicles apparently were enough to stop their pursuers. Our Ohio friends went straight to law enforcement to tell them what happened. The cops took a report and told them they would check it out and be in touch if anything came of it. Of course, nothing ever came of it.

I have a sneaking suspicion that the cops in those parts already knew about such goings-on. I think there may be more than one reason that logging road was disused and overgrown but of course I have no evidence of that. Just call it a hunch. In fact, there are rumors and conjecture that the federal government knows about the bands of feral people in the National Park systems and have even gone so far as to send teams in to eradicate them. That sounds like a shitty movie plot and I don't know how much I believe that. What I do believe is that locals in areas where these sightings occur probably know a lot more about what is going on in the forest than they let on to outsiders.

Hell, there is a story out of Maggie Valley about a family who rented a secluded cabin for a nice vacation. The cabin was wonderful and offered amazing views. The one weird thing they noticed right off the bat was that the owner told them there were sensors on the driveway to warn them if anyone approached the house. The guests found this odd because the sensors were positioned in such a way that an approaching vehicle would not be likely to set them off. Also, why the hell were there some set up at the dead-end part of the drive? What, or who, was going to come visit that they needed to be warned by electronic surveillance? Oh, don't worry they found out.

One afternoon the alarms go off. They go and check but there is nothing there, no cars or animals around so they think nothing of it and continue that day as normal. That night things got not so normal. The family was sitting around a fire with their dogs and enjoying a relaxing night.

On the wind came a strong putrid smell that only lasted a short time until the breeze shifted and it was gone. Then suddenly something hit the cabin, then something else. Someone or something was throwing rocks. They retreated inside. Weeks later the woman came across a documentary about feral people that lived and harassed folks in the same area as the cabin they had stayed at.

This story reminds me more of a Mr. Foot type situation to be honest. The smell and the rock throwing are right up his alley. I included it here because of the reports of ferals in the area and what seems to be prior knowledge of something out there that the owner of the cabin had some kind of a run-in with.

Who are these folks and where do they live? They have to have some kind of dwelling or village, right? The cave systems perhaps?

There's a story about a man, who when he was younger, was in the woods with his grandfather and they came upon a disheveled and dirty man standing in a clearing past a thicket of vegetation. The man was covered in mud and blood and hunched over a deer carcass. The figure did not speak English but his vocalizations were pretty clear to the two interlopers that they should leave him the hell alone and that they did. This same man claims that some thirty years later while hunting, he ran into a woman that had the same dirty unkempt appearance as the one he and his grandfather witnessed so many years before. The wild woman took off and he followed. The chase abruptly ended as the woman jumped down into a hole. The hole was what appeared to be an entrance to a cave system. This certainly is a logical explanation of how these people can seem to come and go so easily throughout Appalachia.

I believe that some of these reports of so-called feral people are probably just generations of families that have lived primitively for years and years and just never had the opportunity or the desire to join modern society. One account I came across was a woman that claimed in the 1980s she would go stay with her grandparents in the Great Smoky Mountains.

One day, they went and loaded up their vehicle with food and supplies and drove to what her grandfather said was her aunt's place to drop off the provisions for them. She says they drove out to the middle of nowhere. Her grandad stopped at an unmarked place on the road and unloaded the supplies and began hiking into the woods. She and her grandmother were forbidden to leave the car.

The woman remembers seeing four teenage boys covered in dirt wearing ragged clothing standing nearby watching the car. She surmised this was her cousins though she was told not to talk or interact with them. I think this kind of thing happens a lot. You got to look after family after all.

There are reports all over the United States that national parks hold populations of people outside of civilized society. I believe we view them just as they probably view us: as outsiders. Something outside the norm. Maybe we are the strange ones in the grand scheme of things.

It is not wise to let your guard down out in the wild because you never know what you may run into. Humans and animals both should be treated with caution and respect. Be kind but be ready and capable to defend yourself if need be. Smile and carry a big stick and all that.

Take care on the trails and in the woods. Be safe y'all.

Happy Hunting.

Dogman

The wolf. An animal that has struck fear in the hearts of humans since the beginning of our coexistence, and which still roams both the land, and nightmares, of man.

I say coexistence in that we walked the same ground. These furry bastards would rip our throats out just as soon as look at us for the first part of our shared time on this rock. They still will!

Some 30,000 years ago at the latest, some wolf looked at some primitive man around his warm safe fire and was just like "hey asshole, give me some of that meat and I'll... Ya knows, maybe keep worse things than me from attacking you." Thus, a friendship was born. We domesticated all kinds of animals and bred them to do our bidding, but I'd like to think the first was dog.

For real. Man's best friend came from some prehistory hunter throwing a piece of venison to a cute pupper and now we have designer dogs that fit in purses and whatever the fuck a pug is.

Tell me a better glow up.

The point is mankind and canines have a long history together. That history is of protection and also destruction. Stories of wolf or dog-like creatures stealing innocent children in the night are scattered throughout our oral and written traditions. Killers that snatch away unsuspecting victims and leave the remains scattered and dripping from the trees of nearby forests are well documented and give insight into the story Of Wolf and Man. (Yes, I made a reference to Metallica's 1992 Black Album.

Bonus points to you if you caught that. You're my kind of people.)

There are tales of the merging of humans and beasts in some brutal union that exists only to terrorize and strike down the citizens of whatever society that ended up cursed with the weirdo that lacked any modern medicine or mental healthcare. So maybe Uncle Kevin who killed all those folks and was found naked in the woods needed to be in prison and not burned because he was a fucking werewolf... but that really doesn't touch on the subject of the dogman does it?

There are the tormented souls shifting into monsters and living such a horrible life by the cycle of the moon. Then there's the good boys out there that are just living their best life.

The point I'm trying to make in here is Dogmen may not have fuck all to do with Lycanthropy. These things may not be werewolves at all per se. They may very well be a thing of their own.

All throughout the Appalachian range there have been reports of tall bipedal creatures covered in fur. This includes our old friend Mr. Foot aka Sasquatch; more importantly though, it includes beasts that possess more canine than ape-like features. Sharp pointed ears and triangular faces. Long snouts with eyes that are said to glow in the dark or reflect the light. If you ask me, that's way more dog-like.

In Eastern Tennessee there is a legend of a dogman stalking trails and lurking in the woods. Scott Carpenter was a well-known (in our circles at least) Bigfoot hunter and investigator. He authored a few articles and books. The man was on a History Channel show for what it's worth, which makes him more of an expert than me. The book he wrote about dogman will be included here later so you can check it out, and let me tell you, it's well worth the read.

Anyway, the story goes he had set out bait traps for Mr. Foot and he was checking the bait to see if anything had disturbed them. He set out looking for a sasquatch but found some absolutely killer evidence of a dogman, instead.

Mr. Carpenter had designed a rig on his pack to film behind him as he moved through his investigations. He was checking his bait traps like any hunter is want to do, and moved through this patch of forest. It wasn't until later, upon checking his footage, that he found he was being stalked. The footage of the camera facing his six o'clock later went on to reveal a furry horror behind him.

In the trees and brush there was a face. Two pointed ears and a snout. Like a black German shepherd peeking out of the woods. But it was high up. Way higher than any man or dog would stand. The footage Mr. Carpenter captured literally gave me chills and made me believe that this whole werewolf/dogman thing may not be bullshit after all.

There are stories of hikers on trails in Eastern Tennessee encountering the dogman. A couple walking their dog along Ramsey Trail near Gatlinburg had their dog stop and whimper. The couple, sensing the tension and the quiet of their surroundings, decided to turn back down the trail to the parking lot. It was on their way out that they caught a glimpse of a seven-foot-tall bipedal wolf-like creature, the sight so terrifying to them, it caused them to never visit that trail again.

Now, I stopped to really think about it after reading their account, and I present to you a situation you can put yourself in, like I did. Follow me now, because it may get a little weird but I want to put you in dogman territory with me and see what happens.

Just imagine:

The woods fall silent and you can tell something dangerous is maybe out there. You look behind you and a black flash in the distance, just between two trees makes you jump. You have heard the stories of things stalking these trails and you have always dismissed them as legends. Cautionary tales to keep children from wandering too far from their parents... In this moment, you're not quite sure what is legend or what's for real. You know you just saw *something*. Something else primal awakens in you. That ancient part of your brain makes you suddenly hyper-aware. Puts you in a state of freeze as you still on the trail and your heart picks up pace, thundering against the inside of your ribs, thumping almost painfully.

The primal fear is warranted as you notice that something has been tracking you. Perhaps a smell catches your nose as the wind shifts and the distinct odor of musk and rot hits you like a brick. It's the smell of a predator. You are no longer the King of the woods. Not now, not here. You may have been out hiking, you may have been out hunting, but now you are the hunted. The surrounding woods are silent and the only thing you hear is the beating of your own rapid heart, the rush of your own blood through your ears as you strain to listen beyond the noise your own body makes to know just what is out there. To pinpoint its location.

You feel it. Watched. *But you don't know where...*

You swear there's a sound in the trees of something else breathing. Heavy breathing. Deep breathing as whatever it is scents you on the air. The snapping of a twig brings your head up to face the dark beyond the trees. The last thing you see is the glowing red eyes and the gaping maw of the creature, lunging out of the dark, jaws snapping at your neck. It slams into you with the force of a truck and there's no time to discern if that is what knocked the wind out of you, or if it was when you hit the compact loam of the forest floor.

It doesn't matter.

It's too late.

They will find your body mangled deep in a holler and far from any trail. The Department of Natural Resources will say you missed your footing, fell, maybe hit your head on a rock. Went unconscious, died of exposure maybe... and that it was scavengers that did the rest. Ravaged your corpse, dined on your flesh... Many will know the truth, but it won't be told beyond conspiracy TikTok's and YouTube channels. Or maybe they won't find you at all, and you'll just become another missing hiker – never seen or heard from again. Either way, that was your fate, you will be gone, and your family, your loved ones, will never know.

Rest assured, if y'all ever find my body torn asunder in the woods. My last words were probably along the lines of "Oh look at you! Such a cute puppers! Who's a good boy? Who's a good boy!"

Either that, or "I can make that jump" or "Here kitty kitty! Psp, psp, psp, psp, psp!"

I'm just that guy. I'm betting a lot of you are too. I figure it's only my kind of people reading this book.

NOT DEER

The vast and dark forests of Appalachia stretch for thousands of miles from the southern states into New England. Reaching the tip of its ancient fingers into the very top of Mississippi and caressing in a swoop across northern Alabama and Georgia like a lover pushing the hair back behind an ear. You may say that those far south borders aren't really Appalachia. I say to you: write your own book.

The Appalachian range is home to many animals and its home to many legends. There seems to be a weird stigma about this region that social media content producers and "influencers" seem to hype. *'Don't go out at night!'* is the call from these folks. Well, I'm here to tell you it's ok to go out at night. It's fine. But don't trust someone calling your name and sure as shit don't trust a deer standing up and walking toward you on its hind legs.

The common whitetail deer is found throughout the United States. The normal ones that don't have twisted bodies and come from the depths of hell are still a pain in the ass for people. They destroy crops, cause damage to property and numerous other crimes.

They all also seem to be suicide magnets; attracted to every vehicle I've ever owned.

They may be cute but they're all bastards is what I guess I'm trying to get across.

Standing on all fours. The whitetail can reach shoulder height to a human and on their back legs they're much taller than many people.

PARANORMAL BY REGION: EAST TENNESSEE EDITION

They'll absolutely fight you. Deer when on the attack will rear back and pummel their victim with their hooves. You can imagine how damaging that can be when factoring in antlers, blind rage, and sheer stupidity. These are all the *non-spooky* ones. Let's talk about the terrifying cryptid known as the *Not Deer*.

The tales of the Not Deer stretch back generations. Deer who behave uncharacteristically. Who stand on their back legs and seem to stare with glowing eyes into the soul of the witness. As with any creature of the crypto zoological persuasion the eyewitness accounts vary. This is a common occurrence. Show a hundred people a rabbit for a few seconds you'll get a hundred descriptions and one will probably claim the rabbit was eight feet tall and had wings. This proves doubly true when emotions are high and people are scared out of their wits by something outside the norm. Paranormal is called that for a reason.

The general similarities between witnesses are that these creatures appear gaunt with elongated limbs and disproportionate body features. The ears are misshapen and pointy or jagged.

In some instances, a large gaping maw opens unnaturally wide containing sharp teeth that have no business being in a deer's mouth. In others, no teeth are bared, but the head itself appears to be much larger than it should be. The eyes glow red and are often described as also being out of proportion. More forward facing like a predator, rather than the prey animal that a deer is supposed to be. This thing is definitely not something you'd see Snow White feeding in a musical number; or maybe you would, if we're talking all those old *original* fairy tales written by the Grimm's.

This thing isn't content on being nightmare fuel on all four, oh no. To make it extra creepy, witnesses constantly say the Not Deer stand on their hind legs and stagger and move like something out of a Romero film. They also reportedly hop as well. I honestly don't know what's more terrifying so see, a drunken zombie deer shambling toward you in the middle of the night or one taking little menacing hops... ok the hopping may be a little funny when you think about it, but probably not with a gaping maw full of sharp teeth and something standing head and shoulders taller than you coming to eat your face.

They generally don't seem to be afraid of people. Flashing headlights, yelling, vehicle horns seem like they don't do much in shooing away devil-Bambi. They tend to observe before they approach, suggesting intelligence. Maybe they just want to help, or they need help? That might not be too far from the truth actually, and we'll get into that in a bit. Through my research, I haven't found any evidence of encounters that ended in harm or death of those unfortunate enough to stumble upon one of these things. I mean, Bigfoot has at least killed a few folks allegedly, (all cryptids are innocent until proven guilty) so maybe step up your game Not Deer!

I jest. I in no way wish any harm on anyone that encounters any unknown entity. I'd certainly need compassion and probably new pants if I ever saw one, myself. I did say they were nightmare fuel, right?

So where do these things come from? An ancient curse that transformed normal deer into grotesque monstrosities? Some deep hidden source of evil in the hills of Appalachia? The government? Wizards? Government wizards?

Maybe misfolded proteins called prions cause a disease that explains a good bit of sightings?

Wait what?

That's right, I'm talking about Chronic Wasting Disease and it's a trip. Buckle up, because there's a similar human disease and you could already have it and have no clue. I'm not a doctor, this is all for entertainment purposes but this is what this here swampbilly's figured out:

Chronic Wasting Disease affects the brain, spinal cord, and other tissues of deer, elk, and moose. The disease causes the animals to experience extreme weight loss, hence the *wasting* part of the name. Other symptoms, according to the Centers for Disease Control and Prevention are: Loss of coordination. Excessive thirst. Drooling. Lack of fear in humans....

Sound familiar?

This is known as a prion disease and there are many that affect different animals including humans. Basically, a protein misfolds and screws everything up and goes on to make others screw up in a cascading failure and *boom*.

You may not be familiar with Chronic Wasting Disease but you have probably heard of its bovine equivalent, Mad Cow disease.

Creutzfeldt-Jakob disease is not related to Mad Cow but it *is* caused by prions and humans *do* get it. There's also *Kuru* that practitioners of cannibalism can fall to, but that's enough about that. I'm not drafting an entry for a medical journal here; I'm writing an entry in a fun book about terrifying creatures that may or may not exist. I do, however, like to present logical explanations when there's one to present, so that's what I found about that.

All I can say, is that I know that if I'm ever in the forests of Appalachia and see a weird ass deer I'm going to avoid I; and I strongly suggest you do the same. Even if it's just a deer with Chronic Wasting Disease, I'd rather not get close… and if it's something worse? Well, I really don't want to get personal with it!

MOTHMAN SIGHTINGS

Here we have another very well-known cryptid. He may not be quite to the level of commercial exploitation of Mr. Foot, but over the years he has certainly become just as popular.

The legend begins in Point Pleasant, West Virginia. The story has been told countless times, but let's give it quick a run down here so we know the basic history before we get into the sightings in Eastern Tennessee, shall we?

Way back in 1966 on a cold November night in Point Pleasant West Virginia in an area surrounded by old WWII munitions bunkers a couple of folks were cruising back roads and having a grand ol' time. That is until they met the monstrosity known now as Mothman.

On the road they came upon an old, abandoned factory that used to produce cement products. Standing on the perimeter they witnessed a hulking humanoid form with glowing red eyes and folded wings. They gunned it out of there but the creature followed. The people claimed the creature moved swiftly through the air without any noticeable movement from its wings. They reported the sighting to law enforcement who held a press conference and eventually the creature was dubbed Mothman.

What followed was a hell of a time for the residents of Point Pleasant. Numerous encounters and sightings, hell even UAP (then referred to as UFOs) and livestock mutilations. This all came to a head on the sixteenth of December 1967 when the Silver Bridge collapsed.

PARANORMAL BY REGION: EAST TENNESSEE EDITION

The Silver Bridge connected Point Pleasant West Virginia to Gallipolis Ohio. It failed and sent forty-six souls to an icy death in the Ohio River. Mothman came to be viewed as either a symbol of warning or the harbinger of the disaster. The sightings fell off but it's been reported around the country. Even right here in East Tennessee.

The Smoky Mountain Mothman mystery comes to us with some terrifying accounts of a winged beast with glowing red eyes.

On a family farm in East Tennessee the father is outside enjoying the beautiful evening when his tranquility is broken by his son running frantically to him. The kid tells his father that he was out at the barn and something huge with wings flew over. It was the size of a person! He claimed.

The dad figures there must have been a huge owl circling around the barn and gave his son a fright. Children often misjudge the size and scope of things, even adults do to be honest, when the situation gets scary. One's mind doesn't not automatically go to Mothman, or anything supernatural. Like any good father, he calms his son down and tells him after dinner he will go check out the barn and the horses and make sure they are safe for the night. This is where the creepy really kicks in y'all.

Dad stays true to his word and goes out to the barn to secure it and make sure his horses are ok. Approaching the barn with flashlight in hand. he hears the horses going crazy.

Now I'll stop here briefly to say that horses being spooked isn't exactly a five-alarm problem. I've personally witnessed a horse freaking the fuck out because a pinecone dropped from a tree. Or a butterfly landed on their nose. Horses are goofy bastards and I love them. However, horses in a barn or their safe space freaking out is a cause for alarm. Something is going on.

Entering the barn he saw a horse in the back was injured. Down the animal's side were slash marks that look like they could have been made by claws. The rational explanation again was that somehow the horse was attacked by a large cat like a mountain lion or even a bear.

The vet that checked the poor thing subsequently agreed. Still, something was off and it was only going to get more so.

A few days later, the daughter of the family is feeding the chickens and getting ready to get them in their coop. Suddenly, she hears the beating of huge wings as a terrifying creature swoops down at her. She flees for her life back to the safety of the house.

The next few days, an eerie feeling fell on the farm like a mountain fog. Something wasn't right. I have to say If I had been through what these fine folks had I'd be uneasy as all hell too.

One night, the calm quiet was broken by the din of chickens in a panic and the family's dogs barking wildly. Dad hears the alarm and rushes out to see what fresh hell has fallen into their laps this time.

When he approaches the chicken coop, all of his dogs stop barking and flee. It can't be comforting when your canine security detail just ups and takes off. I can't really blame them though. The chickens are still going nuts when Dad sees the eyes. Huge glowing red eyes staring right at him. A low guttural growl or hum that is reminiscent of the hum of electrical equipment emanates from the creature. This is the signal to get the hell back to the house as quickly as possible.

There is no doubt now. Strange things are going on and it feels like the farm is under attack by something.

At this point. a rule is set for the family. Nobody for any reason, barring an absolute emergency, is allowed to be outdoors after nightfall. Everyone in the family except the mother has had a run-in with whatever is stalking the property, and this is the safest way to operate for the time being. The mom may have been lucky so far in avoiding an encounter, but her luck is about to run out.

Mom is on a grocery run and she's cutting it close to dusk. She calls the family to let them know that, unfortunately, because of traffic, she won't be home until after nightfall. See where this is going? The road home was like many in the region. It had its curves. Making her way home, she's accosted by a huge, winged creature that seemingly is trying to attack her car. After avoiding crashing her car she stops.

Mom proceeds to do what I probably wouldn't and get out of the car with a flashlight in hand. I think she realized this wasn't the best course of action and quickly got in and sped home. She relayed the harrowing ordeal to her family. Dad made a choice to protect him and his and the next few days were spent reinforcing the house and animal enclosures.

This seems personal to me. This thing appears to have it out for our little happy family. So, what's the deal? Why is it harassing this particular farm? Could it be a message or warning? We'll get into that soon.

The family's neighbors all through this ordeal remained silent or claimed to not have seen anything strange. Well, after these events about when Dad started going all protection mode, some of them eventually admitted to witnessing unusual things in the area. Y'all, *talk to your neighbors*. All we have is each other; *especially* when it comes to otherworldly winged humanoids that attack livestock, little girls, and rural moms on the way home from their grocery runs.

If this was Mothman, or *a* mothman, what was the message he was trying to send? Testimony certainly leads one to think this was something akin to the creature that haunted Point Pleasant West Virginia before the Silver Bridge collapse. Perhaps and hopefully, this thing may be something else entirely. Regardless, at the time of this writing, no further information was available on what's happening to the once quiet farm in the Great Smoky Mountains

Be vigilant and please tell the folks around you, if weird shit starts going down. You never know, it may come back to bless you in the end. Be safe my friends and as always…

Happy trails.

A WEARS VALLEY CABIN WTF

A.J. here! - This story was initially presented to me as a 'Haunted' Wears Valley Cabin, but after hearing and doing most of the write up, this is firmly in cryptid territory. So, to that end, Matt and I discussed and he said I should finish the write up and I said 'ok' but only if he would weigh in at the end with what he thought this thing could be, because honestly, I haven't got a clue! I just know it ain't no ghost.

These events happened to a woman who is now, in 2024, 31 years old. However, at the time of the events she was but seven years old.

It occurred on Thanksgiving Day, when her family drove out to Pigeon Forge and Gatlinburg on Thanksgiving just on a whim. Likely one of the few times of the year that the area isn't completely jam packed with tourists and thus making it a true escape from it all.

As such, they had no hotel reservations or cabin reservations. They just set out in the direction of Cades Cove intending to sightsee with no real plan other than that.

As night began to descend, they started looking for a place to stay – but to their dismay, every hotel and cabin that they would usually stay at was completely booked up due to Thanksgiving. So it was that they felt as though they had lucked out when they managed to score a vacant cabin out on Wears Valley Road.

The girl described this cabin as being a little less like an actual cabin and more that it was just a big house. Which her family didn't mind at all after their difficulties in scoring any type of accommodation in the first place.

Beggars couldn't be choosers after all.

The house was an odd shape, the woman recalls, stating that it was odd, but *huge* – capable of sleeping up to twenty-four people. It was also, again, the only accommodation that her small family could find, so they didn't much care about rattling around in the big old place. They were just grateful to have found anything at all.

The first creepy thing upon entering the big old home was a singular staircase, with walls on either side, leading up to a single door that was closed at the top of the stairs. That wasn't what was creepy in and of itself, but rather it was the metal plaque adhered to that door at the top of the stairs with nothing but the number, 666, emblazoned on it.

(Not sure how much I believe this, I'll admit my skepticism with some of these stories. I'm just here to relate them as I found them, though.)

She said that upon going up the staircase and entering the room, that it just felt creepier and odder. She described it as though it was a sort of Snow White and the Seven Dwarves setup, only a tad less – that as you entered the room at the top of those stairs, there were five twin beds set in a semi-circle or crescent moon shape – just a weird sort of setup, in her opinion, that in and of itself gave her the heebs.

She called her parents to come look, but while they agreed it was a bit odd, they dismissed it as just a garish and weird design choice – after all, it was full dark out there now, and they were staying. Better get used to it.

The family returned to the first floor, and on that floor was a huge jacuzzi tub. Mom, thinking it would be fun, told her daughter to put on her bathing suit, that they would jump in this tub and relax and picture themselves on some warm, tropical vacation somewhere.

Being seven, the girl was super excited for this and thought it was a great idea – so they put on their swimsuits and hopped in the tub, which was situated next to this huge rectangular window looking outside the house. (This is in the middle of nowhere, mind you, and faced no neighbors.)

After a few minutes of being in there, splashing a bit and having a good time, the girl says that her mother starts looking out this window into the dark beyond the glass.

Without warning, her mom lets out this terrifying, bloodcurdling scream. The girl turned, and what she saw sent a frisson of fear down her spine.

She described the creature as being only two to three feet high, with piercing, glowing eyes, and described it as the only thing she could attribute to it – as a gargoyle.

The little girl started screaming along with her mother, jumped out of the tub, and took off running into the house – at which point her dad had reached the bathroom door to find out just what the hell was going on.

I can only imagine this poor guy expecting to see a mouse, rat, or spider to blame for all of the wild shrieking coming from his wife and daughter – but no, both his girls babbled hurriedly what they saw and he just laughed them off, saying they were crazy. That there was no way, and there was no such thing. I wonder if he thought they were trying to prank him, or something – then I wondered if dude had any clue on how to read a room because I can't imagine how scared they were and that that fear was palpable.

Girl and mom weren't joking, though, and their fun in the imaginary sun was dashed. They both changed out of their bathing suits, getting into their pajamas and ready for bed.

A couple of minutes later, the dad comes out of the bathroom and makes a beeline for the bedroom and frantically starts going through the covers and such on the bed, snatching up belongings and hurriedly stuffing them into their bags and said, "We're getting out of here!"

Now *he* was scared which just made the seven-year-old that much more afraid because the woman who was that child today describes her dad as being a man's man. A country boy through and through, an avid outdoorsman who had seen a lot of shit, but here he was freaking the hell out saying, "We're leaving! We're getting out of here right the hell now! Get your stuff!"

It was scary as hell for this little girl who said that her dad wasn't scared of *anything* and that he for certain was terrified by whatever *he* had seen that night.

It was like one o'clock in the morning by this point in her recollection, and super late – so it was even more nuts that all of a sudden, her dad was like: *NOPE! We're leavin'!*

They ran out to the car, loaded up, and took off, driving the two hours plus back to North Carolina rather than stay another minute in that house.

As to what her dad saw to make him want to leave?

The girl doesn't know. To this day, her father resolutely will not speak on the matter. He certainly did see or hear something that night to make him want to take flight and get his wife and child away from that place – but it seems that he is determined to take whatever horror he personally encountered that night to the grave. Perhaps he's one of those people that believes that if he speaks on it, it will make whatever it is more real…

I know I would really like to know… *what was it?*

Matt here!

When A.J. first told me that she had a haunting that took a sharp turn into Cryptid Country I was very intrigued and it turns out rightly so. It's a very interesting story that if I am quite honest, at first, I sort of dismissed until I read the whole thing with the father's actions.

Immediately my mind went to the following: Young child late at night in a creepy unfamiliar house sees an owl or a bobcat out of a window fogged by a hot tub. Case Closed. I will admit that even though I am very much an enthusiast of cryptozoology I try to stay grounded in reality as much as possible. I also refuse to use the Project Blue Book go-to of everything is an owl wrapped in swamp gas. The truth is out there as they say.

What changed my mind, is the account of the father losing his shit and packing up his family and making a swift exit. Surely a dad who was desperate to find lodging and laughed at the mention of a gargoyle would have to have witnessed something absolutely terrifying in order to react that way. So, let's talk about my theories of what this thing could have been assuming it was something outside the normal realm.

Could it have been a gargoyle-like creature that was stalking the woods around the house? Maybe with the whole "666" thing (which I also find maybe a bit fantastical but we are talking about monsters here, so anything goes right?) it could have been something akin to an imp.

A gargoyle, to me, strikes up images of the Flatwoods Monster, a supposed alien that terrified a family in 1952 West Virginia. There are no indications of any kind of UAP or alien activity so that's out but it was worth a mention just to give you an idea of my thought process here.

A.J. suggested perhaps a Rake fit the bill. I have to say this is probably my leading answer on the cryptid side of things. Small humanoid with a large head, sometimes described as having pale or gray flesh. That ticks off some gargoyle criteria right there. I would also like to take this time to confess that, while I am obviously afraid of large creatures, both confirmed and not such as Bigfoot etc., There is something about things human sized or smaller that just give me the creeps. Toddler sized monsters will get a 'no thank you' from me.

Here is where I am going to flip the script a little bit. There have been countless reports of the physical manifestation of a negative energy in a haunted place. I'm not talking just ghosts or intelligent hauntings, no I mean physical *creatures. The several goatmen that haunt cemeteries or bridges across the country. The Pigman legends also come to mind.*

I believe that the place was indeed haunted. The physical presence of the haunting presented itself to the little girl as what she would find most terrifying at the time and that was a "gargoyle."

The dad's reaction of terror and flight lines up with this because this thing showed the dad his darkest imagination. Who knows what he was? Only him because apparently it was enough for him to not talk about it for decades. He never once mentions a gargoyle only that they need to get the hell out of there right then.

This thing may be a demon or some dark entity but it's my opinion that this firmly falls into the category of a haunting. We have come full circle, all the way back to the beginning I suppose.

A.J. this is your problem again, give my best to the terrifying gargoyle demon. I'm off to find something that won't keep me up at night.

A.J. here!

Son of a bitch...

PART 4:
FOLKLORE
&
THE UNEXPLAINED

NORTHEAST TENNESSEE

The Legend of Long Dog

Matt here, and A.J. voluntold me to step into her realm of ghosties for this one. To be fair, she knows me, and knew this one would be right up my alley being the dog lover that I am.

I have long said that humans don't deserve dogs. In our chapter about the Dogman, I mentioned briefly our furry friends' humble beginnings. They have stood dutifully for thousands of years by our side. Best friends indeed. The following tale is tragic but also with a twist of wholesomeness. Leave it to a dog to bring a smile from tears. This is the story about a good girl that became known as Long Dog.

The 1800s in East Tennessee and well in general across the vast reaching lands of the United States were anything but secure. Now, it wasn't exactly a lawless Mad Max landscape but it was kind of close. Thieves and scoundrels ran amok along the roads! Okay so certain rural roads and passages were dangerous is what I'm saying.

The opportunistic thief known as a Highwayman would rob, steal, and kill any all he came across.

(Side note: that's a damn good song, The Highwayman.)

Real highwaymen were absolutely garbage humans. Let's talk about that shall we?

John Murrell was the son of a son of God. The spawn of a preacher. What that man of the Lord brought into this world should revoke any favor of that deity he ever had. The preacher's son ol' Mr. Murrell had a shit load of issues; he had so many issues he could have a subscription to "Fucked Up" magazine. His mamma was a whore. That's not me throwing insults, I support sex workers wholeheartedly, but his mother *was* a prostitute that encouraged little Johnny to come in whilst she was, uh, *plying her trade* so that he could steal the wallets and valuables of her clientele.

The time period and location were just perfect to breed assholes. The biggest one was John. He was said to have been trained in his shitty ways by a real life, no joke, former sea pirate by the name of H. Cranshaw. Murrell supposedly killed many and dumped the bodies into various waterways. He fucked around until he found out; eventually being branded (literally having HS burned into his skin) as a horse thief. For that, he was lashed and imprisoned for a bit.

Now we come to our tragic beginnings of the Long Dog legend:

A Family was traveling along Sage Road near Surgoinsville Tennessee. They made the fatal decision to rest under some trees before continuing on. The two highwaymen Murrell and Cranshaw were waiting for just the chance and came upon the unfortunate family. They left none alive. These two shitheads began loading up the family wagon with their spoils and also the family. Murrell planned to find a spot to dump the bodies as per his usual way.

Then came the member of the slain family that went unnoticed before, a beautiful white dog with little legs. She was a stretchy doggy, long and with stubby little legs. The pair saw this canine begin to chase the wagon as they fled and so they stopped.

The dog walked up to the wagon as if to inquire "hey where's my people" John Murrell saw the pup and thought he may take her for his own. Let's steal the dog of the family I just killed! I told you he was an asshole. He went to grab her and Long Dog tore into his ass! *Good Dog!*

The dog latched on *hard* to John's arm. They struggled and fought. Unfortunately, John's piece of shit partner managed to get a hold of our heroic pup and took her life by choking her. They unceremoniously threw her into a ditch. I did mention these guys were assholes, right?

John eventually met some kind of justice when he was tried for his thievery and other crimes. Murder was not on the list of his official bullshittery because there were no bodies. He had been good at dumping them, you remember. He was sentenced to a decade. That's a light load if you ask me. He should have been keelhauled given his pirate training. Speaking of, I have no clue what became of the dog strangling asshat Cranshaw.

After Murrell was in prison there were strange things reported on the road that the tragic end occurred. Strange but kind of heartwarming in a way.

All along Sage Road people reported a long white dog chasing their wagon. It seemed to be looking for its masters. The dog was a cutie but it seemed to have some glow to it, some ghostly shine. Folks walking down the way were often met with a happy white pupper keen on pets and love. The wagging tail and happy doggy vanished into thin air when the people looked away. Reports of the pup chasing cars and bikes went on until around the 1960s. I'd love to see this benevolent spirit or whatever it was keep on keeping on but maybe it found a way back to its rightful place.

Don't be a John Murrell or a Cranshaw. Be nice to animals.

If you are reading this and you have your very own hero pup close by, tell them I said hi and they are the best pupper in the world.

Be good y'all.

CENTRAL EAST TENNESSEE

OUT OF THIS WORLD

I have a strange affinity for all things extraterrestrial in nature. I have since I was a young boy. It probably didn't help that I was exposed to various media at what could be considered an inappropriate age. I was fascinated by Travis Walton's abduction story when I was a kid. I probably watched the film Fire in The Sky a good dozen times. I'm starting to realize that this may be why I am at my core a science fiction writer before I started investigating crypto zoological mysteries.

I am willing to bet that you have probably seen some strange shit going on in the night sky. You are not alone. East Tennessee seems to be a hot bed of such activity. Unidentified Flying Objects or UFOs, well ok let us use the current nomenclature, shall we? Unidentified Aerial Phenomenon or UAPs are witnessed all the time in these parts.

According to one source I found that tracked reporting metrics, Sevier County had 111 reported sightings of UAP since the turn of the century. If you put that in perspective that's a whole hell of a lot. That's reported, consider all the ones that people are too hesitant to officially say anything about when considering just how prevalent these things are.

Since the Roswell incident the standard explanation for strange things in the sky has been "it's a weather balloon" I have personally watched the launch and flight of several weather balloons and I have to say they can absolutely look strange or scary in the right conditions.

The winds up there can be brutal and the balloons can get going at a good clip.

Knoxville had its own run-in with a balloon back in 2022. Reports flooded in of a UAP but the consensus ended up being it was just a harmless weather balloon. Problem was, who the hell did it belong to? A website that tracks flight data had this thing tagged as being from a certain company but the company claimed they hadn't launched a balloon since the previous year. I was not able to find information on who this thing belonged to. Military? Amateurs? Perhaps little green men going with primitive methods? This incident took place a year before the whole spy balloon fiasco so that's an angle to think about.

The description of a UAP as balloon-like played a part in a rash of sightings involving one of the most secretive and impactful undertakings of all of WWII. The Manhattan project was a combined effort to develop and produce atomic weaponry to give the edge to allied forces. A very important part of this effort took place 25 miles outside of Knoxville at what is now known as Oak Ridge. The secret facilities here worked on separating the isotope Uranium-235 from natural uranium ore. The area was under the most intense security and secrecy but it appears something took an interest to the goings-on and it wasn't foreign agents. They certainly were not earthly foreign agents at least.

On the 13th of October 1950 shit started to get weird around the place. Ed Rymer, a trooper with the security division of the Atomic Energy Commission found himself with one Mr. Moneymaker who worked with Agriculture Research Farm from the University of Tennessee observing some strange lights. The claim was that an unidentified object was flying at upward of fifteen thousand feet making orbits around a "control zone". This object left a vapor trail like a jet. The story goes that this thing just deep dives to the ground. Rymer goes to investigate only for our unidentified aerial assailant to do some wild maneuvering to fly itself out of danger. Zig zagging over a high fence and some trees this thing booked it out of there. The trooper's commanding officer ended up collaborating a good bit of the account. There's more!

A week later on the 20th of October a mysterious radar signal of a cluster of unknown targets prompts the response of an air force interceptor. This is peak science fiction movie stuff y'all. When I read about this my little sci-fi writer's heart almost exploded. This wasn't fiction though this was national security. When the pilot got up there to investigate, he could not provide a positive ID on these things but reported they were between eighteen and twenty-five miles out from Knoxville airport. So much for an alien dog fight but it is still neat to me. They actually scrambled a plane to check this out.

At the same time the pilot was seeing these invaders, we have a witness on the ground who reported observing a balloon-like object whose color he described as gunmetal gray. Security superintendent Larry Riordan gave an account of a ten foot long "balloon" with possibly an object hanging under it. It was hovering over the Agriculture Research Farm. His perspective shifted as he drove around a curve and he stated the object appeared to grow thinner. Due to the simultaneous observations by the pilot and this witness I am inclined to think the interlopers were part of the same group the radar picked up.

A few days later, a radiation sensor was triggered about the same time a witness saw something metallic move over and descend behind a ridge in the control zone. I would think at this point things are a bit intense around Oak Ridge. This was a place of huge national security importance and it appeared to be visited by an unknown force.

Whatever it was buzzing around didn't care if you were off duty either. On the evening of October 24, the assistant chief of security was at a drive in theater watching a movie. I'd like to think he was also trying to unwind after all the goings-on. There's no rest though because in the distance he saw something moving horizontally and flashing multiple-colored lights. His wife and an employee of the theater also witnessed this. Not long after this was going on an air force major at his house watched the same colorful object until it eventually disappeared.

These aren't some rambling stories of drunks out on a boat who saw a strange light in the woods. These are civilian and military personnel with high security clearances at one of the most secretive facilities in the country at the time. The FBI basically threw out all rational explanations after investigating. It wasn't birds, balloons, bees, or folks pulling pranks. They still don't know; they don't publicly acknowledge that they know what happened. I think we all know, they know, ya know?

Quick detour before we continue on our alien journey. Oak Ridge was supposedly predicted forty years before they ever broke ground on the facilities. A fella named John Hendrix claimed voices told him to spend forty nights with his head to the ground out in the woods and the future would be revealed. What folks recall of his prediction was pretty on the money. He claimed there would be thousands of people running around production facilities where they would work on something that would end the greatest war the world had ever known. He also predicted railroads and such leading to Oak Ridge. He was written off as a lunatic and even institutionalized at one point. Maybe this story got a little twisted in history or maybe the voices actually did tell him all that. I know it's not related but we are in the Unexplained section and that was too good not to mention. Ok onwards, or rather upward!

Oak Ridge is about seventeen miles away from the town of Petros Tennessee. That name comes up more than you'd expect in this book. What the hell Petros? While investigating Brushy Mountain State Penitentiary, A.J. met the lead paranormal tour guide and gained so much from the conversation with her. I call her Ms. Jamie; she has a wealth of information on the unexplained phenomenon in the area. The topic of strange lights in the sky came up in the conversation, to which Ms. Jamie replied something to the effect of: "Oh yeah, there's all kinds of things like that around here. We're just on the other side of the mountain from Oak Ridge."

This wonderful lady proceeded to talk about watching orbs in the sky that behaved like nothing she'd ever witnessed before. Darting across the night sky only to stop abruptly then shoot off with amazing speed. These things changed direction on a dime, cutting ninety angles in an instant. This is all classic UAP behavior. She said she thought it could have been military but it certainly wasn't anything they have ever let on about. That's one more check box in the old UAP list. Ms. Jamie stated her grandmother used to enjoy early morning walks. On one of these walks, Memaw witnessed a huge triangular object in the sky make its way slowly overhead. There was no sound at all as this thing silently flew over. She was terrified and until her dying day refused to go for a stroll unless it was daytime.

Then there's the strange goings-on concerning animals around the complex. Mutilated remains were found on the grounds frequently. These gruesome findings had all the telltale signs of classic cattle mutilations. No blood around the bodies, missing organs, and precision cuts. Some animals had no heads or limbs were missing. I'm a big believer in alien contact but I have always been skeptical about animal mutilations. The signs usually can be explained by a scavenger or other predation, decomposition creating what appears to be surgical cuts and a myriad of other things. That's with large livestock though. When dealing with smaller critters it's more difficult to throw away such evidence. My initial thought was ritualistic practices. Some old divination magic involves reading the entrails of a fresh kill. That doesn't really cover the totality of the evidence though. Something happened to these animals and it wasn't natural.

Speaking of unnatural; Ms. Jamie told a story of how a groundhog was found in one of the cages on the premises. She was very clear that it was not a cell. What she called a cage had no opening large enough for the animal to sneak in, according to her not even a rat would be able to. The poor groundhog, which is considerably larger than a rat if you've never encountered one, was freaking the hell out when they found it imprisoned. No one has keys to the place but Ms. Jamie, and she sure as hell didn't put it there. They managed to get it out and set it free. I'm sure the little guy had a wild story to tell his friends, if he had any left. Ms. Jaime said that the Brushy Mountain complex used to be full of 'em, until the mutilations started. Now there are hardly any left at all.

What the hell is going on around those parts? I suppose residents eventually get used to the strange and mysterious. 'Oh, look honey another unexplained light zipping about in the sky, pass the salt please.' Whatever it is, it makes for an interesting story. Big thanks to Ms. Jamie. I wish her all the best.

I wanted to also give mention to some common causes handed out to explain UAP phenomena. These swamp gas and ball lightning. I've seen swamp gas in person. I think it is absolutely the cause for a lot of ghost lights and spooky orb sightings in certain regions but it doesn't cut it for me for the UAP sightings. Ball lightning is insane to watch and could very well be the explanation for some.

The Great Smoky Mountains are no stranger to mystery and this includes that of the extraterrestrial variety. From its northern base nestled in Cades Cove, Gregory Bald reaches 3000 feet into the sky. What sets this place apart though is the bald part. Most mountains in the Appalachians are forested and rocky. Gregory Bald, like other Balds, has a summit largely devoid of trees and any heavy vegetation other than wild grasses.

The following is an anonymous report of strange happenings on Gregory Bald. A man and his two friends decided to hike the mountain together and enjoy the wonderful views the place had to offer. The hike itself is not a particularly difficult one and as they ascended the gentle slope, they talked about the Cherokee legends about how the area was home to a civilization of rabbits who built houses on the grassy summit.

Reaching the top, our friend remembered that a year prior someone told him of a natural spring they had found nearby so he sat out to look for it.

He walked into the tree line beyond the grass listening for the sound of running water. He found something all right but it wasn't a spring.

He claims to have heard something crashing through the trees below him that he thought might have been a bear. What he witnessed would make me prefer the bear to be honest. He described a floating, transparent, sphere moving through the trees. When the sphere touched the ground, it was illuminated by a bright light and what he thought could be two humanoid shapes inside the sphere.

He continued to watch this thing move about when he suddenly found himself discombobulated. He felt as though his mind was in a dream or trance like state. He claims it felt like hours but in reality, only a few minutes had passed. The object moved away and he regained his composure and rushed to tell his friends. His hiking partners had not witnessed the sphere but did say they saw lights and that they believed his story.

The group briefly entertained the idea of trying to track this thing down. The fact that darkness was approaching and they were ill prepared for such an adventure led to the correct decision of just leaving it be. You never want to be caught unprepared, especially after dark. Aliens or not.

I have to say I believe this fella. It just feels like he really saw something out of this world up on Gregory Bald. Why are they bald anyway? What causes this geologic feature around the Appalachians? There really isn't an agreed upon cause. The rock in this area is hundreds of millions of years old so who knows what machinations mother nature was up to. I have heard a theory thrown around that the bald areas are directly related to UAPs and aliens. Kind of like the theory of extraterrestrial bases in Mt. Rainier in Washington State. That's really not an idea I'd hang my hat on though personally.

There's lots of strange things that go on including disappearances. I'll just say this to address the subject. Many reasons exist for folks to go missing in national parks. Some grifters like to exploit this and offer supernatural reasons. While possible I tend to disagree. Could alien abduction or cryptids be snatching people up in the park system of the United States? Sure. Do I think it's a major concern? Not at all. Point is and I've said this a lot in this book. Stay prepared and respect your surroundings.

Oh, one more thing.

Keep watching the skies!

SOUTHEAST TENNESSEE

WHAT HAPPENED TO LOMAX?

A.J. here, and oh, good! You made it here from the Ruby Falls section of the book to hear all about Lomax and what the fuck happened to him in the Ruby Falls Cave system.

Here's the thing about it, and why we're in the Unexplained section of the book: We don't really know.

The story goes that after the discovery of the Ruby Falls Caverns, Lomax set about exploring into the cave systems with a passion and fervor. He tended to go in solo with his chalk or other assorted marking mechanisms, water, and a light, ranging into the caverns further and further making markings all along the way on the cavern walls to know where he had been and to give him a better idea on how to map things.

One day, he set off into a section of the caverns he hadn't fully explored yet, and like anyone with a major passion for anything who gets fully immersed into what he's doing, he ranged into the caves pretty far, and didn't watch his time…

His light failed and plunged him into a pitch blackness that was insurmountable. He was trapped.

After a while, when he hadn't reported back, a search team got together to go looking for ol' Lomax.

Eventually, they found him, but he was in a *state*.

It's said that he was found crouching and terrified against a cavern wall. Babbling incoherently, warning the men, begging them, to go no further into the cavern system.

They had to practically carry Lomax out, and rushed him to a nearby area hospital, where the man who had clearly gone completely mad could hopefully recover from whatever had incapacitated him mentally within the mountain.

Recover Lomax did, indeed, however, at a great personal cost to himself as he refused to talk about what he had seen or encountered down there in the dark and the black. Not only did he refuse to speak on it, he adamantly refused to ever return to the cave system and told anyone who would listen *not to go down there*.

Furthermore, in a physical manifestation of whatever trauma Lomax suffered down there, his hair had supposedly turned completely white from the fright he'd taken.

To this day, no one knows what Lomax heard, possibly saw, or felt down there in the dark after his light went out. For the rest of his days, however, there was no denying; *his light went out*. Not just the one he carried to explore, but the one each and every one of us carries inside.

Whatever it was he encountered inside Lookout Mountain that day changed the man forever, and he completely dropped his passion for cave exploration from that day forth.

The question of *What happened to Lomax?* Persists well beyond his dying day and is why we've entered it here in the *Folklore & Unexplained* section of this book.

The Beast on Lookout Mountain

Matt here, and it's gonna be mostly me for this section from here on out. Let's get into it:

Ghost or cryptid? Cryptid or ghost? Or could this be another phenomenon altogether? There's a reason this creepy crawly is in the 'Unexplained' section rather than up with the 'Critters & Cryptids' and that's that we don't rightly know, friends.

The following eyewitness account can have a few explanations both in the paranormal and the normal. It was so intriguing to both of us that we felt we needed to include it in this book.

Late one night two friends were driving somewhere along Lookout Mountain. The headlights pierced the darkness not much more than fifty feet in front of the vehicle. You all have been there, a dark road barely lit by the lights of your car as you follow the painted lines around bends and curves in the still black void that surrounds you. Just try to keep it between the ditches until you get home.

I personally hate driving in these conditions. I've made the trip down from Tennessee into Georgia way too many times late at night or early in the morning to ever want to do that shit again. I tip my hat to folks who regularly drive those mountain roads on the regular.

Give me a big stretch of I-75 South and I'm a happy camper. There's a much-reduced chance there of me encountering whatever the hell these folks did and that is ok by me. However, driving through the Osceola National Forest in northeastern Florida is a whole different story and one we will eventually tell. Now to continue our story.

In the road ahead of our traveling companions suddenly appears what seems to be a huge animal. Some cross between a wolf and bear. A massive hulking body covered in fur blocked their way. They slam on the breaks and this creature just charges the car full-on . The friends both essentially brace for impact, awaiting the crashing metal and shattering glass but it does not happen.

Right before impact, it disappears into thin air. They both take a breath and confirm that yes there was some monstrous thing in the road. Yes, it just vanished. What the hell just happened?

Here we are folks right back up to the beginning. Is this a ghost or a cryptid? Well, I have some ideas.

This could be an actual entity that haunts that particular road. The origin of such a creature is obviously unknown and without further accounts or witnesses this theory kind of dries up in the sun. There could also be a factor of sleep deprivation or something similar like road fatigue that would lead to hallucinations of something charging the vehicle. Couple this with the phenomenon known as Foile à Deux. This is basically a shared delusion of people in an isolated environment. To me that's a big stretch but I really wanted to mention this possibility to cover all the bases. There is also something that American long-haul truckers call The Black Dog

Trucker legends and superstition abound. It is said that when you are pushing a little too hard and have been awake far longer than is safe, a black dog will appear on the side of the road or walking into the road as a sign the driver needs to find a place to stop and rest. Ignoring the black dog can mean death.

Black dogs have been a death omen for a long time. They are everywhere in English folklore and have roots in Celtic, Germanic, and Norse traditions. This creature that these folks witnessed made me immediately think of the demon dogs. Was this thing trying to warn them of danger? Had they not stopped because of the creature would they perhaps have found themselves in a much worse situation than having a fright in the middle of the road?

I would really like to find more stories involving what appears to be a solid living and breathing animal or creature that suddenly vanishes. Bonus points if it vanishes mid-charge at a witness.

Have y'all ran across anything like this? Let me know. Drive Safe and Happy Hunting!

GATEWAY TO THE SMOKIES
&
GREATER APPALACHIA

FAERIES IN APPALACHIA

The Appalachian Mountains are old. I'm talking older than some fossils, older than bones. Back when all the continents on earth were hanging out in one big mass called Pangea, that's when our rocky friends were formed and these mountains don't just reside here in America as a result.

Back when Mother Earth decided to break up the party and send the land masses that would eventually become the continents we know today in their respective directions, the Appalachians got spread over the eastern half of North America, scattered across and through the British Isles, and finally terminate somewhere on up in Scandinavia.

Those are some of the same places that tell tales of Fae folk and tricksters. That speaks of giants and trolls and elves. It's all the same rock. Tell me there are no Fae living in Appalachia. That there isn't something hidden just behind the veil and that if you are lucky or perhaps unlucky enough you may just catch a glimpse of something that was here long before us and I'd bet top dollar will be here long after the Human race wiped itself off this little blue dot we call home.

The Cherokee have a legend of a race of magical beings they called "The Immortals" or Nunnehi. These human-like Fae folk were said to reside under the earth in vast cities. They approached the tribe offering to let them come and live with them inside the mountains of the Smokies to escape coming destruction. Some settlements took them up on the offer but the majority did not. The Cherokee people were eventually pushed out of the region and were separated from those who chose to live inside the mountains. There is a familiar tone to this story in that tales of races of magical or otherworldly beings living underground or in mountain ranges pop up all over the world.

The Fae could be anywhere and everywhere in these parts.

The evidence could be all around us. Maybe you just have to know what to look for. Rock formations with small openings close to ground level have long been thought to be homes for Fae. Same with trees that are hollow or contain openings. Don't go knocking or messing about or you'll receive the consequences, even if it's a snake bite and not a mystical being cursing you.

Have you ever come upon a circle of mushrooms? Sometimes nothing grows inside the circle other times is just a nice ring in an otherwise normal locale. We always called these fairy circles growing up. My grandmother referred to them as Witch Rings and I think that's a holdover from the German Hexenringe which translates as such. You know what kids like to do with mushrooms? Kick the hell out of them for one. We were taught to never pick, eat or mess with them because of the danger of toxic varieties. The fairy circles, however, we were expressly warned to stay away from and do not disturb or you'd be cursed. I still follow that rule.

Many things are said to happen if you end up pissing off the Fae about their circle. Legends mention people sucked into the Fae realm and forced to dance until they die, some are forced to marry a member of the Fae court, others just straight up disappear. Depending on location and religion the ways to be freed vary. Touching the trapped person with a piece of iron, praying, tricking the Fae or making deals are all on the table. Also, the iron thing is interesting as it comes up a lot with the defense against supernatural enemies. Like silver to vampires and werewolves. Science concludes that these formations are not made by dancing magical mischief makers but by competition for soil resources, nitrogen depletion, even rabbits and their poop come into play. (I read an awful lot about this stuff.) I personally am not taking chances though. Point being, listen to my grandma and leave the damn circles alone!

We talked about a lot of creepy critters in this book. Do any of them fall into the Fae category? Maybe. The serpent has a curse involved.

Mothman has his weird harbinger of doom vibe going for him. It's damn near impossible to find evidence of Mr. Foot; does he slip off into some Fae realm now and then? These are silly questions I know, but it's fun to think about how new and old legends and folklore borrow from each other resulting in the mythology as a whole evolving with humanity. I think that's pretty damn neat. If anything in this book could be categorized as Fae or Fae adjacent, I'd say it's The Squeezer. He was intelligent, easily offended, and quick to turn terrifying. Sounds like a Fae to me, it also sounds like some people I know.

Look at the folks who came here to settle this land. Their traditions and beliefs live on even in current generations. Herbal healers, kitchen witches. I guarantee most of us knew someone's grandma who could take the pain out of a wasp sting or when you hit your finger with a hammer. Hell, as a flatlander growing up in southern Georgia, I had family members that practiced herbalism, cast wards, and made spell jars. The point I'm trying to make is that magic is very much alive. It is tied to the people, the plants, and animals, and especially the earth itself.

Still, there's one story that sticks out in all of this, and unfortunately, neither A.J. nor myself can remember where we read it, but the gist of it goes like this:

There was a creature in the hills and hollers of East Tennessee. A menace, that was almost like a siren but without the water. It would turn into whatever the person so desired to lure them away from civilization and go on to devour its victim. One day, a young lad is out traveling with his single-load rifle and comes across this beautiful blonde woman with slightly pointed ears. He follows her, and she leads him under some pretense to a cave. The boy says something to the effect of coming to, or waking up even though he was already awake - like coming out of a dream, and in a moment of clarity, he wasted no time, unslinging his musket or rifle or whatever over his shoulder, taking up arms, and firing blindly into the beautiful blonde's face.

She hit the ground, although what hit the ground wasn't the beautiful blonde of a moment before, but rather the twisted and grotesque visage of the monster that'd been terrorizing these parts, snatching victims.

What came to mine and A.J.'s mind was this: So, you mean to tell me that no one's put together that obvious faery glamour was used in this instance to lure this teen or whatever, and that when he shot the creature with an old-timey lead musket ball which for sure contained some trace elements of iron that it killed this fuckin' thing; but that no one made the connection that this was some kind of Fae creature?

Thanks to learning all this about Faeries and some of my own pre-existing superstitions, if anyone ever asks to have my name, like the barista at Starbucks, I'm sure to respond with "you may call me Matt." Can't ever be too careful, can you? Coffee shops are the worst about it. I'm convinced that chain coffee places are just a Fae conspiracy to steal people's names and one day they will cash in. How the hell do you think there are so many of them around? I'm only half kidding here, it's like my second favorite conspiracy theory.

All this is to say, and all joking aside: perhaps let's not be so quick to dismiss the thought of Faeries, magic, and unseen worlds. Imagine what an utterly dull world this would be without it all.

Make your own magic and take care of each other; and as always: happy hunting.

ATAGAHI LAKE

Deep in the Great Smoky Mountains, somewhere between Eastern Tennessee and North Carolina, lies a hidden magical lake called Atagahi; according to Cherokee legend. Only those deemed truly worthy will ever have the privilege to set eyes on this mystical place.

The story goes that this lake is kept protected from humans by the animals of the mountain. This is because the body of water is a medicine lake to the wildlife. A bear injured by a hunter could wade into the lake and walk back onto the banks completely healed. Basically, animal paradise, and I don't blame them for keeping humans as far away as possible. Mankind has a way of ruining everything, especially nature.

According to one piece of lore I came across, one person did get to experience the majesty of Atagahi Lake. A young Cherokee man completed the intense process to prove himself spiritually worthy. He prayed and fasted. The young hunter kept vigil all through the night and when the dawn's light broke through the mountain trees the hidden place was revealed.

It was nature in all her immaculate glory. A pristine blue lake stretched out before him. The lake was teeming with all sorts of fish, frogs, and reptiles. The shores were covered in animal tracks and the skies were a flutter with birds. Truly a stunning sight.

Sometime after his peek into the world of Atagahi Lake, the young man found himself in a terrible situation. Driven by desperation from his family's hunger he shot and wounded a bear that ended up getting away. He was never again allowed to visit the hidden lake because of his transgression.

Now, if a random person like you or me were to somehow stumble upon the location of Atagahi Lake, it is said we may hear the wings of hundreds of waterfowl. Investigating the sound would reveal a bone-dry lakebed. No animals. No water. No paradise.

Throughout humanity's global history there are tales of hidden or lost locations. Usually, cities or ancient ruins hold treasure or secrets. El Dorado, Atlantis, etc. this is different though. This may be the most beautiful story of a hidden place I have ever come across. Don't you go looking, you're probably not worthy.

Be careful out there, folks. We don't have a healing lake to take a dip in.

SPEARFINGER

A brave young man sits and rests on the rocks of the river. He holds his baby sister in his arms.

He sits and breathes heavily after hearing the legend of Spearfinger. The legend bothers him but he sits tall in defiance. It's just a legend, after all...

Let us speak about Spearfinger my dear little strangelings.

We can talk about her on our own here, yeah? Anybody afraid of an old woman?

Back to the young brave... he has heard the legend, he knows the stories told by the elders, but though the legend bothers him, here comes an old woman, walking in the woods holding her hand in her shawl. Feeble, nothing to be afraid of...

The young brave gets to his feet, keeping his sister close. He feels the earth shake and move as The Stone Woman approaches up he path. It can't be her... it's just a story... but she's hiding her hands is she not? One hand hides her weakness. One hides her weapon and that finger of hers holds horrible, horrible things.

A stone, sharp edged and foul is produced and elongates from her finger; not quite a claw, but something different. The stone woman's long spear-like finger extends with slow and crackling sounds into an obsidian blade as she grins with malice.

The brave tries his best to protect his little sister but he fails. She embraces the young man tightly, leaving him powerless as she digs the sharp black point into the child, twisting once and extracting her liver with practiced ease. She brings it to her eager mouth to eat. A mouth stained with the old blood and ichor from her previous meals.

She's just a legend... but the brave has learned, legends can be real.

The earth still shakes a rumbling cadence. Fading into the mountains as she departs, leaving him standing horrified, the dead child's body in his arms... his sister, his poor little sister...

What's just happened?

The legend of Spearfinger or the Stone Woman is tied to the rocks and mountains of the Smoky Mountains themselves. She is said to shake the earth as she walks and sings her song about devouring livers. When attacked, spears and arrows break like toys against her skin. In fact, when the plan was hatched to capture and kill this creature, she fell into a pit of spikes unhurt. The tribe who captured her let loose all of their arsenal of spears and arrows to no avail. Spearfinger stood in the pit swiping her sharp finger at the individuals around her and taunting them with her songs.

A Tufted Titmouse, a little gray bird that's cute as a button if you're not from around these parts to know, is said to have been sent from the great celestial beings to give advice on how to destroy Spear Finger. It repeated the word "Heart!" So, the people aimed at the monster's heart but alas again their efforts were fruitless. The elders cut the tongue of the titmouse for lying (hence why it now has a short tongue) and the bird flew back into the heavens.

I kind of feel bad for the little fellers about that; the titmouse wasn't exactly lying but rather just wasn't being specific enough. The heart was indeed the key to Spear Finger's destruction, yet she held her heart not in her chest, but in her closed fist. This information was conveyed by a chickadee, also sent from the heavens. (A lot of information here is given via birds. I'd make a joke about Tweeting but I have far too much respect for the subject matter and disdain for the digital platform to go there except for this little aside.)

Spear Finger was able to be destroyed by killing the heart she clutched so tightly in her fist. It begs the question though; is she somehow still around? Does she wander the dark hills of Appalachia with her blood-stained mouth looking for her next meal? Hell, would you even know her if you saw her?

Chances are no. There has always been a distrust of strangers in these parts because the witch was said to be a shapeshifter in addition to the horror show I described above. As far as legends and lore go, I'm pretty sure ol' Spear Finger is the OG lesson or reason it's said to be unwise to venture out alone. You leave alone and return home, who is to say what really returned is you and that it is not something just disguised as you waiting for the right opportunity to strike?

In addition to the whole stone finger spear and knife thing, it's said she had the ability to move great boulders with ease and shift and morph the earth to her will. Supposedly remnants of her stone building and shifting can still be found through the mountains by way of mounds and other unusual rock formations.

I kind of have to wonder if she was one of the origin stories that breathed life into the urban legends about waking up in a bathtub full of ice, except instead of kidneys, liver seems to be a hot commodity in her world. I mean, I can understand it. It's high in nutrients and often sought out by scavengers and predators. Hell, humans dig it too – liver and onions being a popular dish to help you out if you're suffering from anemia. Polar Bear livers are so high in vitamin A that it can straight up kill a human if you eat enough, and as far as I know, it doesn't take much. So, ya know, maybe skip the Polar Bear liver if you see it on a menu somewhere.

There's another well-known legend concerning the liver. Remember when Zeus got so pissed at Prometheus that he tied him up in the Caucasus Mountains and cursed him so that every day an eagle would eat pieces of his liver and every night it would regrow just to start it all over again?

Funny enough, you can also survive with only part of your liver and it's one of the few organs you can donate a chunk of while you're still alive - so that's fun too; but back to Appalachia and some other interesting rabbit holes of thoughts brought on by the legend of Spear Finger, but I'm going to save that for further on down the line.

THE CUSSING COVER, CADES COVE

Hello, my little strangelings! Did you miss me? A.J. Mason here to bring this one home. So, even though this is primarily Matt's section, we both decided that for this one I was the better candidate to write about it, because even though it's definitely an unexplained phenomenon out of Cade's Cove, it doesn't have much to do with any sort of Indigenous legend or lore and there aren't any cryptids in sight.

No, this one just has to do with people, death, and dying – and possibly life beyond death of a sort, so that is all me and firmly inside my purview, so here we go!

Legend has it, that when Cade's Cove was still a thriving holler with people living in it, there was a couple that lived there by the name of Basil and Mavis Estep.

The legend goes that Mavis was born during a terrible thunderstorm, and for her entire life, she was terrified of them, swearing that one would be the death of her – of course, the locals being the superstitious types didn't help with this, feeding into her fear by essentially telling her, her whole life, that was how shit would go down. It was the early 1900s of it all, my little strangelings and as we all know, people are weird – and not always a good weird. Telling a child that she was born during a thunderstorm and therefore was apt to die during one and drilling that into her conscious and subconscious from an early age is not good weird. We don't do that here. Okay?

At any rate, Mavis was terrified of thunderstorms and the rain to the point she wouldn't be caught dead out in it – and her fear further manifested itself in that she absolutely refused to have a metal bed, or any kind of metal furniture whatsoever in her home, as that was just begging for trouble when the thunder rolled and the lightning struck throughout the Cades Cove Valley, she called home.

Now Mavis Estep had a particular talent for crafting the most beautiful quilts, and she did so with a particular eye for pattern and color. Her favorite of all of her creations, however, was a patchwork quilt made out of one of Basil's old flannel shirts. One she fondly referred to as the 'cussing cover' as it had been the shirt he was wearing during their first, heated enough, marital arguments in which Basil had painted the inside of their cabin up one side and down the other with the most garishly colorful language that Mavis had ever heard him spit.

Mavis ended up preceding Basil in death, but spoiler alert: It wasn't lightning that struck her down, but rather, a protracted illness – which was common for this era and especially in rural Appalachia.

Now Mavis, knowing she had little time left, called her husband Basil to her death bedside. They talked. Traded 'I love yous' I imagine, and Mavis gifted Basil with one thing, telling him to please find happiness, giving him permission to remarry after her passing. Then she made one final request. Well, two really, the first reasonably being that Basil never sell any of her beloved quilts to anyone. The second, that he should never, ever, under any circumstance put any of her beloved quilts on bed with a metal bedframe.

She died, and Basil held true to his promises to her – right up until he didn't.

It was under a year later that Basil Estep remarried, to a woman named Trulie Jane.

Now, Trulie Jane had absolutely no fear of thunderstorms or metal furniture, and was a much younger model, so to speak, than Mavis had been – and thus, Basil may have felt a little pressure to give in to some of his new bride's wishes in order to keep her both happy and from straying out of their marital bend.

One of those wishes was to trade in the couple's wooden bedframe for a new, fancier, metal one.

Basil readily agreed and went against his previous wife Mavis's deathbed request against him ever getting one. A thing Mavis may have forgiven him for – but on a particularly cold night, when the weather was calm and serene but rapidly growing cold with the turning of the season, Truly Jane asked her husband if they might add one of Mavis's quilts to the bed to stave off the growing chill.

Basil thought nothing of it, and told his new bride, Truly Jane, to pick whichever one she would like. She, of course, fell in love and chose the one with a particularly striking red flannel pattern that she found exceedingly pleasing to the eye. It just so happened to be Mavis's favorite, too – the cussing cover.

She went and laid it out over the top of the couple's other blankets to add warmth and make the bed a little cozier during the chillier weather rolling in overnight.

It was strike two, on Mavis's deathbed wishes, and enough to bring Mavis forth from her grave altogether – forget just rolling in it. Truly Jane woke in the middle of the night to the terrifying visage of an angry Mavis, standing at the foot of the metal bed. She said that Mavis looked furious, opened her mouth, and screamed at Truly Jane, who in turn screamed in fright as she watched Mavis disappear before her very eyes.

Basil woke at the terrible cacophony coming from his new wife, and truly upset and terrified, Truly Jane told him all about what she had seen. Basil comforted his bride and told her basically, "There, there, now. You had a nightmare, a night terror, that's all."

Truly Jane had her misgivings, but as her husband cuddled her close and soothed her, she managed to let them all go, and the couple managed to return to sleep, the cold, clear, silent night outside devoid of insect song making it easy in its hushed quiet.

Strike three came shortly thereafter, when out of a clear, cloudless sky, a flash of blue light came, breaking through the couple's bedroom window, knocking Truly Jane clean out of the marital bed, and in that terrible flash of blue light, the smell of burned linens and worse arose, and when Truly Jane came to on the bedroom floor, it was to the horrifying site of the metal bed, the bedding, and her poor husband Basil, a smoking ruin of blackened ash and broken promises.

While there was nothing spontaneous about this particular combustion in the classic sense of the phenomenon – it was a perfect example of a bolt from the blue – and it's been an enduring legend around these parts for decades.

I feel Mavis in this one. It honestly and truly wasn't like she was asking for much. The final promise Basil made to her was broken after her death, when Mavis's remaining quilts were passed down to the Estep children, and those children sold her quilts to varying collectors in the region. Rumor has it, Mavis Estep's quilts are still swirling in quilters circles and collections to this very day – and I like to think they are.

One thing is for sure, with a legend like this attached to her name, no one will be forgetting Mavis Estep any time soon. A legacy I hope this book with its adventures in the Paranormal from ghost stories to legends, to hauntings and cryptids will follow long after both Matt and I are gone.

Until next time, my little strangelings, and the next subject or region…

Happy hauntings and hunting.

AFTERWORD

I know I talked about some pretty spooky things in this book and there's no doubt this area is home to some scary critters and legends. I would like to point out that this isn't meant to stop you from enjoying this wonderful place.

East Tennessee and indeed Appalachia as a whole is home to some of the most kindhearted, down to earth, and just plain ol amazing people in the entire country. Nature here is awe inspiring and everyone should get to experience its wonder and majesty. There is nothing no more inherently dangerous about this place than any other mountain range or forest area. That said the danger does exist. Always be prepared and know exactly what you're getting into when exploring the great outdoors. If you go alone let someone know your timeline and location.

Respect the land, it was here before you and will be here after your bones turn to dust and you become part of it. Respect the folks around you and their privacy. Respect the wildlife and plant life that call this awesome place home.

I have done my absolute best to convey these stories to you as accurately as possible. If I made a mistake, I am sorry. I'm mostly human… er… I'm *only* human after all. I had a blast contributing to this book

AFTERWORD

and I hope you had fun reading it. If you enjoyed it, keep an eye out because we got more coming your way.

Thank you so much and as always…

Happy Hunting

Matt Geist

BIBLIOGRAPHY

BOOK

Baldwin, Juanitta. *Smoky Mountain Ghostlore*, 1st Edition, Suntop Press, 2005.
Brown, Alan. *Ghosts of the South*. 1st Edition, Haunted America, 2021.
Burchill, James V., Crider, Linda J., Kendrick, Peggy, Bonner, Marcia Wright. *Ghosts and Haunts from the Appalachian Foothills: Stories and Legends*, 1st Edition, Rutledge Hill Press, 1993.
Carpenter, Scott. Dogman the Monsters Are Real. CreateSpace, 11 June 2013.
Coleman, Christopher K., *Ghosts and Haunts of Tennessee*. 1st Edition, John F. Blair Publishing, 2011.
Hall, Lynne L. *Tennessee Ghosts: They are Among Us*. 1st Edition, Sweetwater Press, 2006.
Horus, Maren. *Haunted Hikes: Real Stories of Paranormal Activity in the Woods*. 1st Edition, 2017.
Ocker, J W., *The United States of Cryptids*, Quirk Books, 11th Oct. 2022.
O'Rear, Jim. *Tennessee Ghosts*. 1st Edition, Schiffer Publishing, 2009.
Penot, Jessica & Petulla, Amy. *Haunted Chattanooga*. 1st Edition, Haunted America, 2011.
Price, Charles Edwin. *Haints, Witches, and Boogers: Tales from Upper East Tennessee*. 3rd Edition, John F. Blair Publishing, 1999.
Price, Charles Edwin. *Haunted Tennessee*. 1st Edition, The Overmountain Press, 1995.
Price, Charles Edwin. *More Haunted Tennessee: A New Collection of Spine-Chilling Ghost and Monster Tales from the Volunteer State*. 1st Edition, The Overmountain Press, 1999.
Price, Charles Edwin. *Mysterious Knoxville: Ghost Stories, Monster Tales, and Bizarre Incidents from the "Gateway to the Smokies"*. 1st Edition, The Overmountain Press, 1999.
Roberts, Nancy. *Ghosts of the Southern Mountains and Appalachia*. 1st Edition, University of South Carolina Press, 1988.
Russell, Randy & Barnett, Janet. *The Granny Curse: and Other Ghosts and Legends from East Tennessee*. 4th Edition, Randy Russel and Janet Barnett, 2006.
Still, Laura. *A Haunted History of Knoxville: Hanged Killers, Reanimated Corpses, Tragic Fires, Cold-Blooded Murder, and Sweet Revenge*. 1st Edition, Stony River Media, 2014.

TELEVISION

"Brushy Mountain Penitentiary" *Ghost Asylum*, created by Tim Hamilton, season 4 episode 10, Tremendous! Entertainment, 6th Jun. 2016, *Discovery+*
"Cocke County Memorial Building" *Ghost Brothers*, created by Destination America, season 2 episode 5, Pilgrim Media Group/Crybaby Media, 29th, Apr. 2017, *Discovery+*
"Brushy Mountain Penitentiary" *Destination Fear*, created by Kevin Healey, season 1 episode 1, 11 Television, 27th, Oct. 2019, *Discovery+*
"Old South Pittsburg Hospital" *Destination Fear*, created by Kevin Healey, season 1 episode 2, 11 Television, 3rd, Nov. 2019, *Discovery+*

BIBLIOGRAPHY

"Haunted Dam and More" *Paranormal Caught on Camera*, created by Derek Hayes, season 3 episode 9, Meetinghouse Productions, 8th, Sep. 2020, *Discovery+*

"Haunted Crypt and More" *Paranormal Caught on Camera*, created by Derek Hayes, season 5 episode 15, Meetinghouse Productions, 11th, Sep. 2022, *Discovery+*

"Old Historic Harriman Hospital" *Destination Fear*, created by Kevin Healey, season 4 episode 4, 11 Television, 17th, Dec. 2022, *Discovery+*

WEB

Amber, "Haunted Drummond Bridge", *Gatlinburg Haunts*, 13th, Apr. 2021 https://gatlinburghaunts.com/haunted-drummond-bridge/

Amber, "The General Morgan Inn", *Gatlinburg Haunts*, 25th, Jun. 2021 https://gatlinburghaunts.com/the-general-morgan-inn/

Branson, Sara, "Exploring the Eerie: Top 10 Haunted Places in Gatlinburg", *Gatlinburg Hotels*, 24th, Sep. 2023, https://www.gatlinburg-hotels.co/blog/exploring-the-eerie-top-10-haunted-places-in-gatlinburg/

Brown, Alan, "Black Aggie", *The Ghost Doctor*, Date Unknown, https://theghostdoctor.com/black-aggie/

DiRienzo, Daniella, "One of The Most Haunted Bridges in Tennessee, Drummond Bridge Has Been Around Since The 1800s", *Only in Your State*, 06, Oct. 2023, https://www.onlyinyourstate.com/tennessee/haunted-drummond-bridge-tn/

Dodge, Chris. "A UFO Was Sighted in Tennessee in 2022 and It's One of the Most Credible UFO Sightings in History." *Only in Your State*, 01, Nov. 2023, www.onlyinyourstate.com/tennessee/ufo-sighting-tn/

Dodge, Chris, "Out of All the Hauntings Surrounding the Small Jail in Huntsville Tennessee, This One Might Just Be the Creepiest", *Only in Your State*, 25th, Oct. 2022, https://www.onlyinyourstate.com/tennessee/small-jail-haunting-tn/

Fuller, Jessica, "Haunted Tri-Cities: Newport building linked to tragedy, haunting and a conspiracy", *WJHL*, 29th, Oct. 2020, https://www.wjhl.com/haunted-tri-cities/haunted-tri-cities-newport-building-linked-to-tragedy-haunting-and-a-conspiracy/

Gayheart, J.B., "Haunted Gatlinburg Cabin 5150: This Family Never Returned", *The Supernatural Sleuth*, Apr. 2022, https://www.tiktok.com/@thesupernaturalsleuth/video/7360860325090184494

Gayheart, J.B., "The Historic Gatlinburg Inn", *The Supernatural Sleuth*, 8th, Aug. 2023 https://www.tiktok.com/@thesupernaturalsleuth/video/7264953495441263915

Gayheart, J.B., "Greystone Lodge, Gatlinburg, TN: Don't Stay in Room 213!", *The Supernatural Sleuth*, 10th, Aug. 2023, https://www.tiktok.com/@thesupernaturalsleuth/video/7265673754246778155

Gayheart, J.B., "Wheatlands Plantation", *The Supernatural Sleuth*, 14th, Aug. 2023 https://www.tiktok.com/@thesupernaturalsleuth/video/7267322600743882026

Gayheart, J.B., "The Park Vista Hotel", *The Supernatural Sleuth*, 16th, Aug. 2023 https://www.tiktok.com/@thesupernaturalsleuth/video/7268073510868716846

Gayheart, J.B., "Holiday Inn Sunspree Resort, Gatlinburg, TN", *The Supernatural Sleuth*, 18th, Aug. 2023 https://www.tiktok.com/@thesupernaturalsleuth/video/7268754076127481130

BIBLIOGRAPHY

Gayheart, J.B., "Red Ashe Cemetery, Caryville, TN", *The Supernatural Sleuth*, 18th, Aug. 2023 https://www.tiktok.com/@thesupernaturalsleuth/video/7269204781149736238

Gayheart, J.B., "Holiday Inn Sunspree Resort Tower", *The Supernatural Sleuth*, 18th, Aug. 2023 https://www.tiktok.com/@thesupernaturalsleuth/video/7268852401975594283

Gayheart, J. B., "Haunted Gatlinburg: The Edgewater Hotel", *The Supernatural Sleuth*, 15th, Jan. 2024, https://www.tiktok.com/@thesupernaturalsleuth/video/7324494392516021547

Gayheart, J.B., "Gatlinburg's Most Haunted Restaurant: The Greenbriar", *The Supernatural Sleuth*, 3rd, Jan. 2024, https://www.tiktok.com/@thesupernaturalsleuth/video/7319889332121210155

Gayheart, J.B., "Haunted Roaring Fork Motor Trail", *The Supernatural Sleuth*, 2nd, Mar. 2024 https://www.tiktok.com/@thesupernaturalsleuth/video/7341908419416165675

Gayheart, J.B., "Howard Johnson Gatlinburg: Haunted Room 332", *The Supernatural Sleuth*, 7th, Mar. 2024, https://www.tiktok.com/@thesupernaturalsleuth/video/7343639944692387115

Gayheart, J.B., "The Haunted Gatlinburg Inn", *The Supernatural Sleuth*, 27th, Mar. 2024, https://www.tiktok.com/@thesupernaturalsleuth/video/7351038701885017387

Gayheart, J.B., "Haunted Mysterious Mansion", *The Supernatural Sleuth*, 28th, Mar. 2024, https://www.tiktok.com/@thesupernaturalsleuth/video/735140771882293994

Gayheart, J.B., "Haunted Cabin King Branch Rd. Gatlinburg, TN", *The Supernatural Sleuth*, Apr. 2024, https://www.tiktok.com/@thesupernaturalsleuth/video/7361600946587110699

Gayheart, J.B., "Haunted Titanic Museum, Pigeon Forge", *The Supernatural Sleuth*, 2nd, Apr. 2024, https://www.tiktok.com/@thesupernaturalsleuth/video/7353276464680226090

Gayheart, J.B., "Feral People of Cades Cove & Smoky Mountains," *The Supernatural Sleuth*, 9th, Apr. 2024, https://www.tiktok.com/@thesupernaturalsleuth/video/7355878369390595370

Gayheart, J.B., "Haunted Greystone Lodge: Room 213". The Supernatural Sleuth, 16th, Apr. 2024, https://www.tiktok.com/@thesupernaturalsleuth/video/7358468694047001899

Gayheart, J.B., "Haunted Cabin Wears Valley: A Night of Terror [Pt.1.]", *The Supernatural Sleuth*, 17th, Apr. 2024, https://www.tiktok.com/@thesupernaturalsleuth/video/7358849784821615915

Gayheart, J.B., "Haunted Cabin Wears Valley: A Night of Terror [Pt.2.]", *The Supernatural Sleuth*, 21st, Apr. 2024, https://www.tiktok.com/@thesupernaturalsleuth/video/7360431010984561963

Gayheart, J.B., "Smoky Mountain Mothman: It Changed This Family Forever!!," *The Supernatural Sleuth*, 21st, Apr. 2024, https://www.tiktok.com/@thesupernaturalsleuth/video/7360361374809115946

Gayheart, J.B., "Park Ranger's Bigfoot Encounter: Smoky Mountains," *The Supernatural Sleuth*, 29th, Apr. 2024, https://www.tiktok.com/@thesupernaturalsleuth/video/7363463681377799470

Gayheart, J.B., "Haunted LeConte Lodge, Gatlinburg, TN", *The Supernatural Sleuth*, 29th, Apr. 2024, https://www.tiktok.com/@thesupernaturalsleuth/video/7363299548699053355

BIBLIOGRAPHY

Gayheart, J.B., "Strangest Story Ever Told: Smoky Mountain Bigfoot Encounter," *The Supernatural Sleuth*, 30th, Apr. 2024, https://www.tiktok.com/@thesupernaturalsleuth/video/7363739299155660075

Gayheart, J.B., "Warning!!! Haunted Gatlinburg Cabin", *The Supernatural Sleuth*, 1st, May. 2024 https://www.tiktok.com/@thesupernaturalsleuth/video/7364046860325014826

Gayheart, J.B., "Haunted Pigeon Forge Cabin: Employees Refused to Go Back!", *The Supernatural Sleuth*, 2nd, May. 2024 https://www.tiktok.com/@thesupernaturalsleuth/video/7364579211421732142

Gayheart, J.B., "Haunted Pigeon Forge Cabin: This Family Was Traumatized!", *The Supernatural Sleuth*, 7th, May. 2024 https://www.tiktok.com/@thesupernaturalsleuth/video/7366264723119082798

Gayheart, J.B., "Wears Valley Haunted Cabin Nightmare", *The Supernatural Sleuth*, 8th, May. 2024, https://www.tiktok.com/@thesupernaturalsleuth/video/7366632291050736942

Gayheart, J.B., "Haunted Sky Harbor Cabin: Do Not Watch Before Bed!", *The Supernatural Sleuth*, 10th, May. 2024 https://www.tiktok.com/@thesupernaturalsleuth/video/7367400020192087338

Gayheart, J.B., "Haunted Gatlinburg Cabin: Housekeeper's Frightening Encounter", *The Supernatural Sleuth*, 13th, May. 2024 https://www.tiktok.com/@thesupernaturalsleuth/video/7368491261478636842

Gayheart, J.B., "Haunted Chocolate Bear Lodge Pigeon Forge, TN", *The Supernatural Sleuth*, 15th, May. 2024. https://www.tiktok.com/@thesupernaturalsleuth/video/7369242029311741226

Gayheart, J.B., "Haunted Sevierville Cabin: A Night of Terror", *The Supernatural Sleuth*, 20th, May. 2024 https://www.tiktok.com/@thesupernaturalsleuth/video/7371092445280390442

Gayheart, J.B., "Haunted Park Vista Hotel", *The Supernatural Sleuth*, 22nd, May. 2024 https://www.tiktok.com/@thesupernaturalsleuth/video/7371980697998740779

Gayheart, J.B., "Skinwalker at Douglas Lake? Terrifying Tennessee Encounter," The Supernatural Sleuth, 11th, Jun. 2024, https://www.tiktok.com/@thesupernaturalsleuth/video/7379303616668077354

Gayheart, J.B., "Haunted Wilderness of the Smokies, Sevierville, TN", *The Supernatural Sleuth*, 13th, Jun. 2024, https://www.tiktok.com/@thesupernaturalsleuth/video/7380002667759914286

Gayheart, J.B., "Haunted Gatlinburg Cabin King Branch Rd.: A Romantic Nightmare", *The Supernatural Sleuth*, 17th, Jun. 2024, https://www.tiktok.com/@thesupernaturalsleuth/video/7381477276015136030

Gayheart, J.B., "Smokey Mountain Feral People Encounter: The Maggie Valley Terror," *The Supernatural Sleuth*, 1st, Jul. 2024, https://www.tiktok.com/@thesupernaturalsleuth/video/7386672284418788639

Gayheart, J.B., "Smoky Mountain Feral People Horrifying Experience: They Are Cannibals," *The Supernatural Sleuth*, 12th, Aug. 2024, https://www.tiktok.com/@thesupernaturalsleuth/video/7402256075304766766

Gayheart, J.B., "Skinwalker Encounter: Petros, TN," *The Supernatural Sleuth*, 28th, Aug. 2024, https://www.tiktok.com/@thesupernaturalsleuth/video/7407916065088392478

BIBLIOGRAPHY

Kraft, Meghan, "The Red Ash Cemetery Is One of Tennessee's Spookiest Cemeteries," *Only in Your State*, 29th, Oct. 2020, https://www.onlyinyourstate.com/tennessee/red-ash-cemetery-tn/

Kraft, Meghan, "These 11 Haunted Cemeteries in Tennessee Are Not for the Faint of Heart", *Only in Your State*, 21st, Aug. 2022, https://www.onlyinyourstate.com/tennessee/tn-haunted-cemeteries/

Kraft, Meghan, "The Haunted Hike in Tennessee That Will Send You Running for The Hills," *Only in Your State*, 25th, Aug. 2022, https://www.onlyinyourstate.com/tennessee/haunted-hike-tn/

Leonard, Austin, "The Legends of Rotherwood Mansion" *The Kayseean*, 11, March, 2021, https://thekayseean.com/life-and-culture/the-legends-of-rotherwood-mansion/

Murphy, Elias, "Cryptids of the South: The Legend of Old Butler," *East Tennessean*, 31st, Jan. 2023, https://easttennessean.com/2023/01/31/cryptids-of-the-south-the-legend-of-old-butler/

O'Rear, Jim, "GHOSTS OF TENNESSEE - Full-Length, Award-Winning Ghost Documentary," *Ghosts of Tennessee*, 9th, Nov. 2019, https://www.youtube.com/watch?v=n6w490ybgS0

Phillips, Bud, "East Hill Cemetery is the most haunted place in the city of Bristol" *Bristol Herald Courrier*, 30th, Dec. 2013, https://heraldcourier.com/news/local/east-hill-cemetery-is-the-most-haunted-place-in-the-city-of-bristol/article_fac8492e-718c-11e3-9f2c-001a4bcf6878.html

Russel, Lyle S., "The Bleeding Mausoleum", *Tennessee Ghosts & Legends*, 15, May, 2023, https://lylerussell.net/2023/05/15/tn-gl-episode-11-the-bleeding-mausoleum/

Ryerson, Heather, "Inside the Haunted 200-Year-Old Bijou Theatre; Do You Believe?", *Inside of Knoxville*, 31, Oct. 2023, https://insideofknoxville.com/2023/10/inside-the-haunted-200-year-old-bijou-theatre-do-you-believe/

Spivak, Lexi, "Haunted Tennessee: Ghost framed for murder haunts the Drummond Bridge in Coal Creek", *WATE*, 30, Oct. 2022 https://www.wate.com/haunted-tennessee/ghost-with-suave-looks-haunts-the-drummond-bridge-in-coal-creek/

Thomas, Keenan, "Nine haunted places to visit in East Tennessee, if you dare", *Knoxville News Sentinel*, 4, Oct. 2022 https://www.knoxnews.com/story/life/2022/10/05/east-tennessee-haunted-homes-sites-visit-october/

Thomas, Keenan, "From the Bijou to Brushy Mountain: 9 of the most haunted spots in Knoxville, East Tennessee", *Knoxville News Sentinel*, 2, Oct. 2023 https://www.knoxnews.com/story/entertainment/2023/10/02/9-of-the-most-haunted-spots-in-knoxville-and-east-tennessee/

Unknown, "Haunted Cades Cove: The Cussing Cover," *Gatlinburg Haunts*, 2024 https://gatlinburghaunts.com/haunted-cades-cove-the-cussing-cover/

Unknown, "Most Haunted Places in the Great Smoky Mountains," *YouTube*, 3rd, Feb. 2024, https://www.youtube.com/watch?v=2JMEOPw5AJU&t=431s

Unknown, "Most Haunted Places in Tennessee," *Fright Night*, 20th, Apr. 2024, https://www.youtube.com/watch?v=P4u07GhPtbI

Unknown, "Carmichael Inn," *Amityville America & Classic Hauntings*, 25th Apr. 2011, https://amityvilleamerica.blogspot.com/2011/04/carmichael-inn.html

CONTACT

If you have any stories you would like to submit for A.J. & Matt to either cover on their social channels online, or to include in one of the future iterations of these books, you can contact A.J. at soundparanormal@gmail.com and Matt at huntingforcryptids@gmail.com - We promise, we will get back to you!

ABOUT THE AUTHORS

A.J. Mason evolved from the stories she's read, the places she's gone, and the spirits that she's encountered along the way. The Pacific Northwest is where her love and curiosity in all things spooky began; she's brought that inquisitiveness with her in all of her travels. From the paranormal, to urban legends, to all things that go bump in the night, she will dig until she uncovers the truth beneath the lore.

Matt Geist is a self-professed swampbilly from South Georgia. He's loved all things spooky since the beginning but took a hard left into cryptids when he encountered one of his very own in the hills of South Dakota. Today, he leans into this side of the paranormal with gusto and is alright with being 'that cryptid guy.' He brings a certain poetry to the subject, because after all, poetry is where he started.

www.ingramcontent.com/pod-product-compliance
Lightning Source LLC
Chambersburg PA
CBHW070043080526
44586CB00013B/891